THE ECLIPSE OF MORALITY

SOCIOLOGICAL IMAGINATION
AND STRUCTURAL CHANGE
An Aldine de Gruyter Series of Texts and Monographs

SERIES EDITOR

Bernard Phillips, *Boston University*

THE ECLIPSE OF
MORALITY

SCIENCE, STATE, AND MARKET

Lawrence Busch

ALDINE DE GRUYTER

New York

ABOUT THE AUTHOR

Lawrence Busch is University Distinguished Professor, Department of Sociology, Michigan State University. He holds appointments in the Colleges of Social Sciences and the Michigan Agricultural Experiment Station. Dr. Busch is widely published in the areas of the new biotechnologies and the political economy and globalization of agriculture.

ALDINE DE GRUYTER
A division of Walter de Gruyter, Inc.
200 Saw Mill River Road
Hawthorne, New York 10532

This publication is printed on acid free paper ⊗

Library of Congress Cataloging-in-Publication Data
Busch, Lawrence.
    The eclipse of morality : science, state, and market / Lawrence Busch.
      p. cm. — (Sociological imagination and structural change)
    Includes index.
    ISBN 0-202-30621-6 (alk. paper) — ISBN 0-202-30622-4 (pbk. : alk. paper)
    1. Technology—Sociological aspects. 2. State, The. 3. Social marketing.
  I. Title. II. Series.

HM846.B87   1999
306—dc21   99-049622

Manufactured in the United States of America

10 9 8 7 6 5 4 3 2 1

To Lawrence K. Williams
who encouraged me to explore

CONTENTS

ACKNOWLEDGMENTS

No book is the product of a sole author. Bernard Phillips urged me to write this volume as part of the series he edits and provided useful comments as the manuscript took shape. Several of my friends, colleagues, and students read much or all of a draft of the manuscript: William H. Friedland, Joan Dye Gussow, Arunas Juska, Elizabeth Ransom, and Paul B. Thompson. John and Ruth Useem gave the manuscript a particularly thorough reading. To all of them I am greatly indebted for pointing out inconsistencies and inaccuracies as well as conceptual confusion. Over the course of the project, I benefited from discussing my ideas with Frederick H. Buttel, Michiel Korthals, William B. Lacy, Mark Sagoff, Dmitry Shlapentokh, Vladimir Shlapentokh, Christopher Vanderpool, and probably several people whom I have forgotten. Most of my present and former graduate students, including Timothy Koponen, Tonya McKee, Gerad Middendorf, Michael Skladany, and Keiko Tanaka, were parties to discussions of one or more parts of the manuscript. I benefited considerably from their critical comments. Tamar Griffin helped to locate some of the more obscure facts in the library. The Michigan State University libraries staff were helpful and friendly throughout this endeavor.

The Societal Dimensions of Science, Engineering and Technology Program of the National Science Foundation helped immensely by providing me with a Professional Development Fellowship (Grant No. SBR 9514719). That fellowship permitted me to spend several months in the Chicago area interacting with Vivian Weil and David Hull. They guided me through portions of the voluminous literature on ethics. In addition, a sabbatical from Michigan State University provided me with some additional time to write and read. Finally, through this entire endeavor, my wife, Karen Busch, has had the patience to engage in seemingly endless conversations about a very broad topic. She is both my best friend and most severe critic. For that I shall always be grateful.

INTRODUCTION
THE POLITICS OF SCIENCE AND
THE SCIENCE OF POLITICS

The late twentieth century is not a time of optimism. When the cold war was declared ended, a new age was supposed to have dawned. Our leaders told us that we won the war and that we could expect a "peace dividend." With the Soviet threat out of the way, global markets would spring up that would unite the world. Not only were famine and hunger to be done away with, but peace and prosperity were to reign. Information technologies would bring everyone into the "global village." Genetic engineering would feed the world and cure most major diseases. Robotics would eliminate tedious, repetitive work. Liberal democracies of the Western sort would spread everywhere—in the former East Bloc, in the so-called Asian Tigers, and in even the poorest nations of the world. Everyone would be better off, happier, and ready to greet the new millennium with enthusiasm.

Even though I have spent much of my life traipsing around the world, and remained doubtful that complex problems could be resolved so easily, I found myself half-convinced that maybe that really was the case. Maybe a better world was possible and maybe I would be around to see its dawning. But during the last decade my doubts have reemerged. While the Soviet Union is rapidly fading from memory, Russia is all too rapidly falling into chaos. In much of the rest of Eastern Europe, well-stocked shops mask the difficulties of those on the bottom of the economic ladder. In Asia, currencies in Indonesia, Thailand, Malaysia, and elsewhere have collapsed, plunging millions into abject poverty. In Latin America, Brazil teeters on the edge of its own currency crisis. Numerous petty tyrants have seized power or used the end of the cold war to consolidate their positions. Concern about the accidental or terrorist use of nuclear weapons is rising. The remnants of Yugoslavia are still engaged in genocide. In Afghanistan, the Taliban are enforcing a frightening form of Islam that denies to many women the very ability to obtain food for themselves and their families. Civil wars in Sierra Leone, Angola, the former Zaire, and elsewhere go on unabated.

1

In the United States, despite low unemployment and record high stock prices, life is also unsettling. The gap between the rich and poor is growing. Millions have jobs that pay minimum wage—not nearly enough to feed and house a family. Gated communities continue to spring up, protecting the wealthy from those who cannot possibly afford the good life. The United States now has the distinction of having a larger proportion of its citizens in jail than any other nation. Identity politics continues to divide us into ever narrower groups. Information and communication technologies are being used by governments and especially by corporations to inquire into our (no longer) private lives. Genetic engineering is continuing apace, changing us, our environment, and our food—in some cases for the better, in others for the worse. The United States has appointed itself policeman of the world, responding to various crises, not by debate at the United Nations or some other international forum, but by nearly unilateral military action. And the very persons who cheered the waning of state power in Eastern Europe are now similarly enthusiastic about an untested faith in the market.

At the same time, there are cries from various quarters about morality. Somehow it seems as if the entire moral order is under attack. Usually those on the left side of the political spectrum decry the governmental and corporate corruption that have become everyday occurrences. Numerous attempts to create enforceable electoral campaign finance laws have failed, making it possible for large corporations and wealthy individuals to buy lawmakers and sometimes judges, policemen, and other government officials as well. At the same time, those on the right argue that private morality appears to be disintegrating. The president is impeached, not for crimes of state—sedition, treason, disloyalty—but for lying about an extramarital affair. And divorce, kinky sex, homosexuality, and sex and pornography in the media are said to be undermining "family values."

But in this book I shall not chasten each of us for being insufficiently moral. I shall not propose some clever means of resolving all of our social, political, and economic problems. I shall not propose a set of utopian principles that, put into practice, would surely lead us all to righteousness. Nor shall I attempt to show that if certain philosophical assumptions are made, then one can logically deduce right and just behavior or social policy. Instead, this is a book about how faith in science, the state, or the market as a solution to the problem of order rests on unexamined and erroneous beliefs in the existence of autonomous individuals and a reified Society. This individualism, and its collectivist counterpart, lead us to avoid coming to grips with moral conflicts. Each camp offers easy alternatives to moral responsibility.

This is also a book about the origins of modern science. But it is not a history as such. Instead, it traces three approaches to creating a world based on science, approaches that themselves predate our current usage of the very word "science" as well as the seemingly self-evident distinction between the natural and human sciences. Bacon proposed a world based on what we now call natural science, in which use of the proper methods would ensure the emergence of truth. Hobbes proposed a world based on a science of the state, grounded on the model of geometry. Smith proposed a world based on a science of economics, a world in which the "natural propensity to truck and barter" would be used to combat the passions. In each case, science, it was claimed, would lead us to social order, abundance, truth, morality, and social justice.

Many of our contemporary debates hinge on assumptions made in forming these now nearly forgotten "sciences." For example, in the 1960s it was widely argued by those on the left that poverty and crime were the result of society's failures and that individuals were not responsible. Those on the right countered that people were entirely responsible for their own actions.

This is the heart of a debate that neither side can win. For if we are neither fully autonomous nor fully social, then we can neither be entirely responsible for our moral actions as individuals, nor can we be fully responsible as a society either. Moral responsibility lies not in individuals or society, but in the social relations that we create both through our own volition and through choices that society gives us. If, as Adam Smith ([1759] 1982) suggested, we learn the moral sentiments, then failure to learn lies as much with our teacher—society—as it does with ourselves as pupils. The burden of moral responsibility cannot be laid entirely on the shoulders of individuals, where it becomes crushingly heavy, nor can it be laid on society, where it becomes unbearably light.

Finally, this is a book about democracy, not the "thin democracy" critiqued by Benjamin Barber (1984), but about the need to broaden our practice of democracy. For most Americans, democracy is limited to going to the polls once a year and voting for others who will make decisions for us. I submit that this is hardly sufficient to come to grips with the problems that confront us today. We need to deepen our practice of democracy in the political sphere by making it more participatory and deliberative. We need to reinvigorate political debate. We need to reclaim it from the wealthy and powerful. At the same time, we need to build networks of democracy that incorporate other spheres of social life—the arts, the media, the family, education, health care, law, science and technology. Perhaps most importantly, we need to extend networks of democracy to the workplace, for it is there that we spend most of our working hours. It is there that the decisions that most directly affect our lives are made. Moreover, by extending networks of democracy we can reclaim our moral responsibility—neither as an individual duty nor as a societal burden, but as inherent in the networks themselves.

   In the first chapter of this volume I sketch out three sciences of social order. Bacon proposed a world governed by science; Hobbes proposed a
world governed by the state; Smith proposed a world governed by the
market. The next three chapters show how what were initially merely
philosophical treatises on science, the state, and the market became part of
the taken for granted context of social relations. Chapter 5 provides a critique of the three Leviathans. Finally, in the last chapter I suggest some
democratic alternatives—alternatives that are neither utopian nor unitary.
I argue that the resolution of the problem of order cannot be found in philosophical systems, expert knowledge, or blind faith, but only in the daily
democratic participation of everyone in the making and remaking of the
social world.

   One final note: While I have written this book with the United States in
mind, the examples I provide are intentionally drawn from many parts of
the world. After all, Western notions of science, state, and market are now
present, if not universally accepted, in all nations. I leave it to the reader to
determine how and if the democratic alternatives I propose might be implemented elsewhere.

1

DEVELOPMENT AND THE PROBLEM OF ORDER

ORDER

From time immemorial human beings have worried about the problem of order. Ancient primitive rituals were designed to convince their practitioners of the essential order of the world. Stonehenge, the pyramids of Egypt and Central America, the life-size funerary statues in Xian, the innumerable puberty rites that mark the transition to adulthood, the wedding ceremony in a Catholic church, the forms to be filled out to mail a registered letter, the gendered ways in which greetings are exchanged, the analyzed meter readings from a particle accelerator—all reveal our desire to find or create order.

Moreover, as the list above suggests, the desire for order is not limited to any particular form of knowledge. The natural order, the social order, *and* the moral order are equally in need of explanation, of clarification, of security. Indeed, the very distinction between the natural, social, and moral is itself part of the ordering process. Our modern world—indeed, modernity itself—is not exempt from this quest.

This is not to say that there is some genetically determined quest for order that inexorably drives us to try to pin down what is ultimately, at least in part, ineffable. Indeed, all that we can say is that our social nature is not fixed. We require the company of other humans not merely as companionship, but in order to learn who we are. Contrary to Descartes's claim that "I think, therefore I am," we apparently learn how to think and what to think through interaction with others. In so doing, we always first naively accept the world that is given to us and only later (if at all) critique it. Only in critiquing a culture does the problem of order even arise. The well-ordered culture brooks little criticism, for all its members appear to be more or less content. Yet, no culture can perfectly socialize its offspring; no culture is completely uniform in its beliefs; and no culture consists entirely of critics.

5

In the seventeenth century, Britain—and much of the rest of Europe—was suffering from considerable disorder in the form of wars, civil strife, and the collapse of the authority of the Catholic church. Hence, it is not surprising that Britain was the source of numerous critics. Among them were Francis Bacon, Thomas Hobbes, and, somewhat later, Adam Smith.

Bacon critiqued the existing state of knowledge while providing us with the ideal of an administered world in which scientists inform the state of what knowledge is good and what is bad. Hobbes, the veritable archetype for the modern problem of order, critiqued the Schoolmen as well as the republicans, and provided us with a model of the authoritarian state, in which the monarch tells us what is good and bad. Smith, perhaps the most ingenious of the three, dissected the mercantilist myths and provided us with a model in which the market itself tells us what is good or bad.

I have chosen to begin by reviewing these three figures because I believe that they are emblematic of the hopes and the problems that confront us today. As we shall see, caricatures of them and their positions have become rhetorical icons to be held up whenever convenient to justify various policies. Appeals to science, state, and market are commonplace today—but they were once radical ideas that only took on their iconic status slowly.

Furthermore, what these three appeals have in common, and which I shall explain at length below, is that their promises of a better, more abundant, and more orderly world bring with them almost unnoticed relief from much of the burden of moral responsibility outside the domestic sphere. We are told that the state, through the monarch, science, through a scientific body to be known as the House of Salomon, or the market, through its invisible hand, will provide us with a well-ordered society, truth about the world, and justice in the marketplace. Ironically, however, it is by letting the monarch decide what is right and what is wrong, by letting the House of Salomon determine what science shall be carried out, and by letting the market determine of what a societal good shall consist, that Enlightenment ideals such as freedom, liberty, equality, and even autonomy are eclipsed. Yet, we are the heirs to these views.

Of course, another writer might well have picked other persons with whom to make a similar argument. Indeed, non-Western writers might well have chosen to examine the works of Confucius, Mencius, Ibn Khaldun, or any of hundreds of other philosophers and statesmen who have attempted to address these issues in some manner. Alternatively, they might have chosen to focus on more contemporary figures such as Mahatma Gandhi or Julius Nyerere. However, for my purposes here it was necessary to focus on figures for whom science, state, and market are central themes. While Bacon, Hobbes, and Smith, respectively, fulfill those requirements well, I make no claim to their necessary centrality. In fact, I reject the idealist view that the writings of these men somehow transformed the world as they diffused through it. But then what view do I take? Before continuing, a digression on method is in order.

A DIGRESSION ON METHOD

The present work poses several significant methodological problems for me. While I could conceal them within the pages of the text, I believe that it is better to raise them as issues at the outset. The reader can determine whether I have faithfully carried through on my proposed solutions.

Clearly, the simplistic claim that people read Bacon, Hobbes, and Smith and then set out to change the world accordingly is implausible. Thus, if I am going to make a case at all, it must be far more subtle than that. Instead, I shall argue that all critical works of the sort examined here—this work itself not excluded—have necessarily certain features in common.

First, they all begin with a description of the way the world is. Put differently, they advance knowledge claims as to how the world is put together. By definition, no matter how accurate or distorted, such claims are limited in scope by (1) the necessity of summarizing a great mass of details all of which are subject to more or less debate over interpretation, and (2) the spatial, temporal, and social standpoint of the person making the claim. This is not to say that such limitations are insurmountable; as the old saying goes, one need not be an elephant to know an elephant. Nor is it to say that any interpretation is as good or as valid as any other interpretation. Shakespeare's *As You Like It* has been the subject of countless interpretations, but interpreting it as a manual for the repair of washing machines is clearly inadmissible. Contrary to the views of some postmodernists, the world allows flexible interpretation, but only within a relatively narrow range. Were this not the case, communication would be impossible, for every word we uttered would be subject to endless debate over meaning. Nevertheless, these limitations cannot be fully overcome, as we never have "all the time in the world."

Second, the works discussed here all make proposals about how the world *should* be. Some authors make explicitly utopian claims. Thus, following in the footsteps of Bacon, Thomas More, and others, Henri de St. Simon, Charles Fourier, and other utopian socialists of the nineteenth century presented innumerable imagined worlds. They incurred Karl Marx's scorn for what he considered to be their fantasies. But Marx himself had some notions about how the world should be as well—ideas that, while deliberately left vague, helped to spawn several generations of revolutionaries.

But the claim I am making here goes far beyond either avowed utopians or the more vague claims of people like Marx. Bacon, Hobbes, and

Smith considered themselves to be very down to earth, practical men. They were very careful in their examination of the facts (although their notions of what counted as evidence differed markedly). Yet, they made assertions about what ought to be. In each case, they argued that, if one wishes to achieve a good society, that is, a society internally at peace and prosperous, then one must make certain changes in the way things are done. Moreover, they were convinced that all rational human beings would embrace the desirability of such an improved state of affairs. Therefore, a claim about how the world should be was inserted in their analyses, a claim that most surely biased their choices as to which knowledge claims were important and which were not. Put differently, although since David Hume there has been widespread agreement among philosophers that "is" cannot imply "ought," it is well nigh impossible to write about what is without implying what ought to be. This is especially true for those things that are dearest to us. Furthermore, this applies equally well to the present work as it does to those discussed herein. I can think of no way of avoiding that connection.

Third, Bacon, Hobbes, Smith, and others like them were responding to particular concerns that were central to their time at the same time as they were clarifying, modifying, and reordering those very concerns. Their works were neither merely a reflection of their times nor the result of ideas that sprang *de novo* from their respective heads. The same applies for those who have used their ideas to justify, explain, or reject other claims. Thus, I am faced with two potential paths to follow: On the one hand, I could attempt to be true to the original works, trying to clarify what they have to say that my contemporaries would find meaningful, helpful, or useful. On the other hand, I could try to show how their ideas have been adopted, modified, translated, transmuted, restructured, distilled over the last several centuries so as to lead us to take certain institutions and patterns of action as normal and natural. I have decided to take the latter route, although I might well have taken the former. That would have led to a very different book.

Fourth, others have also addressed in print the issues raised by Bacon, Hobbes, and Smith, and have long since been forgotten by all but historians of philosophy. Still others who are now nameless discussed them endlessly in countless salons, coffee- and teahouses, and university classrooms. Those interpretations, both verbal and written, continue to be created even though the original concerns have long since been abandoned. Thus, despite the (appropriately) universal claims made by Bacon, Hobbes, and Smith, their work is the product of their times. A changed world has changed *both* the problems we face and the interpretations we make of their work. Their work was itself part of the process by which the world was changed. Nevertheless, the very fact that at least some of us continue to read their works suggests that they continue to say things that matter to us.

Finally, for many readers the works of Bacon, Hobbes, and Smith were and remain sources of rhetorical icons that can be used for calls to action. They can tell us how the world should be and even offer some advice as to how to make the necessary changes to achieve a desired state. They can be referred to whenever convenient, to serve multiple, even contradictory purposes, to be ready at hand to use in debate, to convince the unconvinced. To do this hardly requires that one even read the works in question—only that one can refer to them or to concepts contained in them. For example, both supporters of environmental movements and large corporations evoke Baconian images of nature in attempts to legitimate their positions. Similarly, conservative economist Milton Friedman invokes the ghosts of both Hobbes and Smith when he tells us that corporations should have only one goal (profit for their shareholders) and that the market will determine which among them are most efficient, while liberals evoke the same ghosts to suggest that corporations should work toward social ends under the watchful eye of the state.

In sum, each begins with a description of the way the world is. Each tells us how the world should be. Each appeals to the concerns of the time, even while transforming those concerns. Each is subject to multiple interpretations. And each has become a rhetorical icon ready to be trotted out whenever necessary. With this as prologue, let us examine each of these figures in turn.

BACON: DEMOCRATIC TECHNOCRACY

First then, away with antiquities and citations on the supporting testimonies of authors, likewise with disputes and controversies and conflicting opinions: everything philological, in short.

—*Francis Bacon*, Novum Organum

The sixteenth century brought with it a crisis of knowledge. The medieval knowledge of the Schoolmen was being challenged and with it all the wisdom of the ancients. The quarrel between the ancients and the moderns was under way, bringing with it a renewed interest in the empirical world, in the rational powers of humankind, and in a new interpretation of the biblical injunction of dominion over the world. At the same time, the Reformation was fragmenting Christianity. It was into this world that Francis Bacon was born.

Like many of his contemporaries who founded botanical gardens in the hope of re-creating the Garden of Eden (Prest 1981), Bacon strove to re-create an ordered world on earth. Bacon was confident that Paradise itself could be regained through the secular advancement of learning (Johnston 1974).

A New Kind of Knowledge

Bacon's approach involved making a plea for a new kind of knowledge— one that dethroned the reliance on Aristotle and other ancients so venerated during the Middle Ages and so transformed by Christian theology. He reasoned that if entire continents were to be found by voyages beyond the known world, then, similarly, an "America of Knowledge" (Feyerabend 1978) was equally needed and possible. As such, he argued eloquently for greater attention to the empirical world, proposing nothing less than a complete revision of the division of knowledge, to be outlined at length in his never completed work, *The Great Instauration*. Furthermore, he challenged the received wisdom of the ancients, arguing that they were really the children of humankind, while he and his contemporaries were those who were old. In so doing he incurred the wrath of some who felt that even the suggestion that the ancients might be wrong tended to undermine the foundations of society.

While in the works published during his lifetime Bacon was deferential in his dealings with the state, in his posthumously published science fiction novel, *The New Atlantis* (Bacon [1605/1626] 1974), we find a world whose very order is sustained by science. Written from the perspective of a sailor lost at sea who discovers a hitherto unknown—and obviously superior— civilization, Bacon explains in considerable detail how his society is organized. It is ruled by a secretive scientific society known as the House of Salomon, itself a model for the research institute he had wished to found in England. The House of Salomon supersedes the state as the highest authority in the land. As a spokesman for the House explains:

> And this we also do: we have consultations, which of the inventions and experiences we have discovered shall be published, and which not: and take all an oath of secrecy, for the concealing of those which we think fit to keep secret: though some of those we do reveal sometimes to the state, and some not. (ibid.:246)

Moreover, Bacon's society is well-ordered in other ways. Despite its distance from Europe, its inhabitants are largely Christian—but free of the cumbersome scholasticism of the Middle Ages. The few who are not Christians are personified by the Jewish merchant that Bacon's sailor meets; he has "a far differing disposition from the Jews in other parts" (ibid.:234). So as not to disturb this Baconian paradise, foreigners are treated politely, but they are segregated for a time from members of the society and then only allowed to visit during a prescribed time and within a prescribed distance of the city.

Bacon's fictional society is quite patriarchal as well, relegating women and servants to the same category.[1] Marriages are conducted only upon the approval of parents. Moreover,

> there are no stews [i.e., brothels], no dissolute houses, no courtesans, nor any thing of that kind. Nay they wonder (with detestation) at you in Europe, which permit such things. They say ye have put marriage out of office: for marriage is ordained a remedy for unlawful concupiscence; and natural concupiscence seemeth as a spur to marriage. (ibid.:235)

In addition, Bacon feels it is necessary to inform his audience that "as for masculine love, they have no touch of it" (ibid.:236), although we are assured that despite this, men form strong, lifelong friendships. In short, Bacon's *New Atlantis* is an administered society. Politics is no longer needed as it has been replaced by technocratic administration. Order prevails. Within the House of Salomon scientists debate democratically, but only members of the elite are allowed to participate in the discussion.

In contrast to this utopian world, Bacon had little to praise about the world in which he actually lived. Bacon attacked the magicians and alchemists for wrapping the study of the natural world in obscure rituals and works. He attacked superstition, old wives' tales, and tradition. But despite Bacon's strong religious beliefs, he reserved his most vituperative attacks for the Schoolmen—so vituperative that he censored much of his own work, realizing that it would make him too many enemies. His argument against the Schoolmen was twofold: On the one hand, he excoriated them for abandoning the Bible—the written work of God—focusing instead on the ancient Greek texts of Aristotle, Plato, and others, and on the huge body of exegetical works that had accumulated over fifteen hundred years of Christianity. But at the same time, he attacked them for abandoning the study of the natural world—the works of God's first six days—accepting instead the received wisdom of the Greeks. As Bacon put it, "Next to the word of God, Natural Philosophy is the most certain cure for superstition and the most approved nutriment of faith" ([1607] 1964:78–79). Thus, the study of the natural world was to be ranked with the study of the Bible as a religious duty. Indeed, the study of natural philosophy would be the remedy for the religious controversies of the day, permitting men "to contemplate the power, wisdom, and goodness of God in his works" (ibid.:97).

Organization and Method

Bacon's approach to the study of the natural world was two-pronged: new organizational forms and a new method. Bacon was unique among his contemporaries in understanding that the project of natural philosophy would require long-term, painstaking research organized so as to make science cumulative. While Bacon never spelled out in detail just what form the new organization might take, various fragments make clear the general outline. Thus, in his plan to reform the universities, he suggested that laboratories be established, that facts be gathered about the world through experiments, and that scientists be required to report annually on the results of their experiments in language that could be understood easily by others. In the *New Atlantis* we learn that his idealized scientific community would consist of a community of scholars sequestered from the demands of the everyday and left to explore the natural world. In short, Bacon envisioned state-financing, an organizational form that permitted long-term research into nature in all its fine detail, and clear language that would permit cumulativity.

Amazingly enough, although Bacon was unsuccessful in his own lifetime, "it took less than half a century to progress from Baconian utopia to reality; the advancement of learning and the institutionalization of research, of which Bacon was the ardent promoter, were officially linked to political power" (Salomon 1973:11). The first college was established along Baconian lines in 1641 (Merton [1938] 1970). By a royal charter, the Royal Society was founded in England in 1660 under the motto (adopted from Horace), *Nullius in verba.* Everything was to be verified by the facts. The Royal Society looked a great deal like the House of Salomon and marked the permanent association of science with the state that is taken for granted today.

But organization was hardly sufficient. The huge task that Bacon set before himself was none other than to develop a new ordering for all knowledge and a new method for arriving at truth. Bacon rejected the reliance on authorities that was the hallmark of the scholastics, arguing instead that "everything must be sought in things themselves" (Bacon [1620] 1994:24). But Bacon was also suspicious of the senses. "For the evidence and information given to us by the sense has reference always to men, not to the universe; and it is a great mistake to say that the sense is the measure of things" (ibid.:22).

The solution for which he argued was a blending of the rational and the empirical: induction. Bacon explained:

> Those who have handled the sciences have been either Empiricists or Rationalists. Empiricists, like ants, merely collect things and use them. The Rationalists, like spiders, spin webs out of themselves. The middle way is that of the bee, which gathers its material from the flowers of the garden and field, but then transforms and digests it by a power of its own. And the true business of philosophy is much the same, for it does not rely only or chiefly on the powers of the mind, nor does it store the materials supplied by natural history and practical experiments untouched in its memory, but lays it up in the understanding changed and refined. Thus, from a closer and purer al-

liance of the two faculties—the experimental and the rational, such as has never yet been made—we have good reason for hope. (ibid.:105)

To Bacon, induction meant aiding the senses with instruments, much as the telescope allowed Galileo to find Jupiter's moons. Even more importantly, experiments would do for the senses and the mind what mechanical inventions do for the hands. Experiments would permit one to examine "nature pressed and molded." This would be likely to yield results that remain concealed in "nature untrammeled" (ibid.). Such results would be cumulative as well, since the conditions by which nature was to be "pressed and molded" could be varied so as to understand how nature reacted under a variety of circumstances. Moreover, rather than starting from generalizations, Bacon thought it necessary to start with particulars. Even first principles were to be put forward for careful examination. At the same time emotion was to be banished from natural philosophy as it was always a source of error.

Moreover, Bacon was convinced that, unlike the methods of the Schoolmen, alchemists, and magicians, his method would open learning to all. "For my method of discovering knowledge places men's natural talents almost on a level, and does not leave much to their individual excellence, since it performs everything by the surest rules and demonstrations" (ibid.:125). Thus, one only need to follow the new rules—rules that can be taught in the schools—to produce results by induction.[2] Following the new rules would create "a blessed race of Heroes or Supermen who will overcome the immeasurable helplessness and poverty of the human race" (Bacon [1603] 1964:72).

In *The Advancement of Learning* ([1605/1626] 1974), Bacon developed an argument for empirical knowledge. Against the Schoolmen, who argued that Adam's fall from grace took place precisely because of the quest for this sort of knowledge, Bacon made a quite different claim:

> It was not the pure knowledge of nature and universality, a knowledge by the light whereof man did give names unto other creatures in Paradise, as they were brought before him, according to their properties, which gave the occasion to the fall: but it was the proud knowledge of good and evil, with an intent in man to give law unto himself, and to depend no more on God's commandments, which was the form of the temptation. (ibid.:6)

Using the biblical story of King Solomon as support, Bacon argued that it was completely within the divine plan for humans to systematically gather empirical knowledge of the world. Such knowledge would serve the dual function of increasing human understanding of the world and improving well-being through mechanical invention. Such knowledge would glorify the work of God:

Inventions come without force or disturbance to bless the life of mankind, while civil changes rarely proceed without uproar and violence. . . . And indeed it is this glory of discovery that is the true ornament of mankind. In contrast with civil business it never harmed any man, never burdened a conscience with remorse. Its blessing and reward is without ruin, wrong or wretchedness to any. For light is in itself pure and innocent; it may be wrongly used, but cannot in its nature be defiled. (Bacon [1607] 1964:92)

Note that in this passage Bacon simultaneously made two claims that were later to become widely accepted. First, he argued that technologies themselves are always good, although they may be "wrongly used." Furthermore, Bacon contrasted the harmless work of invention with the often harmful work of civil society. Since empirical learning merely revealed the work of God, it was innocent of sin and could only serve to make for a more humane society. Thus, science and technology were removed from society; they were merely the revealing of the work of God.

This is not to say that inventions have no social effects. Indeed, Bacon insists that they do. In his *Thoughts and Conclusions* he uses the examples of printing, gunpowder, and the nautical compass to make his point clear:

These three . . . have changed the face and status of the world of men, first in learning, next in warfare, and finally in navigation. . . . In fact, no empire, no school, no star seems to have exerted a greater influence on human affairs than these mechanical inventions. As for their value, the soonest way to grasp it is this. Consider the abyss which separates the life of men in some highly civilised region of Europe from that of some savage, barbarous tract of New India. So great it is that the one man might appear a god to the other, not only in respect of any service rendered but on a comparison of their ways of life. And this is the effect not of soil, not of climate, not of physique, but of the arts. (ibid.:93)

Thus, inventions always have positive effects. They make Europeans appear as gods—surely a reference to Cortez's reception among the Aztecs—but not because Europeans are inherently superior. Their superiority is only due to their superior inventions. One need not go far beyond this to see a justification for the entire colonial project: Europeans, following Bacon's method, will bring the benefits of Christian religion and science to the heathen, thereby showing them both God's written and natural works.

But in order to create this new earthly paradise, Bacon had to add another twist to the argument. For experimental methods would also help to reveal God's *moral* plan. The key was to obtain knowledge not "with an intent in man to give law unto himself," but to reveal knowledge empirically using the proper method. In so doing not only would temptation be ended, but the physical and moral well-being of humankind would be improved. Once we begin to use the method provided, "then right reason and sound religion will govern the exercise of it" (Bacon [1620] 1994:131).

This explains the seemingly contradictory position that Bacon takes with respect to power. He is quite aware that the knowledge he longs for is also power—dominion over the natural world. But this power is benign since it springs from the works of God. Thus, in Bacon the ancient union of the good and the true is preserved. The physical power to change the world is also the moral power to improve it according to God's wishes. Bacon gives some hint as to how this is to be accomplished in *The Advancement of Learning*:

> How, I say, to set affection against affection, and to master one by another; even as we use to hunt beast with beast, and fly bird with bird, which otherwise percase we could not so easily recover: upon which foundation is erected that excellent use of *praemium* and *poena* [i.e., reward and punishment], whereby civil states consist: employing the predominant affections of fear and hope, for the suppressing and bridling of the rest. For as in the government of states, it is sometimes necessary to bridle one faction with another, so it is in the government within. ([1605/1626] 1974:164)

Put differently, like Smith several centuries later, Bacon believed that the passions could be controlled by setting them against each other.

Conclusions

In sum, for Bacon, science was to open the doors to technical change, to increasing creature comforts, and to a far greater knowledge of the natural world. As Bacon realized, so doing required freedom of inquiry, freedom of speech, and a kind of democratic decision-making among scientists about the facts of the natural world. It required abandoning the scholastic obsession with words and reverence of the ancients. Much of Bacon's world came to be. As philosopher John Dewey (1859–1952) put it nearly a century ago:

> Unrestrained faith in Nature as both a model and a working power was strengthened by the advances of natural science. Inquiry freed from prejudice and artificial restraints of church and state had revealed that the world is a scene of law. The Newtonian solar system, which expressed the reign of natural law, was a scene of wonderful harmony, where every force balanced with every other. Natural law would accomplish the same result in human relations, if men would only get rid of the artificial man-imposed coercive restrictions. ([1916] 1961:92)

But at the same time, the faith in science required that everyone be relieved of the moral responsibility of control over technology and its consequences. Science and the technologies it produces were deemed innocent, merely the discoveries of the works of God. As such, science, technology, and their products were best left untouched by governments, by questioning citizens, and even by scientists themselves. Although the religious trappings have long since been discarded, contemporary arguments for science and technology continue to take this same form.

HOBBES: THE MORAL RESPONSIBILITY OF THE STATE

> *Legitimate kings therefore make the things they command just, by commanding them, and those which they forbid, unjust, by forbidding them. But private men, while they assume to themselves the knowledge of good and evil, desire to be even as kings; which cannot be with the safety of the commonweal*

—*Thomas Hobbes,* Man and Citizen (De Homine and De Cive)

If for Bacon the solution to the problem of order was to be found in science and technology, for Hobbes (1588–1679) it was to be found in the state. Hobbes lived during an extraordinarily turbulent time in England. He survived the overthrow of the monarchy, the short-lived commonwealth, and the restoration. He fled with Charles to France to avoid the antimonarchical forces and published *Leviathan* by sending sections of the manuscript to a printer in London. He saw his books banned by the church and by Oxford University. He was accused of atheism. And yet he was a staunch supporter of monarchy.

Like Bacon, Hobbes's central concern was the maintenance of order. In a world in turmoil—the state under attack, the church collapsing before his eyes—Hobbes had good reason to be concerned about order. How could order be maintained in this war of each against all? He spent much of his life attempting to answer this question.

Hobbes was a colleague of Bacon and was strongly influenced by Galileo. He was particularly impressed by Galileo's understanding of inertia, and felt that everything was caused by motion. Moreover, he was particularly taken by Galileo's method of explaining the observable as the result of a combination of unobservable factors and showing how their logical combination would achieve the expected result. His self-imposed task would be to take society apart, divide it into its simplest elements—individuals—and then show how their interaction would necessarily lead to certain observable results.

Furthermore, like most of his educated contemporaries, Hobbes was convinced of the mechanical nature of the universe. Individuals were themselves reduced to mechanical apparatuses. Indeed, he even complained that his contemporary, René Descartes, was not mechanical enough (Matson 1964).

Hobbes attempted and largely succeeded in producing a comprehensive framework that was at once a theory of knowledge, morals, and action.[3] Four central and (for Hobbes) undeniable problems supported Hobbes's edifice: (1) Each human being has an equal need for food, clothing, and shelter. (2) Goods in the world are scarce. (3) Each human being has the power to kill another. (4) Altruism exists but it is limited; some persons would take advantage of a situation and exploit others (Rachels 1993). A social contract would rectify these problems by producing equity, justice, and certainty.

The Search for Truth

As Shapin and Schaffer (1985) have shown, Hobbes was convinced that true knowledge could only be had about things that were produced entirely by humans. Hence, he made geometry his ideal. But at the outset of *Leviathan*, Hobbes informs us:

> For by Art is created the great LEVIATHAN called a COMMON-WEALTH, or STATE, (in latine CIVITAS) which is but an Artificiall *Man*; though of greater stature and strength than the Naturall, for whose protection and defence it was intended; and in which, the *Soveraignty* is an Artificiall *Soul*. (Hobbes [1651] 1991:9; emphasis in original)

In short, according to Hobbes, since the Leviathan is produced entirely by man, and is "but" an artificial man, it may be known with a certainty that cannot be granted to knowledge of the natural world. Moreover, once knowing it, it becomes possible to improve it. But his method and the turbulent reality of his times required that he start by postulating autonomous individuals as undeniable observables.

Hobbes's men and women are driven by innate appetites such as hunger as well as by passions. The passions may lead them to do things that are even contrary to their best interests. Yet, Hobbes does point out that people are not at all like ants or bees: The agreement among bees is natural while that among people is artificial. People compete with each other for honor and dignity. They are vain; they seek glory. They distinguish between the common and the private good. Moreover, the passions are greatest in those with the most material concerns. Thus, increasing wealth will bring with it increasing passions.

However, all people are capable of reason, which may be used to tame the passions. All persons wish to preserve their own lives. This desire is the starting point and goal of reason. It sets limits to both liberty and obligation. But reason is not infallible. It must be understood within the context of language, which is used to transform mental discourse into verbal discourse. Language permits one to distinguish truth from falsehood as these are not the properties of things but of language itself. Language also makes possible communication. It gives us the ability to measure. Furthermore, it makes it possible to command and to understand commands.

But language is a two-edged sword. It also permits the passing on of errors and lies. It permits one to deceive others by using words metaphorically.[4] It even permits self-deception. It allows one to describe absurdities such as round quadrangles and to create sentences that refer to nothing at all, such as those of the Schoolmen. Moreover, all debate and discourse are mere matters of opinion and cannot end by revealing facts.[5] The conclusions of discourse are always dependent on the premises with which they begin. Nor is the Catholic church a source of true knowledge; it has no means of enforcing its orthodoxy. Furthermore, the Protestant notion that all can decide for themselves is even more dangerous as it leads to the fragmentation of authority.

However, certain knowledge is nonetheless possible, at least insofar as it concerns things that we make ourselves. Thus, for Hobbes, geometry provides the ideal. Geometry produces certain knowledge because it is designed to do so by virtue of the principles we apply to produce it. For example, no plane triangle can have interior angles that sum to more or less than 180 degrees. (In contrast, while tennis also has rules, only practice determines the outcome of a match.) Only a fool would argue that any other form of plane triangle exists. Similarly, reasons Hobbes, "politics and ethics (that is, the sciences of *just* and *unjust*, of *equity* and *inequity*) can be demonstrated a priori; because we ourselves make the principles" ([1658] 1991:42; emphasis in original). Thus, the certain knowledge necessary for universal assent and civil peace is attainable.

However, politics and ethics make little or no sense in a state of nature. Left to their own devices, individuals in such a state would engage in a war of each against all. Such individuals would be moral beings, but as they would be utterly autonomous and fearful of each other, they would be unable to develop a common rule of good and evil:

> For these words of Good, Evill, and Contemptible, are ever used with relation to the person that useth them: There being nothing simply and absolutely so; nor any common Rule of Good and Evill, to be taken from the nature of the objects themselves; but from the Person of the man (where there is no Common-wealth;) or, (in a Common-wealth,) from the Person that representeth it; or from an Arbitrator or Judge, whom men disagreeing shall by consent set up, and make his sentence the Rule thereof. (Hobbes [1651] 1991:39)

Thus, for Hobbes, people measure other people and all things by themselves. The good is that which is desired no matter how it may be defined (Gert 1991); the bad is that which is to be avoided. To be honorable is tantamount to being honored. To be honest is be recognized as honest. The worth of a man is determined not by any intrinsic property, but by what others would *pay* for his power.

In a state of nature each may decide for him- or herself what is good and what is bad. Only in civil life does a common standard emerge, for in civil society it becomes possible to enforce through power a single standard of goodness, of morality. Even God is to be obeyed because of his power, not because of his goodness. Thus, in one stroke Hobbes institutionalizes the sharp division between public and private. "For just as every citizen hath his own private good, so hath the state its own public good" (Hobbes [1658] 1991:69–70). Moral responsibility in the public sphere is shifted to the sovereign, while moral responsibility in the private sphere is thoroughly relativized. To attempt to determine what is good in the public sphere oneself is to attempt to be like a king, behavior that surely will endanger the commonwealth. Hence, Hobbes resolves what he sees as the problem of moral relativism by relieving everyone of the burden of moral commitments in the public sphere, and by placing that burden on the Leviathan.

Justice, therefore, cannot exist independently of the covenant that permits the formation of the state. Injustice involves the breaking of the contract to which one had (implicitly) agreed. Thus, morality is made objective (in the same way as geometry?) by making its ultimate goal the preservation of all in a state. Natural rights are surrendered, as they detract from the achievement of the goal of preservation. Moreover, the sovereign cannot be unjust or make unjust laws (although a given law may well be immoral—violating a higher law passed on by God).

Following his mathematical metaphor, Hobbes sees justice as of two kinds: commutative and distributive. Here Hobbes reveals himself as clearly in the modern camp: Commutative justice is found in the market. "For neither if I sell my goods for as much as I can get for them, do I injure the buyer, who sought and desired them of me; neither if I divide more of what is mine to him who deserves less, so long as I give the other what I have agreed for, do I do wrong to either" ([1642] 1991:139). Indeed, the value of things is not intrinsic to the thing itself, nor is it dependent on the labor that went into its production (as in the medieval notion of a "just price"), but it is merely what others will pay for it. In contrast, distributive justice is based on worthiness. But such worthiness can only be determined by the state, since—contra Aristotle, who claimed that some men were made to rule and others to obey—all men are equal. Class and status are conferred by society; they are not inherent in the nature of things.

The State

Having assumed the existence of autonomous individuals, Hobbes must also posit the existence of the state. But for Hobbes the state or commonwealth is a human product. It is an artificial person where the sovereign is the head. Ministers, therefore, represent the person of the commonwealth in the very literal sense of representing the sovereign. Civil laws are artificial chains connecting the lips of the sovereign to the ears of the subjects. They are commands made by the sovereign and, as such, can never be against reason. These chains of law are weak, but they are dangerous to break as the state punishes those who break the laws. Thus, the laws themselves do not govern; men do, through fear of other men.

Hobbes identifies three types of state: monarchy, aristocracy, and (representative) democracy. He quickly admits that none are perfect, but he argues that monarchies are best since the public and private desires of the monarch are one, which is not necessarily the case in other forms of government. Moreover, he notes that the monarch cannot disagree with himself and can take secret counsel. And, in a monarchy whosoever lives a quiet life need have no fear of persecution. Precisely these advantages that he sees in monarchy, he sees as disadvantages in aristocracy and democracy. Both forms are as good as monarchy in demanding authority, but subjects have no more liberties in a democratic than a monarchical state. Furthermore, aristocracies and democracies may be fraught with factions. The desires of a given member of the ruling elite may make him put his personal good over that of the state, using the state to further his own ends. For this reason, too, for Hobbes, the division of powers is dangerous and is likely to lead to collapse.

But people must be educated to come together in a state. After all, they come together in a state not out of love for others but out of self-love. The state must help to do away with superstitions and false prophecies (although actual states often encourage such beliefs). The state must also tell everyone what right reason is. It must determine and remove those doctrines that are detrimental to it. It must tell everyone what the right religion is. Indeed, Hobbes *defines* the church as the company of men united under the sovereign.

Equality has a special importance for Hobbes, as it explains simultaneously the actions of people in a state of nature and the role of the state. Hobbes makes no claims about intellectual or moral equality. All persons are equal for Hobbes because the weakest can kill the strongest. Thus, in a state of nature, equality is a problem: Two men who desire the same thing can become enemies and one can kill the other. The creation of a state brings with it inequalities through the establishment of civil laws. In what he surely knew was a direct assault on the received wisdom, Hobbes even goes so far as to assert that servants and lords are equal except insofar as civil law makes them unequal. He also argues that the same applies to inequalities between men and women. Although in a state of nature mothers have dominion over their children, men usually have power in commonwealths and families. This, he observes, is the case because states were erected by fathers. Furthermore, since one cannot have two masters, either man or wife must dominate in the family.

In addition to establishing inequalities among persons, the state also must establish itself as the one institution to which other institutions are subordinate. But following his logic for the relationship between the sovereign and his subjects, Hobbes sees all other institutions as civil persons who must be represented by a spokesperson:

> A Person, is he, *whose words or actions are considered, either as his own, or as representing the words or actions of an other man, or of any other thing to whom they are attributed, whether Truly or by Fiction.*
>
> When they are considered his owne, then is he called a *Naturall Person*: And when they are considered as representing the words and actions of an other, then is he a *Feigned or Artificial person.* (Hobbes [1651] 1991:111; emphasis in original)

Thus, for Hobbes institutions have no existence independent of whosoever is their spokesperson, whoever *represents* them. In addition, institutions—from the state to the family—have no internal structure other than obedience to a single personal authority as implied by a social contract. A division of powers can only result in chaos. "A Multitude of men, are made *One* person, when they are by one man, or one Person, Represented; so that it be done with the consent of every one of that Multitude in particular" (ibid.:114; emphasis in original). Thus, families, churches, and merchant companies are also civil persons and subordinate to the state.

The state provides numerous benefits for its subjects. Most important of these is the avoidance of civil war, the "greatest incommodity." But the state also offers defense against foreign enemies, safety for its subjects, peace at home, wealth, and prosperity. Moreover, subjects are free to enjoy what he calls "harmless liberties." Hobbes is quite clear in noting that complete liberty is absurd as it would reestablish a state of nature. People would be free to do whatever their strength and wits permitted. Thus, the only liberty that is possible is that in which regulated action is permitted: the liberty to buy, to sell, to contract, to raise one's children and such other liberties as are not restricted by laws.[6]

Nevertheless, Hobbes's state has its limits. For example, he argues that states should share their tax burden equally (in the interests of peace). Too many laws are deemed undesirable. All who break the laws should be punished in the same ways. Counsels who give undesired advice should not be punished. Judges must not be corrupt, but must understand the principal law of nature: equity. They must hold hearings before sentencing, divest themselves of passions, and not punish the innocent. One must be able to sue anyone—even the sovereign if he breaks his own laws. Finally, no one may be expected to obey commands that would lead to eternal damnation or that would do ill to oneself. Therefore, one cannot be made to testify against oneself. One can even run away in fear of death or punishment, although this behavior may be deemed dishonorable. But actual states are not perfect. Hobbes's state is no utopia. Hobbes notes that states, like mechanical inventions, require time to perfect.

In contrast to the relations among persons within a state, states themselves are in a state of nature. Thus, contracts between states—in the form of treaties, alliances, agreements—are invalid as there is no means of enforcing them. Moreover, unlike humans, states are not equal; some are far more powerful than others.

Nevertheless, despite his emphasis on the role of individuals, Hobbes was not a psychological egoist. He argued that men were motivated by self-interest, but not all men at all times. Thus, most men will obey the law at any given time, while a few will not. It is because of this few that the state is necessary.

It should also be noted that, although Hobbes argued that nothing in his work was contrary to the word of God, to good manners, or to civil order, his books were banned by both Oxford and the Anglican church. So irritating was his work that a bill introduced in the House of Commons to ban atheism and profaneness specifically mentioned his work. Happily for Hobbes, it did not pass the House of Lords; as a result he was spared from punishment. But the furor he aroused through his work was hardly limited to England. French Catholics were equally angered by *Leviathan* as it challenged the authority of the church.

Conclusion

In sum, Hobbes attempted to resolve the problem of order by simultaneously inventing both the calculating citizen and the modern concepts of power, interest, and politics (Latour 1993). Hobbes's citizens are calculating both in the sense of operating in the market where mathematical calculation is essential as well as in their use of reasoned action to attain their personal ends (cf. Replogle 1987). As Dennis Wrong (1994) has observed, they are undersocialized; they are so self-interested that only a coercive state will hold them together. Hobbes's sovereigns have enormous moral power—the very power to determine what is good and what is evil. Yet, ironically, while Hobbes preached obedience to the sovereign, he denied to the sovereigns of his day the justification they so greatly desired (MacPherson 1985). Moreover, for Hobbes, nature and society are fully separate while both are removed from the divine world.

SMITH: THE MORALITY OF THE MARKETPLACE

This system, with all of its oppositions and tensions, comprises Smith's solution to the problem of order, or of the organization and control of the economic system.

—Warren J. Samuels, "The Political Economy of Adam Smith"

Like Bacon and Hobbes before him, Smith (1723?–1790) was also concerned with the problem of order, but Smith rejected the paths already taken. Smith believed that new technology would improve the lot of humankind, but he saw nothing in it that would tend toward either order or disorder. It was simply not of much concern to him. On the other hand, Smith certainly saw a role—indeed, a strong one—for the state, although not the autocratic one envisioned by Hobbes. Yet, however necessary to Smith's approach, neither technology nor the state had the capacity to resolve the problem of order. That role was to be reserved for the market.

When Smith wrote in the eighteenth century, Britain was already a market society. What Bacon had hardly foreseen and what Hobbes had only vaguely envisioned was a reality by the time that Smith began his career. This new form of society was already seen by Smith and his contemporaries as the normal, natural type of human organization. Yet, it needed philosophical grounding both to legitimate it and to ensure that justice prevailed. It was this task that Smith set out for himself.

The Social Nature of Morality

Smith was a key figure among a group who have come to be known as the Scottish Moral Philosophers. A key theme uniting this group was that people are not born human, but derive their humanity from society itself. Thus, Thomas Reid argued that only by virtue of their social life are people more than mere biological organisms. For him, individuals raised outside society would be incapable of exercising any form of moral judgment or reason. Similarly, Francis Hutcheson maintained that human care of and concern for others was learned through contact with society. And Adam Ferguson argued that humankind exists only through the social; without it the very concept of humanity made no sense.

For Smith, too, most human traits are derived from interaction with society. In particular, Smith argued that human conscience itself is social in its origins. Like Hume and Hutcheson before him, Smith argued that through society each person was provided with a conscience. That conscience took the form of an "impartial spectator" found inside each of us. Unlike ourselves as agents, who may act impulsively on the basis of passion, this spectator maintains a certain level of objectivity, of distance from action. As such, argues Smith, it provides us with sympathy for others, an ability to understand their plight. It is the (almost) incorruptible policeman inside us who prevents us from wronging others, who makes us strive to be virtuous, or who tells us we are guilty even when others are unaware of our guilt.

In some ways Smith's impartial spectator is the forerunner of the symbolic interactionism of George Herbert Mead (Shott 1976). Smith's impartial spectator appears much like Mead's "me." But, as we shall see below, although Smith argued that we are socialized into society (to use a modern term and not Smith's), he failed to note an important implication of this view: that any extant society must be therefore the result of previous social interaction. This led Smith to naturalize the institutions and individualized behavior he saw around him at the same time as he maintained the social character of morality and ethics.

The mode of production also played a pivotal role in Smith's philosophical framework. He believed that each mode of production—hunting and gathering, herding, settled agriculture, and industrial society—had its own division of labor, its own technologies (each building on those of previous generations), and its own moral sentiments. Observing his own time, Smith noted that, unlike a century or two earlier, there were substantial numbers of different occupations, each occupying a specialized niche. He saw the origin of this division of labor in a natural propensity to truck and barter, thus reading into history the unique characteristics of the market society of his day. The object of this bartering was also naturalized as the motivation of men to better their condition by increasing their fortune (Hirschman 1977). But this posed enormous problems for Smith, for how could people not living in small villages, not in face-to-face contact with each other daily, learn to behave morally? Would not the vast scale of industrial societies create the conditions for the collapse of moral order? Smith's answers to these questions can be found in his two greatest works. Let us examine each of them in turn.

Moral Sentiments

Unlike Bacon and Hobbes, Smith began his career by examining in great detail the place of morality in his system of order. In *The Theory of Moral Sentiments* ([1759] 1982) Smith attempts to derive the phenomena of the moral world from a single principle in a manner resembling that of Newton's derivation of the principle of gravity (Raphael and Macfie 1982). Smith begins with the Stoic teaching that life should be lived according to nature. But he interprets this as meaning conformity to natural law. Indeed, Raphael and Macfie argue that "ethics for him implied a 'natural jurisprudence,' and his economic theories arose out of, indeed were originally part of, his lectures on jurisprudence" (1982:8).

In a manner somewhat reminiscent of Hobbes, Smith argues that the first task required of us by nature is self-preservation. But unlike Hobbes, who sees only isolated individuals, Smith sees social beings who are able to place themselves in others' shoes. Thus, sympathy is the means by which social control is maintained. Sympathy, as expressed through the impartial spectator, causes people to control their potentially offensive actions in two ways: (1) by imagining what it would be like to be the recipient of those actions and (2) by causing us to avoid the disapproval of others. Thus, judgments of our own conduct always refer to the (implicit) feelings of some other human being. Put differently, for Smith sympathy permits us to retain an objective view of our situation, to get outside ourselves so to speak.

Like symbolic interactionists Charles Horton Cooley and George Herbert Mead a century later, Smith starts with the child who must be educated such that the social self emerges. Smith even notes that small children lack the ability to recognize others' views of them. As the impartial spectator develops, children learn to view themselves as others see them. They acquire a form of objectivity about their own situation. But, in a certain sense, Smith goes beyond the symbolic interactionists for he puts sympathetic *feelings* at the center of his analysis. Thus, both rational and affective behavior are governed by the impartial spectator, a social product.

Like earlier thinkers from Machiavelli to Hobbes, Smith reserved the passions to the wealthy, who, freed from material concerns, could afford to let their passions run wild. In contrast, ordinary men were far more concerned with their material improvement. Yet, like Hobbes, Smith believed that all men were motivated by vanity. Indeed, the quest for material improvement—an instrument of vanity—was for him reinforced by all the noneconomic passions. Power, ambition, even respect, could be obtained through economic improvement.[7] The passions would be expressed in the desire for things that belonged to others—a uniquely human capacity. As such, the passions could be kept under control if a means were devised to pit them against the interests (Hirschman 1977).

The key, then, was to establish a society in which social order would be maintained by encouraging respect for the rich and powerful. This could only be accomplished by subordinating the passions to moral rules, by developing socially acceptable norms of conduct that could be enforced by some superior authority. How this would come about would await his second and much more empirical major work, *An Inquiry into the Nature and Causes of the Wealth of Nations*.

The Wealth of Nations

While the *Moral Sentiments* attacked the problem of order from the vantage point of the feelings and behavior of individuals, the *Wealth of Nations* (Smith [1776] 1994) complemented it by attacking the problem as one at the level of the nation-state. As Hirschman (1977) has observed, the *Wealth of Nations* established a powerful justification for the pursuit of economic self-interest. For Smith, feudalism was a period of continual war, ending only when the widespread rise of commerce introduced order. Thus, the problem that Smith sets out for himself is to understand how commerce produces order and how that order both can be made more widespread and can be improved. Therefore, the *Wealth of Nations* is not a volume of abstract theory; indeed, it is a detailed empirical account of the situation of his time together with a series of suggestions for improving it (cf. Thompson 1971). But Smith is no utopian. He is ambivalent toward capitalism. His institutions are neither inevitable nor the culmination of human improvement. Instead, they are subject to change and redesign (Samuels 1977).

As is well-known, central to Smith's vision is a market economy. The market economy breaks domestic linkages and replaces them with those of the market. The market, unlike the state or science, is a mechanism that permits the establishment of order without the need for elaborate central direction. Consider the premisses on which Smith builds his market economy: First, he assumes that all individuals have the same desire for exchange. Second, what people want to exchange is not the result of individual preferences; if such were the case, then each might desire something different. Instead, for Smith exchange is the result of copying the tastes of others. This is the case because through the impartial spectator we see ourselves as others see us. In particular, Smith notes that those things desired by the wealthy are wanted by the poor as well, because the poor wish not to be seen to be poor. Moreover, the things desired are rare, so competition to obtain them ensues. But note that the competition of which Smith speaks is a kind of perpetual independent striving, not that of many producers each with a small share of the market (Scherer 1970). Such competition does not lead to ruin, but to perpetual progress. Thus, rather than being concerned with utility, Smith is concerned with order. As Samuels puts it, "The market is *above all* an institutional mechanism to compel men to pursue self-interest in social rather than anti-social ways" (1977:196; emphasis in original).

Nevertheless, Smith claims that his invisible hand also ensures that markets actually give people that which they desire. As long as competition is atomistic, Smith argues that markets will provide people with the goods they want at a low price and in the proper quantity.

However, this does not eliminate the need for power. Indeed, for Smith the economy, like the state, is a system of power. Moreover, "market order is achieved only within the structure of power" (ibid.:192). To the extent that it works as it should, the price system itself is coercive; it ties self-interest to the social good. In addition, the market must be regulated by the state, whose role is to support the market's moral framework. The state must ensure that competition is atomistic. It must prohibit certain social relations that otherwise would form by banning professional associations and corporations. The state must provide public goods such as roads, bridges, and canals. It must set a legal framework for the protection of private property and the rule of law.[8]

Conclusions

Far from being an ideologue, as he has been painted by contemporary proponents of the free market, Smith was searching for the means to better order society. He wished to tame the passions, to increase the likelihood of peace and prosperity. He was not concerned with optimality, with partial equilibria, with laissez-faire, or with utility (Coase 1976). These ideas were developed later by other economists. He was not an apologist for the bourgeoisie; furthermore, he rejected the corporate world as an abomination.

Smith firmly believed that if the state produced the right preconditions, the market would serve to produce order. Yet, as Robert Heilbroner (1961) has remarked, "The *Wealth of Nations* is a program for action, not a blueprint for Utopia." Thus, Smith's system allows considerable future institutional tinkering so as to produce a more just and a more well-ordered society, a society in which the passions will be more fully subordinated to the interests.

Yet, Smith's insistence on the need to remove all restrictions from the trade in corn (grain) seemed to justify the repeal of laws that set aside grain for the poor (Thompson 1971). Less than twenty years after he wrote the *Wealth of Nations* (a caricature of) his view of the market was so taken for granted that philosopher Edmund Burke could rail against "an indiscreet tampering with the trade of provisions" so as to feed the hungry. For Burke, "the moment that government appears at market, all the principles of market will be subverted" ([1795] 1881:154). A half century later, the sacrosanct character of the market would be so unassailable as to permit the British government to let a million Irish die (see Chapter 4).

THREE PATHS TO ORDER; THREE PATHS
FROM MORAL RESPONSIBILITY

In short, Bacon, Hobbes, and Smith provide us with three paths to social order. Each in his own way attempted to solve the riddle of social order by providing an organizing principle. For Bacon science and technology will produce order by telling us what is natural and, hence, right. Politics will become administration, with administrators obeying the natural laws revealed by the scientists. For Hobbes the monarch will tell us what to do. Order will be imposed by a social contract that somewhat arbitrarily grants the king the power to impose order. For Smith a properly designed marketplace will produce order by balancing the passions and the interests. Order will emerge out of the strivings of atomized individuals, each competing to gain the most wealth in the marketplace.

Paradoxically, all three succeeded in simultaneously creating both autonomous individuals and Leviathans. If Bacon and Hobbes saw individuals as autonomous and in need of a Leviathan (science or the state) to watch over them, Smith saw individuals as in need of *being made* autonomous such that the Leviathan of the market would tame the passions. Together, they instantiated individualism in (at least) three ways:

1.   Political Individualism.   Hobbes was convinced that only a monarch could ensure stability for the state, for in a monarchy private and public interests would be identical. But he left the door open for democratic or aristocratic regimes. Indeed, his only point of difference with modern representative democracies was his assertion that the Leviathan select his or its own successor. While the Western democracies and (with few exceptions) their Eastern imitators have rejected the self-perpetuating Leviathan of which Hobbes wrote, representative democracy in effect cedes one's decision-making in the political sphere to others. These others act on behalf of the electorate, but like Hobbes's monarch, follow their own conscience. Once elected, the electorate can rest easy knowing that someone else will shoulder the moral burden. James Madison (1751–1836), one of the founders of the American republic, knew what he said when he noted that the United States was to be a republic and not a democracy (Madison, Hamilton, and Jay [1778] 1966). Moreover, each member of the electorate is now one of many equal political beings whose attitudes can be measured in opinion polls, but whose individuality fades into mass politics.

In this world of political individualism, scientists act, much as Bacon suggested, as advisors to the state, revealing what the world of nature has to say. They engage in the apolitical politics of expertise. They claim to provide answers to the political questions of the day, sometimes manipulating the politicians and sometimes being manipulated by them.

2.   Economic Individualism.   Whether the product of a state of nature or an atomizing market, "Economic Man" is a rational, calculating individual who only enters into relationships as necessary to further his own ends. His worth is determined by the marketplace, over which he has little or no control: "The *Value*, or WORTH of a man, is as of all other things, his Price; that is to say, so much as would be given for the use of his Power" (Hobbes [1651] 1991:63). As a worker he cedes his rights to the corporate Leviathan—the corporate CEO in whose name he works. Though he may be a citizen, his rights as a citizen end at the door to the workplace.

As consumers, we are equally individualized. But "consumption is less a refuge of personal freedom in an organized society, and more a system of values, a site for social control" (Mcintyre 1992:53). Consumption has become a duty, more a rite than a right. Not only are sales relationships increasingly depersonalized and anonymous; consumers are becoming actively involved in the work necessary to permit consumption. At supermarkets and discount stores we obediently collect the goods and place them in shopping carts and on conveyor belts. As patrons at fast food restaurants, we stand in line to be served and we bus our own dishes. At automated teller machines, we pay for the privilege of entering the digits into the bank's computers. In addition, as consumers, we are (re)assured in knowing that the Leviathan of the market, Smith's invisible hand, will produce, as Jeremy Bentham (1748–1832) suggested somewhat later, the greatest good for the greatest number. In both cases, as workers and as consumers, we are massified, anonymous, interchangeable, equal.

3. *Social Individualism.* We have also come to perceive ourselves as isolated individuals. Age-old traditions have come apart at the seams. Where once we were born into traditions, we can now choose which traditions we will follow. Or we can invent new traditions and just as easily abandon them. The nuclear family separates the generations, and even the nuclear family is hardly stable. Divorce rates in many nations are rising. Age segregation separates parents from children.

Moreover, the products of the science that Bacon envisioned surround us now. The modern automobile, air conditioned, sound-proofed, silent, with stereo music piped in, creates a wall between its occupant and the rest of the world. The high-rise apartment buildings of our cities as well as the private homes of our suburbs create and even encourage anonymity. Shopping malls replace the disorder of downtown. At the mall one only meets nice people. There are no vagrants, no sideshows, no street vendors. There is no violence, no passion. There is nothing to disturb the sound of money changing hands.

Similarly, chain stores ensure a certain stability by reassuring the anonymous customer that the products on display and the service provided in one store will be much the same as those in every other store. Television allows one to view the entire world as a spectator. But unlike spectacles of old, the spectacles of television demand no commitment. Indeed, even as they bring wars to our living rooms, for us they produce no disorder or violence, only indifference. If they become distasteful, they can be easily dismissed by turning off the set. All of this and more reinforces one's feelings and action as an isolated, atomized individual subject to an impenetrable, reified social structure. Social relations are reduced to instrumental rationality (Habermas 1971), to pure calculation.

Yet, for all their differences, Bacon, Hobbes, and Smith agreed on several things. They were all weak constructivists; they saw society as a social product subject to reform and renegotiation. Yet, while they each rejected the old order, they accepted hierarchy as natural. They also agreed that the solution to the problem of order lay in intellectual activity, not in demo-cratic discourse. They each claimed to have found a singular, unique, and logical solution to the problem of order, although they disagreed on just what that was. Finally, even as they attempted to develop moral, ordered, and affluent societies, they believed that moral responsibility was too dan-gerous to be left in the hands of ordinary people. Of course, moral duties to God and family were left intact by each of them (although Hobbes did suggest that the family must also have its own "monarch"). But God and family in both their philosophical systems and in actual practice were in-creasingly restricted to the realm of the private. In a Protestant world, re-ligious belief could no longer be the province of the state; both Protestants and Catholics would be compelled to practice toleration. Even Hobbes, who argued strongly for a state religion, admitted that individuals could not be compelled to believe. Furthermore, in the modern world, medieval notions of fealty were limited to the family. Thus, the family, too, was rel-egated to the private sphere.

But this left a huge lacuna. If moral responsibility was confined to the private sphere, what would hold society together? The apparent solution was to find some *external* force that would ensure moral order. Bacon ap-pealed to nature, Hobbes to the stick, and Smith to the carrot. Each was quite willing—indeed, eager—to relieve individuals of most moral responsibili-ty so as to achieve moral and social order. Virtually all moral responsibility beyond God and family was shifted to nature, the state, or the market. Put differently, the age-old link between morality and order was severed.

But the theories of Bacon, Hobbes, and Smith did not remain theories. Since they described and prescribed simultaneously, they were both mate-rialized in the world and provided rhetorical icons that could be drawn on when necessary, even when the names of Bacon, Hobbes, and Smith were no longer conscious memories for those drawing on them. In several of the chapters that follow, I shall attempt to provide a series of examples of how the ideas initially described/prescribed by these men were developed, modified, transmuted, and materialized.

Of course, lived history is far more complex than any story that I (or anyone else) might recount here. Each story of the Baconian legacy might be retold as a Hobbesian or Smithian tale. For example, I have chosen to re-count the history of the Soviet Union as a Baconian narrative where Soviet statism and suppression of markets form a backdrop to untrammeled faith in science and technology. But another writer might well have empha-sized the importance of the state or recounted the numerous failed attempts to establish markets. There are several reasons for this. First, proponents of scientism, statism, and marketism have failed (and I believe will contin-ue to fail) to force the world into the box provided by the theory. The more they have tried, the greater the resistance they have encountered. Thus, no pure instances of science, state, or market exist. Second, logic-in-use is not the same as reconstructed logic (Kaplan 1964). When I do something, I may have certain ends in mind. When asked to justify it later, I may refer to an entirely different and far less messy set of ends. Thus, a politician might condemn a particular person because she or he sees that person as a personal threat. When asked to justify the action, however, an appeal might be made to nature, to the state, or to the market. As a result, no person and no institution can be fully consistent with any particular system of ordering in all aspects of life. Finally, historians present different narratives because they ask different questions. Some ask who the great men were. Others ask how daily life was lived. Still others focus on politics or economics. The question I pose in the three chapters below is as follows: How and with what consequences did the perspectives so brilliantly described by Bacon, Hobbes, and Smith, respectively, become institutionalized in various places at various times? Let us begin by examining the legacy of Bacon.

NOTES

1. As Keller (1985) has noted, Bacon's work is replete with sexual imagery, nearly all of which emphasizes the domination of both women and nature.
2. Bacon argues that while anyone can use the method, the common man cannot fully understand the results, "since they cannot be brought down to the common man's comprehension, except through their effects and works" ([1620] 1994:129).
3. One might argue that knowledge, morals, and action are facets of the same problem: that of maintaining order in society. For Hobbes it is necessary to define what shall count as knowledge, what shall be considered good, and what actions people shall take. Hobbes argues that a Leviathan is necessary to define each. See MacPherson's (1985) introduction to the *Leviathan* for a review of Hobbes's logic.
4. It is astonishing to the modern reader that Hobbes seems unaware of the numerous metaphors that he uses to make his case.
5. In this matter Hobbes was in full agreement with most of his contemporaries. As Shapin and Schaffer note, "At the Restoration it seemed clear that all free debate bred civil strife. It seemed less plausible that some forms of free debate might produce knowledge which could prevent that strife" (1985:290).
6. MacPherson (1962) has argued that Hobbes's state is a fundamentally capitalist state. Whether or not this is the case, it is certainly clear that Hobbes's views were fully compatible with capitalist understandings of states and markets.
7. Note how modern this idea is. In the Middle Ages power and respect derived from rank, not riches.
8. At the same time, it should be noted that Smith was well aware that state power could corrupt. He wished not a minimal state but a limit on state power. And even a limited state would not necessarily deliver humankind from war (Hirschman 1977).

Reprinted with permission of the Special Collections Library, University of Michigan.

2

THE TECHNOLOGY OF POWER AND
THE POWER OF TECHNOLOGY

The conclusions of natural science are true and necessary, and the judgement of man has nothing to do with them.

—Galileo *(quoted in Jerome Ravetz,* Scientific Knowledge and Its Social Problems*)*

Modern science . . . is a threat to democracy, the quality of human life, and even the very capacity of our planet to support life at all.

—Sal Restivo, *"Modern Science as a Social Problem"*

The Baconian view of technology soon became the accepted wisdom, although the claim that it would allow one to better know God's works soon faded into the background. Science rapidly became an end in itself, a substitute for moral reflection, a justification for all sorts of radical upheaval designed, ironically, to create order. Consider the thoughts of some of its main proponents through the centuries.

Andrew Ure, self-proclaimed apologist for the factory system, noted:

> The blessings which physico-mechanical science has bestowed on society, and the means it has still in store for ameliorating the lot of mankind, have been too little dwelt upon; while, on the other hand, it has been accused of lending itself to the rich capitalists as an instrument for harassing the poor, and of exacting from the operative an accelerated rate of work. (1835:6–7)

According to Ure, by embracing science, all manual labor would be eliminated. The tasks of workers would be reduced to "the exercise of vigilance and dexterity" (p. 21). For Ure, the ten-hour day would infringe on the rights of workers to work as they saw fit. Moreover, it would intervene in the transformative progress of science.

Furthermore, if Ure was concerned to justify the factory system through science, Charles Babbage, inventor of the analog computer, attempted to make the case for large-scale government funding for it. In his 1830 volume *Reflections on the Decline of Science in England and Some of Its Causes*

33

([1830] 1970), Babbage explained the importance of "abstract" scientific advance as a means for economic growth. He further noted that instruments could be used to do away with judgments. A few years later, Babbage noted how machines could be used to do away with inattention, idleness, and even dishonesty. But, in an ironic twist to Ure's view, he also noted that strikes had the desirable effect of advancing technological improvements, thus strengthening national industry (Babbage 1835).

Moreover, if all the phenomena in the world could be explained by technoscience,[1] then all human differences could be explained in the same way. Not many years later technoscience would be used to justify slavery, racism, and colonial empires. Africans, native Americans, Indians, and Asians were clearly inferior to Europeans. They sorely needed the paternal hand of the West, which would Christianize them, make them into good (read "easily exploited") trading partners, and integrate them into the grand European plan of the Enlightenment. This contrasts markedly with earlier accounts. For example, the Dutch sailors who arrived in Benin about 1660 described the city in glowing terms (Dapper [1660] 1975). Somewhat later, Cadwallader Colden ([1727] 1902), the lieutenant governor of the Province of New York, praised the five Indian nations of New England for their wisdom and government. Soon after the British conquered India, European travelers there told of its wonders.

Indeed, they had good reason to marvel at some of the products of the civilizations they encountered. For example, Chinese science and technology had furnished Europe with porcelain, gunpowder, the magnetic compass, and printing. Moreover, it had produced a highly productive agriculture capable of continuous cultivation over centuries without soil degradation. India developed the number system currently used around the world (often mistakenly identified as of Arabic origin) and with it major advances in geometry as well as algebra. Indian astronomers mathematized planetary motion long before Galileo. China and India both made contributions to the technologies of ocean sailing as well as to medicine (e.g., Goonatilake 1982). Furthermore, members of all the societies conquered by Europeans had intimate knowledge of the flora, fauna, geography, climate, and other conditions of their regions. Europeans quickly appropriated this knowledge while rarely acknowledging its importance. Yet, in many cases, without such knowledge, Europeans would not have survived in the conquered lands at all (Crosby 1986). All this had to be suppressed for the myth of European superiority to flourish.

But once established by science, the alleged inferiority of non-Europeans was used to justify genocide and laws prohibiting or limiting formal education. Nor were colonized peoples the only ones to be deemed inferior and condemned to second-class status. The handicapped, homosexuals, and women were all "demonstrably" inferior. Indeed, well past the middle of the twentieth century, racial and ethnic inferiority was preached and taken seriously. Even today, pseudoscience such as *The Bell Curve* (Herrnstein and Murray 1994) is taken seriously in certain quarters.[2]

THE UNITED STATES

Unlike the nations of Europe, the United States enshrined invention in its founding constitution. Among the powers specifically granted to Congress was "to promote the Progress of Science and useful Arts, by securing for limited Times to Authors and Inventors the exclusive Right to their respective Writings and Discoveries" (Article 8.8). Although the founders were not of one mind with respect to rewards for discovery, there was widespread agreement that scientific progress and technical change were desirable for the new republic.[3] Benjamin Franklin (1706–1790) was convinced that experimental science should be made to serve the public good (Campbell 1999). Franklin's experiments with electricity as well as his inventions of stoves and chairs have become virtual founding myths of the nation. Jane Colden, daughter of Cadwallader Colden, compiled the first botanical codex of North American plants. Others, such as Jefferson, were equally keen on invention. The new republic was envisioned as part of the newly emergent republic of science.

Moreover, from the first days of the republic, the link between scientific understanding and technical development was established. The case of Oliver Evans (1755–1819) is illustrative. Evans was responsible for inventing the first continuous-flow flour mill in 1783. His mill used all three types of continuous conveyors: belts, screws, and bucket chains. It drastically reduced labor needs at the same time as it reduced waste. It was soon widely adopted— in part because Evans's patent claims were largely ignored—and remained the standard for flour mills until the invention of roller milling in the 1880s.

Of particular note was that Evans felt compelled to write *The Young Mill-Wright and Miller's Guide* (1795), a 440-page, self-financed book of which fully 140 pages were an explanation of Newtonian mechanics. Clearly, Evans did not see the science as a mere afterthought but as central to his technological innovations. The use of science in this manner served him well as he invented a high-pressure steam engine that became the model for nineteenth-century factories and a steam-powered wagon (that was too heavy for the poor roads of the day) (Ferguson 1980). Nor was Evans alone in his belief that theoretical knowledge and practical application were intimately linked. In 1830 the Franklin Institute engaged in a detailed study of the relative efficiency of waterwheels. British commissions visiting the United States in the 1850s were impressed by the theoretical knowledge of American mechanics (Reich 1985).

Moreover, Evans's invention took assembly line technology, already in existence for several hundred years in other industries, to its logical conclusion. It shifted the production process from one in which manual labor was used to aid the machine to full automation, where workers are machine tenders. As further described below, his work paved the way for later innovations both in assembly line technology (Ford) and in scientific management (Taylor) (Giedion [1948] 1975).

By the mid–nineteenth century, Americans had established an unshakable faith in scientific progress: "Everyone invented, whoever owned an enterprise sought ways and means by which to make his goods more speedily, more perfectly, and often of improved beauty" (ibid.:40). By 1875 the Pennsylvania Railroad had hired a PhD chemist to check the quality of the materials it purchased. Three decades later the chemistry staff had jumped to thirty-four (Reich 1985).

However, by the late nineteenth century, the United States was no longer a fully agrarian society. The granting of huge tracts of land to the railroads during the Civil War—an area fully as large as England and France combined—had contributed to the rise of large-scale industry. The war itself, bringing demands for mass-produced arms and uniforms, also transformed the nation. By the last quarter of the century many of the problems long apparent in Europe were beginning to be felt in the United States as well. Farmers and workers were beginning to challenge the newfound wealth of the robber barons (Josephson 1962) by becoming populists or socialists.

Science and organization appeared to many to provide both an explanation and the antidote to the ills of the time. The passage of the Hatch Act in 1887 provided funds to each of the states to establish agricultural experiment stations. This was the first large-scale infrastructure for research of any kind in the United States. It was justified on the grounds that problems on the farm could be resolved by science. Several attempts were made to create engineering experiment stations as well, but these failed as opponents argued that industry had the resources to do its own research.

Of greater ideological significance, if of less practical value, was the embracing of what came to be known as Social Darwinism. Central to that movement was sociologist Herbert Spencer (1820–1903). Social Darwinism "offered a comprehensive world-view, uniting under one generalization everything in nature from protozoa to politics. Satisfying the desire of 'advanced thinkers' for a world-system to replace the shattered Mosaic cosmogony, it soon gave Spencer a public influence that transcended Darwin's" (Hofstadter 1955:31). Although Spencer was English, his works were serialized in the newly founded *Popular Science*. Spencer soon became an American household word. In popularizing the notion of "survival of the fittest," Spencer combined the invisible hand of Smith with the natural selection of Darwin. He argued that competition was the natural order of things from micro-organisms all the way to business enterprises: He further argued that change must be slow; revolutions or sweeping reforms would veer off the evolutionary course. "The process cannot be abridged; and must be gone through with due patience" (Spencer 1906:367). Even state intervention in the economy was viewed as dangerous (Spencer 1890). Indeed, in his *The Man Versus the State* ([1916] 1945), he provided both a classic libertarian account of freedom and an amazingly accurate view of the results of state socialism. Even moral decisions could be gleaned from a proper reading of the evolutionary process.[4] Thus, Spencer argued against government relief for the poor on the grounds that it merely allowed the unfit to live longer. In contrast, private charity was acceptable as it built the character of the giver.

Conveniently, Spencer's views justified the newly ascendant business establishment. The authority of employers could now be justified on the basis of their success in business. Soon, Andrew Carnegie (1835–1919) became his most ardent admirer (Peel 1971). John D. Rockefeller, Sr. (1839–1937), was quick to pick up on Spencerian terminology: "The growth of business is merely a survival of the fittest" (quoted in Hofstadter 1955:45). But Rockefeller disagreed with Spencer when it came to free competition. Like Karl Marx, Rockefeller believed that competition would lead to either ruin or monopoly, and clearly monopoly was a far more comfortable position in which to be. [Of course, Marx saw monopoly as a mere way station on the road to socialism. To Rockefeller, it was large-scale private planning units that would best manage the economy instead—units such as his beloved Standard Oil (Chernow 1998)].

Rockefeller was very much part of what came to be known as the Progressive era. He was firmly committed to science as the solution to the problems of the day. Although he initially took part in the technical operation of his company, he soon decided to leave that largely to experts. He spent most of his time engaged in financial and administrative matters. As he himself put it, "I never felt the need of scientific knowledge, never have felt it. A young man who wants to succeed in business does not require chemistry or physics. He can always hire scientists" (quoted in Chernow 1998:180). In this respect his position was little different from that of radical economist Thorstein Veblen, whose *Theory of the Leisure Class* (1912) critiqued the class and lifestyle of which Rockefeller was a part. In his *The Engineers and the Price System* (1921), written in the middle of the red scare of 1919, Veblen suggested that Rockefeller was indeed right: Engineers were the ones in charge of the day-to-day operation of industry. Therefore, Veblen reasoned, if the engineers so desired they could summarily dispose of the "absentee ownership" and claim the factories for the public good. A

Council of Engineers, a "Soviet of technicians," would oversee the full employment of both people and resources. The engineers would plan to use the most advanced production methods to create an abundance of everything, rather than controlling supply as monopolists did. While this might not occur in the immediate future, there was little doubt in Veblen's mind that it would surely happen soon. In sum, both Veblen and Rockefeller saw technical progress as necessary and apolitical. They merely disagreed as to who should control it.

Rockefeller's commitment to science and organization was perhaps nowhere more apparent than in his choice of philanthropic projects. The General Education Board would provide funds to teach farmers to farm scientifically. It would also reform medical education to make it more scientific (ironically driving out the homeopaths that Rockefeller himself used). The Rockefeller Institute would finance medical research so as to eliminate epidemic diseases. The same would hold true for the Rockefeller Foundation: "Like the family's other philanthropies, the Rockefeller Foundation was attuned to the optimistic, rational spirit of the Progressive era and drew on its new class of technocrats. Science would be the magic wand waved over any project to show that it was sound and objective, free of favoritism or self-interest" (Chernow 1998:568). I shall say more about these projects below. Suffice it to note here that none of his philanthropies would encourage that dreaded dependence of which Spencer and others warned. The process of evolution would go on, but with a little help from its friends.

Business interest in science and technology was hardly limited to Spencerian theories. Of equal or perhaps greater interest was the use of science and technology to spur industrial progress. By the late 1880s, Arthur D. Little was already telling companies of the importance of science-based inventions. Moreover, the passage of antitrust laws made industrial innovation an attractive goal for the control of the market, which was no longer accomplishable by other means. As a result, industrial research laboratories were created by many of the larger corporations. Among the first was that established at Menlo Park by Thomas Edison. Edison believed that he could routinize research and regularize invention. He saw his electric lamp as not only technically, but morally and aesthetically superior to gas lamps (ibid.).

Soon large research labs were established at General Electric and Bell (later American Telephone and Telegraph or ATT). Both companies established large programs in physics and chemistry as applied to particular products and processes including telephony, radio, electric lighting, and electron tube technology. General Electric also rapidly established linkages with appropriate departments at the Massachusetts Institute of Technology. In both cases, attorneys peered over the shoulders of scientists quickly patenting anything that might keep competitors out of the picture. By 1920, nearly a quarter of the articles in *Physical Reviews* were authored by industry scientists (Reich 1985).

Nor was science to be used merely to create technologies. It would also transform the organization of work. Frederick Winslow Taylor (1856–1915) was an engineer whose science of industrial efficiency was a page ripped right out of Bacon. Although Taylor was oblivious to the mind-numbing effects of his approach to work, it would be a mistake to see him as merely the lackey of the elites. Indeed, throughout his life, Taylor saw his work as emancipatory. As Taylor himself put it, "In the future it will be appreciated that our leaders must be trained right as well as born right, and that no great man can (with the old system of personal management) hope to compete with a number of ordinary men who have been properly organized so as efficiently to cooperate" (1911:6–7). If Taylor was an apologist for anyone, it was for the engineering and managerial classes.

Taylor's grand idea was that the interests of employers and employees were really the same. All wished to maximize income. What was required was a competent engineer to show them how to do so by coordinating their activities in a harmonious manner. The solemn duty of the engineer—as manager of things and people—was to replace the rule of thumb used in industrial production.[5] The single most efficient way to produce things would be revealed by scientific methods. Workers would be studied as if they were machines so as to determine the best way to accomplish their tasks. Work would be rearranged as a result of time and motion studies, output would soar, and prosperity would not be far behind. Workers would be paid more and company profits would climb as well. Thus, unions and collective bargaining could be dispensed with. Class conflict would end. Science would determine what constituted a fair day's work.

Nor was Taylor alone in his newfound stress on efficiency. The conservation movement of that time shared many of the same beliefs. The conservation movement was closely linked to the major engineering societies; its proponents consisted largely of scientists and engineers (Hays 1959). Conservationists argued for the development of management tools that would permit extracting a maximum sustainable yield from nature. Their views contrasted greatly with those of preservationists. For example, naturalist John Muir (1838–1914) wished the government to preserve certain natural areas from development *of any kind*. In contrast, prominent conservationists such as Gifford Pinchot (1865–1946), first director of the Forest Service, encouraged logging as long as enough trees were replanted to ensure that forests could be harvested and rangelands grazed indefinitely. Moreover, while Muir and his supporters emphasized government intervention to protect the aesthetic beauty of the wilderness, Pinchot wanted government control in order to protect against unbridled growth. The end result was the creation of two separate governmental units in two different departments: The National Park Service in the Department of the Interior and the (much larger) Forest Service in the Department of Agriculture.

At the time, Pinchot's position played well with President Theodore Roosevelt. "The President, Pinchot, and Garfield[6] carried their interests in efficiency into a variety of fields other than natural resources. They emphasized, for example, the value of large-scale business organization, and warned that anti-trust action might impair increased production" (Hays 1959:126). But Pinchot was quite willing to challenge whoever might detract from his quest for efficient use of forest resources. Laissez-faire strategies were as unacceptable to him as the inefficiencies of the large trusts. He advocated public control over cutting on *private* lands. Finally, he was fired by President Howard Taft as a result of his challenge to the coal barons. Moreover, his position was soundly rejected by the American Society of Foresters, who were far more sympathetic to the aims of the large trusts than Pinchot (Frome 1971). To the end Pinchot staunchly believed that "this union of research and administration underlies the progress of forestry and the morale and efficiency of the Service. To separate the two would ruin the Service" (quoted in Schiff 1962:2–3).

The nexus of science, organization, and efficiency is also apparent in the work of the Country Life Commission. The Commission's Report ([1909] 1911) was arguably the principal statement of a group consisting mainly of agricultural scientists that historian David Danbom (1979) has dubbed the "urban agrarians." Although at the time most Americans were farmers, they were unrepresented on the commission. Moreover, although most farmers of that time produced for the market, they certainly did not see farming as a business and they were not particularly concerned about increasing agricultural productivity.

Perhaps no one summed up the urban agrarian position better than Eugene Davenport, dean of the College of Agriculture at the University of Illinois:

> Many individuals will be crowded out as agriculture exacts more knowledge and skill. . . . The great laws of evolution and the survival of the fittest will continue to operate, and in the interest of progress, they ought to operate. Progress is not in the interest of the individual, and it cannot stop because of individuals. Everything must surrender to the central idea that this is a movement for the highest attainable agriculture in the fullest possible sense of the term. (quoted in Danbom 1979:40)

If Davenport's criticisms of those who were inefficient were oblique, A. F. Woods pulled no punches. In his Presidential Address to the American Association of Land-Grant Colleges in 1925, Woods argued, "The low-grade inefficient farmer who has demonstrated inability to learn and cooperate with others must be eliminated. These produce the surplus by slovenly methods and do most of the howling" (quoted in Hardin 1955:201). In short, the focus on organization and efficiency was portrayed as not merely a particular way of thinking and acting, but as an inherent part of nature itself. Knowing nature provided the clear path to action, the only action that was possible for reasonable people. The disorganized character of country life, the lack of adequate planning, and the ignorance of natural processes were barriers to be overcome through science, education, and administration. Those who did not conform were to be consigned to the dustbin of history.

The Country Life Commission recommended that extension services be provided throughout the nation so as to help farmers become more organized, more scientific, more rational. Business interests, especially bankers who loaned money to farmers, also encouraged the formation of extension services. More efficient and scientifically oriented farmers would repay their loans on time. They would purchase the newly developed farm inputs such as artificial fertilizers, tractors, and improved seeds. Those who refused to adopt the new techniques were often denied credit. Not surprisingly, many farmers were suspicious if not hostile to the self-appointed preachers of what historian Samuel P. Hays (1959) called "the gospel of efficiency."

Paralleling the Country Life Commission was the beginning of agricultural extension work under the Rockefeller-financed General Education Board. Seaman Knapp (1833–1901), an early champion of extension work, quickly aligned himself with business interests to show the effectiveness of the new extension approach. Later, the Smith-Lever Act—supported largely by business and agricultural scientific interests—provided federal funds to help put extension workers in every county in the nation. But unlike virtually all other programs of the federal government, extension programs were to be financed by federal, state, and private funds. Moreover, extension agents soon found that the most effective way to reach farmers was to organize them into groups—groups that soon became known as Farm Bureaus. Not surprisingly, those farmers who shared the urban agrarians' concern for organization and efficiency were the most likely to join the new organizations.

By 1921, the link between extension and the Farm Bureaus had become a national scandal: Government funds were being used to create a private organization. The federal government demanded that the link be severed, but a new lobby group for (wealthier) farmers had already been formed: The American Farm Bureau Federation.[7] The Farm Bureau was more than happy to support the goals of organization and efficiency advocated earlier by the Country Life Commission. In many states, Farm Bureau offices continued to be located in the same buildings as those of various agricultural agencies of the government. Moreover, even in states where resis-

tance to the Farm Bureau was strong, deans of colleges of agriculture tended to be sympathetic to the ideals of organization and efficiency (e.g., see
Beardsley 1969).

Of course, there were critics. Some rural sociologists began to criticize
the Country Life movement. A few scientists complained that there was
more to life than organization and efficiency. For example, in 1933 the
noted pomologist Ulysses P. Hedrick observed:

> There is a flood of literature urging the industrialization of agriculture. From
> it one would glean that the object of life is to obtain efficiency. Some of the
> happiest, most worthy, and most influential farmers in the State are dread-
> fully inefficient. A self-respecting freeman is a more desirable citizen than a
> slave to industry. (quoted in Danbom 1979:143)

Yet, in fact, there was little organized resistance to the technological juggernaut. For most farmers, and certainly most of the nonfarm population,
"the new machines, plants, fertilizers, and all the new developments were
looked on as undiluted goods" (McConnell 1953:14).

Followers of Taylor soon introduced his notions of scientific management to schools, homes, and farms (Jones [1916] 1917). Nutritionists embraced Taylor in their attempts to develop home-cooked meals that were
more nutritious and required less labor (Levenstein 1988). Psychologist
Hugo Munsterberg took Taylor's ideas of management and began to design tests of memory, dexterity, and attention for job applicants (Spring
1972).

In education, school boards and university governing bodies would be
pared down to size and run by businessmen following efficient business
principles. A new class of trained school administrators and educational
leaders would take over from scholars. Knowledge was to be utilitarian,
preparing students for jobs in industry. Elementary and secondary schools
were to be run like factories, their product an endless supply of trained students (Callahan 1962).

The Country Life movement advocated the consolidation of rural
schools, a logical extension of its progressivist position. School consolidation was hardly a new idea, having been voiced as early as the 1850s.
Consolidation, it was claimed, would create great economies in school purchasing and management, help rural schools keep up with their urban
counterparts, provide greater variety for students, improve the quality of
teachers, and (to play on nativist prejudices) keep new immigrants from
taking control of the schools (Rosenfeld and Sher 1977). Virtually no one
contested the claims at the time as they seemed self-evident. Yet, these inflated claims proved largely illusory. The high cost of transportation often
offset any supposed benefits of consolidation. Centralized purchasing
often was accompanied by higher distribution costs. Benefits of small

schools—local control, closer relations with the community, far more students who were able to participate in school events—were never considered by the proponents of consolidation. In short, "by consolidating, rural communities relinquished the advantages of smallness and received little in return" (Sher and Tompkins 1977:75). Although resistance continued throughout the interwar period, by the end of the Second World War, school consolidation was a reality. In short, Taylor and his followers intended to do within the factory, the school, the local government, the home, and the farm precisely what Bacon had proposed doing for the nation-state: factory politics would be replaced by smooth running factory administration. Workers and managers, housewives and students, farmers and government officials would be subordinated to the scientifically organized industrial system.

More recently, Taylor's ideas have been reborn in the fast-food industry. There, Taylor's scientific management is paired with the use of highly sophisticated cooking technologies (but without the higher wages that Taylor recommended). Indeed, as late as 1973 one manual on the food service industry quoted Taylor with admiration (Reiter 1991).

Many of the supporters of the Country Life movement were also linked to the growing interest in genetics in the late nineteenth century. At that time, no distinction was made between genetics and eugenics. For example, statistician Karl Pearson (1857–1936) believed that the problem of mental retardation could be easily resolved through genetic research, while geneticist William Bateson (1861–1926) thought racial betterment was possible (Rosenberg 1967). The prominent horticulturist, Liberty Hyde Bailey, was active in both the Country Life Commission and the American Breeders' Association (ABA), as was Willet Hays, assistant secretary of agriculture under Theodore Roosevelt. Eugene Davenport, Alexander Graham Bell, and Luther Burbank were all active on the ABA's eugenics committee, the goals of which paralleled that of the Country Life movement. Eventually, the ABA was reorganized as the American Genetic Association and became a strong advocate of the use of eugenics to improve humankind. As that occurred, and as genetics as a discipline became more institutionalized, many scientists backed away from the eugenic claims. Nevertheless, the association between genetics and eugenics remained for some time (Kimmelman 1983).

The infatuation with science and technology as the solution to all the problems of humankind was widely shared among American scientists. In the biological sciences it involved reconceptualization of biology along mechanistic lines—what historian Philip J. Pauly (1987) has called the "engineering ideal." Much as plant breeders and other agricultural scientists of the late nineteenth and early twentieth century had focused on manipulating and controlling the traits of plants, other biologists began to attempt the same with other organisms. They found their philosophical ideal in the physics of the day.

German-born biologist Jacques Loeb (1859–1924) was a harbinger of the new biology. He maintained close ties with physicist Ernst Mach (1838–1916), writing to him that "the idea is now hovering before me that man himself can act as a creator even in living nature, forming it eventually according to his will. Man can at least succeed in a technology of living substance" (quoted in Pauly 1987:51).

Upon arriving in the United States, Loeb soon joined the faculty of the University of Chicago, where he became fast friends with philosopher John Dewey and a strong supporter of the ideas of Thorstein Veblen. Indeed, Loeb's work became the model for Dewey's image of scientific inquiry. He devoted much of the rest of his career to developing a form of biology that was based on engineering rather than analysis. In 1909 he moved to the Rockefeller Institute at the invitation of Simon Flexner (1863–1946). In turn, Flexner reorganized the institute so as to triple support for the kind of basic research for which Loeb was known. Flexner's hopes were realized some years later when Loeb developed a technique for the commercial production of insulin. Moreover, the influence of Loeb's engineering approach was widespread: Biologist Hermann Joseph Muller attempted to control the evolutionary process. He induced mutations in fruit flies (*Drosophila melanogaster*) by exposing them to x-rays. Gregory Pincus, a student of John William Crozier, who in turn was a student of Loeb, developed the first oral contraceptive. Psychologist John Broadus Watson employed Loeb's approach to the control of human behavior. B. F. Skinner, also a student of Crozier, developed behavioral psychology (Pauly 1987).

But Loeb was only at the tip of the proverbial iceberg. In addition to supporting Seaman Knapp through the General Education Board, the Rockefeller Foundation began to support practical applications of research of various sorts. Here, too, rationalization, organization, and promotion of efficiency were central concerns. Under Warren Weaver, the Rockefeller Foundation picked up several strands of Loeb's research and attempted to develop what was variously known as "mathematico-physico-chemical morphology," "experimental biology," "new biology," and "molecular biology."

By 1932 the United States was in the midst of its worst depression. Many blamed the depression on the vast increase in production brought about by scientific and technical change, and especially the physical sciences. They argued that such technical change had resulted in overproduction of farm and industrial products, lowered prices, and, eventually, economic collapse. Weaver was quite cognizant of this and directed his attention to creating an alternative. He explained:

The challenge of this situation is obvious. Can man gain an intelligent control over his own power? Can we develop so sound and extensive a genetics that we can hope to breed in the future, superior men? Can we obtain enough knowledge of the physiology and psychobiology of sex so that man can bring this pervasive, highly important, and dangerous aspect of life under rational control? Can we unravel the tangled problem of the endocrine glands, and develop, before it is too late, a therapy for the whole hideous range of mental and physical disorders which result from glandular disturbances? Can we solve the mysteries of the various vitamins . . . ? Can we release psychology from its present confusion and ineffectiveness and shape it into a tool which every man can use every day? Can man acquire enough knowledge of his own vital processes so that we can hope to rationalize human behavior? Can we, in short, create a new science of Man? (quoted in Kohler 1980:263)

If the modification of the physical world was problematic, then the solution lay in modifying people to fit the new society. Perhaps mental retardation, criminality, and social deviance could be wiped out by applying the successes of applied physics to biology.

Between 1932 and 1957 the Rockefeller Foundation funneled ninety million dollars into molecular biology and related programs. The foundation's largesse legitimated the use of physical technologies in biology while undercutting anatomical and evolutionary research programs. Biologist Linus Pauling's work was supported for over twenty years. In the 1930s, the biology department at the California Institute of Technology was headed by the eminent biologist Thomas Hunt Morgan and emphasized genetics. It was supported as a whole by the foundation. Other prominent men of science such as Hermann Joseph Muller, Erwin Schrödinger, Max Delbruck, and Francis Crick were also supported.

At the same time, in 1932, a group began meeting in Britain that called itself the "biotheoretical gathering." The group, made up of prominent biologists and physicists, including J. D. Bernal, began to theorize about what it called "mathematico-physico-morphology," a position that its adherents saw as a response to reductionist tendencies. The Rockefeller Foundation soon heard about the group and began to provide it, too, with financial support. Ironically, the foundation refused to support the work of two key contributors to the field, Conrad H. Waddington and Joseph Needham, whose political views were considered too radical by the foundation. By 1938 the foundation was using the less cumbersome term "molecular biology" in its annual reports (Abir-Am 1987).

But Weaver's program was quite radical in yet another way. Not only did it propose to treat biology like physics. It also applied the new principles of management to science itself. No longer would the foundation merely support scientists who appeared to have promising ideas; it would develop its own program with its own goals and pursue those goals by coordinating the work of numerous scientists in the United States and abroad. In a word, it would bring organization, efficiency, and control to the hitherto seemingly unorganizable process of generating new knowledge (Yoxen 1981).

Nor was the restructuring of the social world to be left entirely to the physical sciences. The social sciences as well were to be restructured to emphasize the new approach. In 1923 the Rockefeller Foundation created the Social Science Research Council, the aim of which was to make social science research more scientific. A foundation officer, Beardsley Ruml, had a mandate to spend twenty million dollars in a single decade so as to make social science more scientific. In order to avoid bad publicity, the Rockefeller tie was initially kept secret, with funds funneled to the council via a special committee. Social control was a central feature of the council's research. Its first project was an examination of the problems of migration into the United States. Eugenics played a significant role in the project (Fisher 1990).

Arguably the high point in the unquestioned faith in technoscience was the Century of Progress Exhibition in Chicago in 1933. There, in the midst of the worst depression to date, an entire fair was devoted to technical progress. The motto of the fair, almost fascist in tone to contemporary ears, was "Science Finds, Industry Applies, Man Conforms." To emphasize how technoscience would transcend ordinary human comprehension while guiding us to some unimagined yet well-ordered future, the fountain in the Hall of Science contained two life-sized human figures, dwarfed by a robot twice their size (Staudenmeier 1989).

The post–World War II years were both the best and worst of times for science and technology. On the one hand, the detonation of the atomic bomb burst the illusions that anyone might have had about the inevitably positive nature of science and technology. While the bomb had helped the Allies to win the war in the Pacific, its terrible destruction left a mark on humankind that was unlike any previous weapon.

But soon after, Vanevar Bush (1945) prepared the definitive document describing the glories of *Science, the Endless Frontier*. Bush set out an image of science as a never-ending quest for knowledge that would improve the human condition. Government would provide the funds, but scientists would determine the research priorities. His report set the stage for the first massive funding of scientific research by the United States government. The National Institutes of Health and the National Science Foundation benefited especially from this newfound and newly justified government largesse.

Moreover, a little more than a decade later, United States science got another boost. When the Soviets launched Sputnik I in 1957, Americans quickly decided that they were behind in the "space race." Thus, the American space program was launched largely as a response to Soviet technical development. American action was as much designed to bolster flagging prestige as it was to protect against military threats. Ironically, President Dwight D. Eisenhower—formerly a general—was far less convinced of the necessity to increase spending for space and military research than were members of Congress. Yet, reluctantly, in 1958 he signed legislation creating the National Aeronautics and Space Administration (NASA). The language of the times was largely that of catching up, of races, as if technology moved linearly and one could spread the nations of the world neatly across some sort of time line.

Similarly, when a group of U.S. engineers visited the Soviet Union in 1961, they were shocked to discover that the Soviets had trained nearly as many engineers as had the United States. Immediately they began to argue that the United States had to step up its training of engineers. If it did not do so, some unspecified but ominous fate would clearly befall the American nation: "Unless we exert ourselves and put forward our best efforts, the gap between us will disappear all too soon, and we shall find ourselves behind—in second place—with all that can mean to our future welfare" (Engineers Joint Council 1961:87).

Modernization theory, widely accepted in the social sciences at the time, made much the same argument for the entire world. Economist Walt Whitman Rostow's *Stages of Economic Growth: A Non-Communist Manifesto* (1960) used an airplane metaphor to explain social change. All nations supposedly begin on the runway until they build up (or fail to build up) sufficient technological change to permit "take-off." Thus, from this perspective, contemporary Uganda would be merely several hundred years behind Great Britain on the same path of change.

But Americans were hardly alone in their faith in technoscience. Citizens of most of the major powers of the twentieth century shared Americans' beliefs. Nevertheless, one nation stands out among all others in its obsessive quest for technical and scientific progress: the Soviet Union. It is to that nation that I now turn.

THE SOVIET UNION

Here indeed we see the opening of a golden age of technique, where there are no traditions, no sentimentalities to paralyse the gigantic scale of planning and the daring of creation. Here, "to want," "to act," and "to be able" are merged into one unity of incredible dimensions.

—Professor M. Bonn, quoted in V. V. Prokofyev, Industrial and Technical Intelligentsia in the U.S.S.R.

Perhaps no nation in this century embraced science and technology with quite the uncritical passion as did the Soviet Union. Two centuries earlier,

Czar Peter the Great (1672–1725), by force, had attempted to introduce modern technology to Russia both to permit industrialization and to build a modern military. Similarly, from the very creation of the Soviet state, Soviet leaders extolled the virtues of the technology that would propel the nation's level of living far beyond its capitalist neighbors. Without doubt, the Soviet position arose as much from the destruction wrought by revolution, civil war, and world war, which left the country's relatively weak industrial infrastructure in ruins, as from the legacy of Peter. Thus, the Soviet obsession with technoscience emerged at least as much out of necessity as out of theory.

Marx and Engels were not the only starting point. The Soviets found another more thoroughly Russian, but more obscure and more millennial figure to whom to turn for advice: Nikolai F. Fedorov (1828–1903). Fedorov "saw in technology the chance for a victory over the blind forces of nature, a victory that could lead to mankind's mastery of the universe and even resurrection of the dead. Furthermore, he believed that humanity's domination of the universe should be its main goal" (Shlapentokh 1997:302).

Fedorov envisioned that all of humanity would eventually be collectivized under the czar, who as an autocrat best represented the relations between father and son. What was needed was a common cause grandiose enough to capture the imagination of all mankind. That cause was none other than the resurrection of the dead. Through the use of science and technology, death would be overcome; the Orthodox Christian goal of resurrection would be achieved not by prayer or salvation but by the power of work and technology. As Fedorov put it, "Under the circumstances, what is needed is not economic reform but a radical technical revolution bound up with a moral one" (1990:62). Fedorov's ideas were widely accepted after the 1905 revolution and continue to be of importance even in contemporary Russia.

Initially, the Bolsheviks rejected Fedorov's position. But Fedorov's distaste for Western democracy and praise for the conquest of nature played well in the world of millenarian enthusiasm ushered in by the 1917 revolution. V. N. Murav'ev—who was initially opposed to Bolshevism—introduced Fedorov's ideas to Leon Trotsky, who found them quite appealing. To Fedorov, the army was the epitome of collectivization; it was also Trotsky's base of support. (Later the army would be seen as a means for ensuring Russian domination of the world.) Trotsky tried and failed to militarize the trade unions after the Civil War ended. But he was more successful in transforming the concentration camps into collectivized work organizations in Fedorovian style.

As historian Dmitry Shlapentokh notes, "The Bolshevik leadership also promulgated the idea that while in the hands of the capitalists technology would be the damnation of humanity, in the hands of the Bolsheviks the same technology would become humanity's blessing" (1996:438). Consider, for example, the position taken by Anatolii Lunacharskii, one of the most educated of the Bolsheviks. Lunacharskii became minister of education in the 1920s. He believed that the path to immortality began by working for the creation of socialism on earth.

Of even greater import was the prestige heaped on Konstantin E. Tsiolkovskii (1857–1935), who had been coached in mathematics by Fedorov when a student (Koutaissoff 1990). Tsiolkovskii extended Fedorov's desire for immortality. By the last decade of the nineteenth century he had already written a book proclaiming that the cosmic expansion of humanity and technological development would go hand in hand. Rocket ships would be constructed to explore space. Million person volunteer armies would transform the earth. But Tsiolkovskii was not merely an idle dreamer. He was trained in physics and astronomy and devoted his career to pioneering research in rocketry and wind tunnel design for aerodynamic studies. By the early 1920s, Tsiolkovskii was revered as a genius and space exploration was made a central feature of the Russian national technoscientific agenda.

During the 1920s Fedorov was widely revered among the Soviet intelligentsia, including most engineers and technicians. Universities began training engineers to build the most grandiose projects conceivable. Fedorovism "was based on the following philosophical paradigm: humanity's victory over nature and technological progress necessary for accomplishing this were possible only in the context of collective, organized labor—this required a strong despotic government" (Shlapentokh 1996:443).

Furthermore, Soviet socialist technoscience would be no different than capitalist technoscience. It would simply serve the class interests of the proletariat rather than those of the bourgeoisie. Thus, with few exceptions, the Soviet state could borrow all the knowledge that had been accumulated by the West. As Stalin put it, "In the sphere of technique we are the pupils of the Germans, the English, the French, the Italians, and, first and foremost, the Americans" (1932:44). Furthermore, for them, since only one technological path existed, it was easy for Lenin and Stalin to justify the elimination of any semblance of workplace democracy and to establish *by law* one-man control over each unit. Even the scientists and engineers who had been connected with the old regime could be utilized in this manner, as long as they renounced their older ties.

Of particular note was Alexei Gastev (1882–1941), founder and head of the Central Labour Institute and a major popularizer of scientific management in the Soviet Union. Like Taylor, Gastev had been a skilled worker before becoming an engineer and manager. He shared with Taylor the notion that there was a single best way to do a job. By 1918 he had convinced

the state to introduce the piece rate in factories as a way to spur productivity. In 1919 he organized a school of "social engineering" in the Ukraine.
While Lenin had been initially somewhat suspicious of Taylorism, Gastev
helped to convince him of its centrality to the goal of increased production
and productivity. In 1921 Lenin granted Gastev's institute the princely sum
of five million gold rubles, despite the weak financial condition of the state.
Gastev promised to do no less than reorganize Soviet industry along Taylorist lines and to create, as he put it, a "Soviet Americanism" (Bailes 1977).

Gastev proposed a "labor obligation" similar to a military one, complete
with labor champions who would receive medals for their heroic feats of
production. Moreover, he firmly believed that workers themselves would
become increasingly standardized and mechanized, so much so that they
would become anonymous and could be managed by machines. His views
were largely accepted by both Lenin and Stalin despite resistance by
unions and claims by some that he was ignoring worker psychology as
well as physiology. Nevertheless, until both he and his institute were
purged in 1938, Gastev and his associates were the last word on the link
between technology and management. Indeed, he was ironically prophet-
ic when he said:

> The metallurgy of this new world, the motor car and the aeroplane factories
> of America, and finally the arms industry of the whole world—here are the
> new, gigantic laboratories where the psychology of the proletariat is being
> created, where the culture of the proletariat is being manufactured. And
> whether we live in an age of super-imperialism or of world socialism, the
> structure of the new industry will, in essence, be one and the same. (quoted
> in Bailes 1977:377)

Lenin agreed. During the civil war period alone some forty new technical institutes were established, largely on Lenin's authority (Bailes 1978).
Scientists at the institutes were quite free to determine what were legitimate topics for research. For Lenin, socialism was merely a matter of who
was in control of the means of production, not how they were organized
or what technologies they employed. Thus, he could argue in 1917, "Socialism is nothing but the next step forward from state capitalist monopoly. In other words, Socialism is nothing but state capitalist monopoly *made
to benefit the whole people*; by this token it ceases to be capitalist monopoly"
(Lenin [1917] 1932:7; emphasis in original). Only a year later he took this
position to its logical conclusion writing:

> The possibility of building socialism will be determined precisely by our suc-
> cess in combining the Soviet government and the Soviet organization of ad-
> ministration with the modern achievements of capitalism. We must organize
> in Russia the study and teaching of the Taylor system and systematically try
> it out and adapt it to our purposes. (1937:341)

By 1931 Taylorism was used as the means for determining wages through-out most of Soviet industry (Bailes 1978).

Lenin enthusiastically and uncritically embraced electrification as the icon to represent technological progress in industry, noting in rather cryptic fashion that "communism means the Soviet power plus the electrification of the whole country" (quoted in Pearce 1952:19). In agriculture as well, electrification and increased scale were essential: "The superiority of large-scale farming in this very important respect has been fully established" (Lenin 1938:219).

Nevertheless, there were tensions between "reds" and "experts." The older generation of engineers, while clearly necessary to the building of the Soviet state, might still be loyal to their old capitalist and czarist masters. They might be experts, but they might not be sufficiently red. However, show trials, like those of Shakhty and the Industrial party, in which prominent engineers were tried on charges of conspiracy, could be fabricated so as to ensure that the technical intelligentsia remained—whether out of fear or patriotism—loyal to the new regime.[8] Indeed, one of the prominent leaders of the Industrial party, P. I. Pal'chinsky, was an admirer of Herbert Hoover, then at the forefront of American engineering. Pal'chinsky had even translated Hoover's book into Russian (Bailes 1974). Whether they were loyal Soviets or not, they undoubtedly shared the Soviet belief in the power of technoscience. Yet, as Stalin put it, "The engineer, the organizer of production, does not work as he would like to, but as he is ordered, in such a way as to serve the interests of his employers" (quoted in Bailes 1974). In short, just as the Soviet state would command the technologies of capitalist production, so would it command the engineers.

Stalin, too, enthusiastically embraced Fedorov's fascination with technological mastery of nature and his belief in the authoritarian state. Stalin's slogan was widely repeated through the late 1920s: "Technology in the period of reconstruction decides everything" (quoted in Bailes 1978:160). Like Fedorov, Stalin used the army as a metaphor for collectivization:

> Now we have passed from the fronts of the civil war to the industrial front. In keeping with this we shall need new industrial executives, good directors of factories and mills, good heads of trusts, business-like syndicate workers, level-headed planners of industrial construction. It has now become necessary for us to train new commanders of regiments and brigades, new heads of divisions and army corps of industry and commerce. We cannot move a step forward without such people. (1932:39)

Moreover, for Stalin technology was not merely individual machines but a grand system for redesigning society with ever-increasing returns to scale. Consider, for example, his admiring clarification of Lenin:

As you see, when Lenin speaks of the electrification of the country, he means not the construction of isolated power stations, but the gradual "transformation of the economic life of the country, *including agriculture,* on a new technical basis, the technical basis of modern large-scale production," which one way or another, directly or indirectly, is bound up with electrification. (Stalin 1932:16; emphasis in original)

Furthermore, Stalin encouraged scientific research focused on extending life. He supported the claim of agronomist Trofim Lysenko (1898–1976) that species could be transformed by changing their environments. All biologists who held contrary views were purged.[9] He encouraged film director Sergei Eisenstein (1898–1948) to produce propaganda films that showed collectivized humanity's victory over nature. He rapidly built the Soviet aircraft industry using aviation as a metaphor for what Soviet technology could accomplish (Bailes 1978). Several novels, popular among young people, glorified the work of engineers (Bailes 1974).

Stalin demanded both blind obedience to the state *and* social change. And Fedorovism provided the ideological justification necessary to obey the state, to collectivize everything, while at the same time preaching change. Indeed, the Stalinist state offered hope not merely of a better life, but of mastery of the laws of nature, eventually permitting immortality. As one historian has noted, "Fedorovism became an ideological Leviathan which controlled not only the political and economic life of society, but the laws of nature and the cosmos itself" (Shlapentokh 1996:452).

The influence of Fedorov did not go unnoticed by more widely known and respected Russian philosophers. Nikolai Berdiaev was strongly influenced by both Marx and Fedorov. At first, he saw the 1917 revolution as too much like Western European revolutions to be Fedorovian. He found it to be too materialistic, too democratic, and too similar to capitalism. But when Bolshevism became more authoritarian, Berdiaev found in it the Fedorovian potential. Berdiaev soon began to sympathize with the Eurasian movement, which advocated a totalitarian state, looking eastward (rather than to the West) for social and spiritual guidance, and most importantly, a central role for technology. Berdiaev proclaimed the Russian Revolution as the start of a new era. In his 1924 volume, *New Middle Ages,* he singled out Fedorov as the source of intellectual guidance for the new regime. Ultimately, however, he rejected the emphasis on technology, arguing that it would control human life. Only through mystical revelation would humans affect the fate of the universe. In short, despite his rejection of technology—his works were banned by the Soviet authorities—Berdiaev saw it as an irresistible force, independent of human will (Shlapentokh 1997).

In the now somewhat outdated Marxist-Leninist philosophy, it was claimed that technical progress and political revolution were the driving forces of historical change. To the Soviets, technology was viewed as an all but unstoppable force, unidirectional in character, unleashed by the transformation to socialism. As Friedrich Rapp put it, "Taken on the whole, in Soviet philosophical discussion of the causes of scientific and technological change the prevailing approach is that of scientific-technological determinism" (1985:144). This determinism meant that (1) the central task for planners was the forecasting of technical change, (2) engineers would play a key role in incorporating new technologies into the Soviet industrial machine, and (3) any already extant Western technologies could merely be borrowed by Soviet engineers.

Many Western observers were as enthusiastic about Soviet technoscience as were the Soviets themselves. For example, an American engineer, Walter Arnold Rukeyser, one of many brought to the Soviet Union to help in the vast public works of the postrevolutionary period, felt compelled to write a book on his experiences in the Soviet Union. He noted that when he first arrived, "I had not yet fully grasped the fact that what I had been brought over to do for this one comparatively small industry was but part of a gigantic plan preconceived in every humanly possible detail for each and every industry in the Soviet Union" (1932:26–27). In 1932, at the height of the Great Depression, surely the full employment and rapid economic growth in the Soviet Union must have stood out in stark relief.

American agriculturalists, many the victims of the collapse of farm prices after the end of World War I, also were enamored by the Soviet experiment. With the largesse of the Rockefeller Foundation, agricultural economist M. L. Wilson had established Fairway Farms, a huge experimental wheat farm in Montana. The farm was to be the first step in the industrialization of agriculture. Experiments would determine the optimal size for farm machinery. When offered the chance to design a collective farm, Wilson jumped at the opportunity. Sitting in a Chicago hotel room for two weeks in 1928, he and two other men designed a one-hundred-thousand acre wheat farm to be created on the Russian plains. On it, people and equipment would work in one massive, carefully regulated system to produce huge wheat harvests. Soon after, they got the opportunity to put their ideas into practice. Huge orders of American farm equipment were delivered, but problems emerged almost as soon as Wilson arrived. The Soviets were resentful of their American teachers and often angry at those who forced collectivization on them as well. Few of them had any experience in operating or maintaining equipment. Infrastructure was largely lacking. New equipment that should have lasted a decade was scrap iron in a year or two. Spare parts took months to arrive. However, despite Wilson's frustrations he remained convinced to the end that, once the organizational problems were worked out, the Soviet Union would export two to three hundred million tons of wheat per year in direct competition to the United States (Fitzgerald 1996).

Even twenty years later at least some Western visitors still clung to the Soviet technoscientific megamachine. A pamphlet issued in Britain in 1952 entitled *Man Conquers Nature* featured the text of speeches made by a number of British citizens who had visited the USSR including the well-known physicist and historian J. D. Bernal. Bernal was enraptured by what he saw in the Soviet Union, noting that

> This is really a revolution in engineering that has been achieved by increasing the scale and power of operations. Now for the first time men are working on the scale of nature itself. They have passed beyond the scale of merely modifying existing drainage systems here and there, and are approaching the time when they will design them over a whole area of a continent, to suit human needs. (1952:26–27)

Others who visited the Soviet Union with Bernal were equally impressed. They talked of the great afforestation projects, huge new irrigation schemes, vast hydroelectric complexes, the complete electrification of agriculture, enormous livestock farms, windbreaks across the Soviet prairies hundreds of miles in length, vast increases in worker productivity, and the "large-scale experimentation made possible by a socialist economy" (Dunman 1952). One writer even suggested that the collective farms were too small and would have to be grouped together to effectively use the new technologies.

During the regimes of Khrushchev and Brezhnev, the Fedorovian ideal continued to be central to both Soviet ideology and practice. It was especially apparent in the continued support for and eventual success of the space program. Sixty-five percent of the members of the Central Committee had a technical education by 1966 (Bailes 1974). Brezhnev himself was a metallurgical engineer. The dispute between "reds" and "experts" ended by the production of red experts from the Soviet schools.

Of course, there were always critics of Fedorovism, but until more recent times, most were silenced by the Soviet regime. One such critic was playwright Mikhail Bulgakov. Unsuccessful in emigrating after the 1917 revolution, Bulgakov decided to pursue a career in the Soviet Union. But he soon concluded that beneath the facade of Soviet ideology was a Kafkaesque bureaucracy. In his play *The Fatal Eggs* he described a future world in which a red ray of life is discovered, only to be wrested from its discoverer by party officials. The result is a catastrophe reminiscent of Michael Crichton's more recent novel *Jurassic Park*, where giant reptiles are loosed on the world (Curtis 1991). Not surprisingly, the play was quickly banned by the Soviet regime. Boris Pasternak's critique of the Soviet regime in *Doctor Zhivago* was also anti-Fedorovian in its theme. Similarly,

Aleksandr Solzhenitsyn rejected the technological juggernaut, idolized village life, and urged withdrawal from Western worldliness.

Only in the 1980s did it become possible to offer an alternative within the confines of the Soviet state. Yet, the power of Fedorovism is reflected in the fact that even its critics felt it necessary to drape their alternative in Fedorovian banners. In particular, the writers of the "Village school," such as Valentin Rasputin, who later became a member of Gorbachev's Presidential Council, were critical of attempts to dominate nature. Rasputin argued that such attempts would eventually crush both the state and the nation. But to make his case, he had to argue for a new interpretation of Fedorov as a humanistically oriented ecologist—a position in direct contradiction to Fedorov's approach (Shlapentokh 1996). Only with the collapse and discrediting of the Soviet regime has the appeal of Fedorov begun to wane. Whether it will appear again in a new form in the future remains to be seen.

In sum, Soviet Russia embraced the Baconian ideal of technoscience—albeit in secular clothing—with unparalleled enthusiasm. Technology would not merely permit the building of the Soviet state, but would define its very character. Like Bacon, the Soviets believed that technoscience would tell everyone what the truth was; it would provide guidance as to how to act by providing both means and ends, thereby replacing politics by administration. Thus, virtually no thought was ever given to a specifically socialist technoscience, based on alternative ways of providing public goods. One might have expected that a socialist state would have, for example, focused on developing the world's best public transportation. Instead, even the American obsession with private automobiles was copied by the Soviet state. In other domains as in transport, Soviet technoscience focused on following the Western path. As Stalin put it, "We must do everything in our power to catch up with and outstrip the technical development of the advanced capitalist countries" (1932:34). In a tragic failure of the imagination, no thought was ever given to an alternative path of development. The goals of development were fixed by technoscience; they were never in doubt. Moreover, Soviet firms could be run by engineers, who would supplant workplace politics by finding the best way to produce a given good.

Ironically, the very faith in the power of technoscience proved to its adherents the rightness of their claims. If only one path to the future existed, then there was no point in trying to find alternative paths. The similarities between Soviet and Western technoscience only proved the linear character of technical advance: How could there be any other path, if two opposing systems produced the same technologies? Furthermore, if economies of scale were endless, then there was no point in building on a more human scale. And, since the centralized Soviet state controlled all the major institutions of society, there was little room for opposition. Of course, faith in science combined with faith in the power of the state did not create Bacon's utopian society. Instead, the world the Soviets made was one of gigantic, often monstrous, projects, of poor copies of Western technologies, of bureaucratic nightmares, and of shattered dreams.

FROM THE GREEN REVOLUTION TO THE GENE REVOLUTION

> *It is not the plant breeders' job to "transform" the distribution of income and power. Yet their hopes and motivations, and those of the financial backers of aid to international research, have always centred on the belief that increased and more stable food production would mean less poverty and hunger. Can this be achieved without the "transformation"?*

> —Michael Lipton and Richard Longhurst, New Seeds and Poor People

> *Modern rice and wheat technology, which triggered the green revolution, were in fact developed for production environments considered optimal for these commodities.*

> —Per Pinstrup-Anderson, Agricultural Research and Technology in Economic Development

The unconditional acceptance of technoscience spread during the latter half of the twentieth century, especially in the domain of agriculture. Whereas faith in technoscience was largely limited to the Western world prior to World War II, the postwar period was one in which the Baconian spirit spread rapidly to what became known variously as the developing nations or the Third World. The Green Revolution was variously touted as the technoscientific solution to problems of hunger, poverty, national security, population growth, and the specter of communism.

As noted above, agricultural research helped to transform U.S. agriculture beginning in the late nineteenth century. At the end of the second world war, the United States was alone among the major industrialized nations to have its infrastructure intact. Yet, two new problems arose: How would Europe and Japan, ravaged by the destruction of the war, rapidly reindustrialize and once again feed themselves? Moreover, how would the former colonies of the imperial powers, now rapidly gaining independence, be put on a firm foundation? How might they, too, produce adequate food supplies and become prosperous and industrialized rather than "go communist"?

From the vantage point of U.S. officials, these questions were more than academic. On the one hand, without a prosperous Europe and Japan, the United States would have no way of trading with the rest of the world. On the other hand, instability in the newly independent nations might provide an avenue for communist insurgency. Indeed, Chiang Kai-shek was gradually being pushed out of mainland China by Mao Zedong and the Red Army. Indian leaders, too, had socialist ambitions.

Clearly, helping Europe recover from the war was the first priority. The Marshall Plan provided a smorgasbord of aid programs designed to speed recovery. In Japan, the U.S. occupation forces imposed democratic government and aided industrial recovery. But in these nations trained technical personnel already existed. Industrial and agricultural recovery could be largely confined to provision of raw materials and manufacturing equipment.

What would later be called the Third World posed a far less tractable problem. Those newly independent nations lacked trained manpower. Their leaders had little experience in governing and often leaned toward leftist causes. Their populace was largely illiterate and engaged mainly in farming. Their infrastructure was poor and in some cases nearly nonexistent. It appeared that they were ripe for communist agitation, for red revolutions.

Enter again the Rockefeller Foundation. Guided by a conviction of the benefits of technoscience, the foundation had begun work on crop improvement in China in the 1920s. However, with the growing chaos of civil war and the Japanese invasion, foundation staff had been forced to leave China. In 1943 they established a presence in Mexico. Ever since its revolution, Mexico had been engaged in land reform. The great estates of the nineteenth century had been broken up and given to groups of smallholders who farmed their holdings (*ejidos*) communally. The Mexican government also had been hostile to the United States, nationalizing the holdings of foreign oil companies—including Standard Oil, the source of the Rockefeller fortune—and otherwise complaining of Yankee imperialism. The foundation officers decided to take a very different approach. Looking at Mexican agriculture, they compared it to the United States in the 1880s (Dahlberg 1980). It was characterized by large numbers of smallholders, each barely carving out subsistence without any of the benefits of new technologies.

Elvin Charles Stakman, a plant pathologist from Minnesota, led the Rockefeller team that examined the Mexican agricultural situation. Stakman had already demonstrated his credentials by executing a barberry eradication program—barberry was a host for wheat stem rust—in the United States. While Stakman on the surface might seem to have been an unlikely candidate to lead such a team, in fact he had many of the necessary qualities. As John H. Perkins explains:

> Even though the barberry eradication campaign was very different from the foundation's work in Mexico, they were joined by a common theme: the relentless, systematic planning of land use by experts and policy makers to extract maximum agricultural production through the use of modern science, to build a strong industrial state. (1997:92)

The team recommended that a Mexican Agricultural Program (MAP) be established. In 1943, three U.S. experts were dispatched to Mexico. Two of them, Norman Borlaug and J. George Harrar, were students of Stakman and shared many of his views. The Rockefeller program was marked by a desire to transform Mexico into a modern industrial state by reducing the proportion of the population working on the farm. Moreover, the focus was to be on individual farmers rather than villages. This would be the foundation's response to the potential threat of socialism or fascism in Mexico.

The Rockefeller program fit well with the needs of Mexico's elites, too. Mexico's population was growing rapidly and food imports were a drain on scarce foreign exchange. Moreover, many wished to industrialize as their neighbor to the north had done. Indeed, Mexican grain production had declined in 1943 just as the foundation started its program, although this was due more to the U.S. request for certain industrial crops for the war effort than to any change in Mexican agriculture (Perkins 1997).

After consultation with the Mexican government, Rockefeller staff decided to focus on developing rust-resistant wheat varieties. Although foundation reports emphasized the reduction or elimination of poverty, the choice of wheat over maize reflected middle-class food preferences. Maize, after all, was the food of the poor. It also reflected the foundation's conviction, shared by officers of the Ford Foundation, that more prosperous farms would have to be larger and that surplus labor would have to be moved to the cities to work in the emerging industrial economy. Moreover, unlike maize, wheat had long been traded internationally. Mexican government officials saw the potential of eliminating imports and even of exporting any surplus that might be produced. Mexican industrialists felt the pressure on wages caused by expensive imported wheat as well. Finally, the more highly capitalized Mexican farmers saw the potential for higher profits in wheat.

Borlaug soon realized that wheat was being grown in two very different locations: In El Bajío wheat was grown by smallholders while in Sonora and Sinaloa it was grown on large farms. Despite the claim of alleviating poverty, Borlaug was convinced that it was necessary to work with the large farms as they would have the necessary capital to purchase seeds, machinery, and agrichemicals. The varieties that were produced were usable in both locations, but clearly the better capitalized farmers had a considerable advantage over their poorer compatriots. Borlaug soon obtained a semidwarf variety that had been identified some years before in Japan. It had both the stiff straw and short stature that permitted greater grain yields without lodging (i.e., falling down in the field). Indeed, the straw was so stiff initially that it was difficult to cut without machinery (Thiesenhusen 1971). Moreover, the short-strawed varieties could not be used for thatching roofs, a concern to smallholders but not to their better endowed competitors.

The significant increase in the productivity of wheat transformed the Mexican economy, although perhaps not entirely as the scientists and planners had envisioned. As a consequence of the success of the Rockefeller program, Mexico was able to reduce and even eliminate grain imports for a number of years. But, at the same time, Mexico City became the world's largest city. Women found the move to the city particularly difficult, as jobs for them were hard to find.

But if foundation and government support for plant breeding was initially motivated by economic theories about the development of modern industrial states, that view was eclipsed later by another view that emphasized the "population problem." Late in the eighteenth century, economist Thomas Robert Malthus ([1798] 1959) had warned that population growth would eventually outstrip available food supplies. The discovery of the three major plant nutrients—nitrogen, potassium, and phosphorus—by agricultural chemist Justus Liebig in 1840 was motivated largely by that concern (Krohn and Schafer 1983). Economist John Maynard Keynes had raised the population issue in a somewhat more optimistic vein early in the twentieth century.

In contrast, plant breeder Edward Murray East, already known for his work in developing hybrid corn, wrote about it in dire tones in his book *Mankind at the Crossroads* (1923). Echoing Malthus, East noted that if birth rates did not decline, the world's population would surpass the ability of the earth to produce food, leading to war and famine. Moreover, as East saw it, the white race was intellectually superior to all other races. Perhaps as a result of that alleged superiority, it had a duty to ensure that all humans developed their capacities: "What is needed in each country is a population compatible with a sound economic system, where every member of society has the opportunity of developing to the full extent of his or her capacity" (ibid.:13). Birth and death rates had already declined in Europe and the United States, but they remained quite high in the rest of the world. In short, while scientific agriculture was desirable, without population control humans were condemned to a life of war and misery for, echoing Bacon, "Nature's laws will make no allowance for human desires" (ibid.:40). As a result of the work of East and others, by the end of the Second World War, demographic concerns were well established in foundation and government circles and population control programs were high on the agenda.

The Malthusian conclusions of these theories gave cause for concern among Rockefeller Foundation officials: Was increasing food production merely setting the stage for a worse catastrophe in the future? As early as 1929 demographer Warren S. Thompson had noted that in the industrialized nations, birth rates were falling faster than death rates leading to slower rates of population growth (Szreter 1993). In 1945 Frank W.

Notestein and Kingsley Davis of the Princeton University Office of Population Research presented much the same information at a conference on postwar food supplies. They theorized that in poor agrarian societies additional children meant additional hands to work in the fields and provide social security in one's old age. Moreover, in such societies high infant and child mortality rates were common. Therefore, there were considerable incentives to have many children. In contrast, in industrial societies the state provided social security, infant and child mortality rates were low, and the costs of raising children (who were prohibited by child labor laws from working in industry) were high. As such, in industrial societies, birth rates declined. It appeared that only industrialization and improved public health would bring about a "demographic transition," eliminating the Malthusian problem (Szreter 1993).

Notestein's work fit neatly with the concerns of the day. On the one hand, it provided seemingly straightforward justification and direction for massive postwar development programs to alleviate poverty and establish liberal democracies in what was soon to be known—as the result of the work of another demographer—as the Third World (see Wolf-Phillips 1987). On the other hand, it employed up-to-date statistical methods that appealed to policymakers by virtue of their apparently scientific rigor. In 1948 Notestein traveled to East and Southeast Asia with Marshall C. Balfour and Roger F. Evans of the Rockefeller Foundation on a fact-finding tour. By the end of the tour he was advocating widespread family planning programs so as to reduce fertility and thereby speed the transition (Szreter 1993).

However, demographic transition theory was fraught with problems, most of which were ignored by its supporters (Teitelbaum 1975). Most importantly, the proponents of the theory jumped to evolutionary conclusions. What happened in the industrialized West would happen in the rest of the world if only industrialization proceeded apace. Second, proponents used ecological data—data about units such as nations—to draw inferences about the behavior of individuals and to make causal connections, a highly suspect approach. Finally, despite years of follow-up research, the demographic transition is only partially supported by the data even within the industrialized nations. It remains merely an empirical generalization. In contrast, theoretical evidence to explain it remains fraught with difficulties. Indeed, the editors of a recent volume on the subject note that "we do not intend to lend credence to the sometimes misguided body of theory that has developed around it, be it in the form of crudely economic determinist explanations, or equally crude evolutionary or modernization theory, or narrowly focused diffusion theory" (Jones and Douglas 1997:4). Regardless of its weak theoretical underpinnings, the demographic transition, shorn of its explicitly racist origins, became the conventional wisdom by the 1960s.

However, with the beginning of the cold war, national security also became a concern. Indeed, soon after the Rockefeller team returned from Asia, the Chinese nationalist regime of Chiang Kai-shek was toppled by the communists. Coupled with the understanding of demographics, this suggested what Perkins (1997) has called the Population–National Security Theory (PNST). In brief, poverty and misery were now said to be caused by population growth. This, in turn, led to discontent and political instability. The instability could be and was used by the communists to provoke revolutions. The solution to the problem lay in increasing agricultural productivity so as to permit widespread industrialization and a prosperous agriculture at the same time as fertility decline would be encouraged through dissemination of birth control methods and devices. Birth rates would decline, poverty would cease to be a major problem, and communists would have little support. By the 1960s officers at the Ford and Rockefeller Foundations argued that "new technology in agriculture was to create a breathing-space for education, rising welfare, and contraception to bring down family size" (Lipton and Longhurst 1989:346). Foundation agronomists—whether in Mexico or South Asia—could now couple increasing the food supply with fighting communism. The Green Revolution would surely defeat those bent on red revolutions.

The U.S. government soon picked up both the theoretical framework and the practical applications that were pioneered by the Rockefeller Foundation. Truman's Point Four program suggested that the spread of communism would be fought by helping the newly independent nations of the world to become similar to the United States. Hunger and overpopulation would be eliminated and with them would go the threat of political instability and, worse, communist insurgency. American aid programs were established with a strong emphasis on increasing agricultural productivity. Both the Ford and Rockefeller Foundations joined in, creating complementary programs in many of the larger nations. What had happened in Mexico was repeated with varying degrees of success in a number of other nations including India, Indonesia, and the Philippines.

To accomplish the immediate goal of developing and putting to use high-yielding varieties, it was necessary to hedge one's bets. Varieties were developed not for the poorest regions but for those regions already served by irrigation systems, with better soils, better infrastructure, access to fertilizers and other agrichemicals, market-oriented farmers, and therefore most likely to have the wherewithal to rapidly adopt the new technology packages. Thus, the potentially destabilizing issues of land reform, landlessness, usurious money lending, and isolation could be and were sidestepped.

Although most of the breeders and other scientists active in the initial stages of the Green Revolution were unfamiliar with either the special issues raised by tropical climates (e.g., fragile soils, erratic rainfall) or the diverse cultures and peoples of those climes, they plunged ahead. One consequence of their efforts is the litany of environmental problems associated with use of the new varieties: salinization, declining water tables, deforestation, abandonment of crop rotations, soil compaction, and declining genetic diversity among others.

The Green Revolution was in many respects a moral crusade (Perkins 1997). "Miracle grains" were to be spread through the countryside. Nobel Peace Prize winner Norman Borlaug talked of "wheat apostles" (Shiva 1991). Yet, oblivious to their own moralizing, its proponents claimed to be value-free, neutral. In this sense they differed little from the majority of American agricultural scientists. As philosopher Paul Thompson has argued, most U.S. agricultural scientists came from farm backgrounds characterized by a naive utilitarianism in which all innovations were considered good. To this they added a positivist training in science, which stressed value neutrality. "The two dogmas thus form the basis for a productionist paradigm, a world view characterized by total confidence in production enhancing agricultural technology" (Thompson 1995:60).

Despite its scientism, the Green Revolution did have its successes. Supporters can rightly claim that yields of wheat, rice, and to a lesser extent maize were raised markedly in some regions, making it possible to feed a growing population. Family planning permitted millions of women to avoid unwanted pregnancies. Thousands of scientists and university faculty were trained in the United States and Western Europe. Similarly, thousands of Americans and Europeans went abroad. Together they constituted an enlarged group of persons with experience in more than one culture, a group that for all its problems remains essential for mutual understanding in the complex world in which we live today (see, e.g., Porter 1987; Useem and Useem 1955). With the support of foreign governments and private foundations, dozens of new universities and research centers were established in the newly independent nations. For the United States, with its isolationist heritage, the Green Revolution and associated development efforts marked a sea change in domestic university education as well.

While the debate over the consequences of the Green Revolution continues, one thing is clear: Farmers had little say in its development or implementation. Indeed, the Green Revolution was not merely a change in seeds. "All other aspects of agriculture—cropping, irrigation, and cultivation—were expected to change to meet the requirements of the new seeds. Finally, those social and economic relationships that inhibited the introduction of new seeds were seen as impediments to be overcome" (Dahlberg 1980:58). As a result, even as yields rose, many farmers lost their farms entirely and became part of the rapidly growing shantytowns, *bidonvilles*, and *favelas* surrounding the large cities of the developing world.

Women were particularly affected as they often found that whatever independence they had in the countryside was eliminated in the city. What few jobs existed went to men. When women were employed they were often paid less than their male counterparts. Similarly, many farmworkers lost their jobs, especially as weed control was shifted from labor to herbicides. Those who were fortunate enough to stay on the farm found themselves wealthier, but dependent on the suppliers of inputs—seeds, machinery, chemicals, water—that were necessary to ensure the higher yields of the new varieties.

Despite the range of problems identified with respect to the Green Revolution, the lessons have apparently remained unlearned. Recent advances in biotechnology permit far more radical changes than those produced by the Green Revolution. In particular, the new biotechnologies permit transfer of genetic material across species lines, thus making any cross possible in principle. They also permit fine tuning of crops and animals to meet specific industrial needs. Thus, canola with high lauric acid content (for cosmetics) and rabbits that produce pharmaceuticals for humans in their milk are now realities.

Many developing nations have jumped on the biotechnology research bandwagon with enthusiastic financial support. India, Brazil, Mexico, Thailand, and Egypt are among them. As with Green Revolution technologies, claims that biotechnology will eradicate hunger and poverty are heard. Once again, distributional and environmental issues are often brushed off as of little or no consequence. This is not to say that biotechnology is irrelevant to the poor. To the contrary, as activist Henk Hobbelink writes, "As with the Green Revolution, the question is not whether biotechnology will reach the poor, but how and with what consequences" (1987:6). Few social or environmental scientists are connected with monitoring the consequences of the new projects, either in industrialized or developing nations. And, perhaps most importantly, once again virtually no one has bothered to ask the public if this is indeed what they want. Even farmers have rarely been given an opportunity to participate in determining which biotechnologies, if any, should be created and used. We are all expected to be the passive recipients of these new, undiluted goods.

OTHER NATIONS

Although the examples here have been necessarily limited to a few cases, the Baconian spirit can be found throughout the world today. To take but two examples, consider the seemingly opposing views on technology of technological enthusiast, Antoine de Saint-Exupéry, and pessimist, Jacques Ellul. In both his novels and personal accounts, Saint-Exupéry

(1900–1944) paints the picture of technology as an idealized liberating force. As a pilot in the early days of aviation, Saint-Exupéry piloted hundreds of flights across the Sahara and the Andes. He was exuberant about the potential of technology and marveled at the fact that it was possible to forget that the machine was not part of the natural world. Machines for him were perfect precisely because with continued use they permitted one to forget their contrived, goal-oriented, and mechanical character. They blended into nature. Like Bacon, he believed that "the machine does not isolate man from the great problems of nature but plunges him more deeply into them" (Saint-Exupéry [1939] 1965:42). Moreover, machines could bring people closer together, thereby annihilating time and space. Finally, technologies would show us how things really are. As he noted in wonder and awe, "The airplane has unveiled for us the true face of the earth" (ibid.:62).

In contrast, political scientist and theologian Jacques Ellul (1912–1994), in his 1964 volume *The Technological Society*, argued that technique had become autonomous and was no longer tied to tradition. Although Ellul insisted that his position was nondeterministic, he wrote that "there is no choice between two technical methods. One of them asserts itself inescapably: its results are calculated, measured, obvious, and indisputable" (1964:80). For him, technical progress required concentration of capital, bureaucratic decision-making, widespread adherence to the same economic norms, and the subordination of the state to techniques. Furthermore, he argued that the world was converging toward a single set of techniques since "it is efficiency and success that lead history to adopt a certain direction—not man who in some sense makes a decision" (ibid.:183). He argued that as propaganda techniques became more effective, a new reality is created in the minds of citizens, one from which escape is impossible.

Yet, as different as Saint-Exupéry and Ellul were, they shared the Baconian myth. For Saint-Exupéry, technology was liberating as it opened new vistas for human contemplation. For Ellul it was constraining as it took control away from human beings. But for both, technology was a force in itself, detached from the context of invention and use. For both, technology was to be obeyed. For both, technology itself was a moral force.

THE CRITICS

This is not to suggest that technoscience was without its critics. Among the first was Jonathan Swift (1667–1745), who in *Gulliver's Travels* satirized the unbridled optimism of experimental science in a manner that still rings true today. When Gulliver arrives at the extraordinary land of Laputa, an island in the sky, he notes:

In these colleges the professors contrive new rules and methods of agriculture and building, and new instruments and tools for all trades and manufactures, whereby, as they undertake, one man shall do the work of ten. A palace may be built in a week, of materials so durable as to last forever without repairing. All the fruits of the earth shall come to maturity at whatever season we think fit to chose, and increase a hundredfold more than they do at present, with innumerable other happy proposals. The only inconvenience is that none of these projects are yet brought to perfection, and in the meantime the whole country lies miserably in waste, the houses in ruins, and the people without food or clothes. By all which, instead of being discouraged, they are fifty times more violently bent on prosecuting their schemes, driven equally by hope and despair. (Swift [1726] 1947:227)

Swift then details the many endeavors in which the scientists are engaged: the extraction of sunbeams from cucumbers, building houses from the roof down, condensing air into a dry substance, softening marble, and preventing the growth of wool on sheep. Finding nothing of interest in Laputa, Gulliver soon continues his travels.

Similarly, a century later, Thomas Carlyle (1795–1891), in a widely read article, noted that while material prosperity had arrived, wealth was becoming more and more concentrated. The mechanical metaphor, so eloquently described by Bacon, had transformed more than the material: "Not the external and physical alone is now managed by machinery, but the internal and spiritual also" (Carlyle [1829] 1878:188). Institutions, government, religion, and taste were now explained away as mechanisms.

Arguably among the most perceptive of the critics was economist Clarence Edwin Ayres (1891–1972). Ayres was particularly aware of the dependence of modern science on machines, a dependence that made it as interesting to financiers as to faculties. In his book *Science: The False Messiah*, he argued that "machinery begins by altering the day's routine, and ends by altering the cosmos" (Ayres 1927:121). Indeed, the precision and repeatability of scientific experiments, noted Ayres, derives directly from their unnoticed dependence on machines, on instruments. Moreover, as the size and cost of the instruments of science rose, the industries built on scientific discoveries or inventions—he saw no difference between the two—would become ever more concentrated (Ayres 1944).

Among the more recent critics, perhaps geologist David Sarewitz deserves special attention. He observes:

Knowledge and innovation grow at breathtaking rates, and so does the scale of the problems that face humanity. Science-based revolutions in areas such as communication and information technologies, agriculture, materials, medical technology, and biotechnology are accompanied by global weapons proliferation, population growth, concentration of wealth, declining biodi-

versity and loss of habitat, deterioration of arable land, destruction of strato-
spheric ozone, and the potential for rapid changes in the earth's climate.
(Sarewitz 1996:3–4)

Despite this, he notes that U.S. federal government support for research
and development grew an astonishing four hundred percent *after inflation*
between 1960 and 1990.

Sarewitz chronicles what he describes as the myths of science commonly believed today:

- The myth of infinite benefit asserts that research is separate from society and exists merely to provide a constant flow of benefits to all. Yet,
the benefits of research are often available only to those with the wherewithal to exploit them. Moreover, research creates new and often unimagined social problems to solve.
- The myth of unfettered research suggests that scientists are detached
from the concerns of daily life, unrestricted such that they may pursue
their imaginations and busily work on various experiments each of
which will contribute equally to advancing the frontiers of knowledge
and benefits to society. In practice, science is and must be restricted by
funding priorities. It is funded unevenly across fields of science because, whatever their reasons, legislators believe that some fields are far
more interesting and important to society than others.
- The myth of accountability is the claim that scientists' obligations are
fulfilled if they maintain their intellectual integrity and produce research products that meet scientific standards. However, such a view
excludes outsiders—including those who pay for the research—from
making their own judgments about the usefulness and importance of
scientific research. As philosopher Sandra Harding suggests, "Why
should society, in the face of competing social needs, provide massive
resources for an enterprise that claims itself to have no social consequences? There is a vast irrationality in this kind of argument for the purity of science" (1991:38).
- The myth of authoritativeness asserts that science can bring closure to
political debate by providing the last word on a given subject. Yet, as
others have noted, it is precisely the most contested areas of science that
are likely to be the subject of lengthy political debate (e.g., Nelkin 1984).
When the scientific community is largely in agreement, the rest of society agrees as well. Global warming is a case in point in two ways: The
initial "solution" proposed by politicians was to pass it on to scientists
for further study. This avoided the need to make difficult political decisions. Then, as consensus among scientists increased, so did international willingness to confront the issue.

- Finally, the myth of the endless frontier implies that all good ideas orig-
  inate in basic science, are eventually transformed into new technologies,
  and finally are embraced by the public at large. But, in point of fact, science and technology are today inextricable in several ways: First, new
  problems for science often emerge from new technologies. For example,
  empirical observations in astronomy and the invention of the steam engine set in motion whole fields of science (Cardwell 1971). More recently, the invention of the digital computer made possible whole new
  fields of science, such as computational biology. Second, most scientific work is thoroughly dependent on technologies. One need only wander through a laboratory building on almost any university campus to
  see the enormous variety of machines that undergird the entire scientific enterprise.

CONCLUSION: BACON LIVES!

Yet, despite harsh criticisms of its limits and attention to its pitfalls, Bacon's belief that science would permit us to build an ideal society still holds
many in its grip. For example, the eminent entomologist, Edward O. Wilson (1998), in his recent book *Consilience,* tries to make the case for the
fundamental unity of knowledge. There is little to quibble with in his
lamenting the fragmented character of contemporary knowledge. Similarly, Wilson is certainly correct in noting that all human activities must have
biological (and even physical) origins. He is also correct in asserting the
need for greater contact between biologists and social scientists.

But, unfortunately, Wilson does not stop there. Wilson begins his book
by asserting, "When we have unified enough certain knowledge, we will
understand who we are and why we are here" (ibid.:6–7). Wilson is fond
of noting that the social sciences will have come of age when they are able
to predict events, thus reducing politics to administration.

Like Bacon several centuries before him, Wilson is convinced that by
linking the social sciences and the humanities to biology, it will be possible to determine what the right and the good are. The new science will
bring an end to the ideologies that now reign—whether postmodern or
Marxist. Yet, in his embrace of neoclassical economics and contract theory,
Wilson fails to recognize precisely the kind of ideological commitments he
claims to eschew.

Moreover, in Wilson's new world of unified science, art and moral philosophy will be subsumed under the biological umbrella. However, one
must ask how demonstrating that morality has a biological basis can in any
way help us to resolve the difficult moral problems of our time. Can biology (even linked with the social sciences) tell us whether abortion is moral-

ly right or wrong? Can biology tell us whether to remake the human body through genetic engineering? Hardly.

The Baconian ideal was recently expressed yet again in a recent *New York Times* article. Staff writer John Tierney, in an article entitled "Technology Makes Us Better," opined that the current technological changes we are experiencing are all for the good. While we may currently find that they are annoying or even harmful, this is merely a feature of the first-generation technologies. Just wait a few years and all will be well. A new age of cooperation, peace, and justice will prevail, at that same time as we gain more and more individual control over our lives and bodies, all thanks to the benefits of technology. Most surprisingly, we find that Africa's autocratic regimes will be undermined because "Africa's leaders can control newspapers, but citizens in remote villages are now getting uncensored news from Africa Online" (Tierney 1997). Where these internet connections are is unclear. Only one million Africans have internet access, and eighty percent or more of them are in South Africa (Useem 1999). In fact, on average there is only one *telephone* for every fifty-seven households in sub-Saharan Africa. In Uganda and Mali only one household in 435 has a telephone (International Telecommunications Union 1994).

Moreover, glowing endorsements of anything and everything deemed scientific continue to pour forth from the highest levels of government. In President Clinton's report on science and technology we find little guidance as to what scientific research should be funded. But we are told that "such investments drive economic growth, generate new knowledge, create new jobs, build new industries, ensure our national security, protect the environment, and improve the health and quality of life of our people" (Clinton 1997). Nor is the executive branch alone in its unbridled enthusiasm. The recent report of the House Committee on Science (U.S. Congress 1998) also embraces science as an undiluted good.

In sum, more than three hundred years after Bacon's death, the belief in the power of science and technology to resolve not merely technical but moral problems lives on. But whereas Bacon had proposed a program that was radically new, today the proponents of scientism merely recite the well-worn phrases of a past time. So opaque has faith in science and technology become that many who believe in it often do not even notice that they hold beliefs. To them, scientism is so self-evident that criticizing it is absurd. However, scientism is but one of the proposed paths to social order and perfection. Let us turn now to the state.

NOTES

1.   Following sociologist Bruno Latour (1987), I use the term "technoscience" to describe the interpenetration of science and technology. Today, we have both technologically embodied science and scientific technologies.

2. For critiques of *The Bell Curve*, see Duster (1995), Hauser (1995), and Taylor (1995).

3. In the early years of the republic, granting and enforcing patent rights were quite difficult affairs. See Bathe and Bathe (1935) and Federico (1945) for accounts of one such case. On the other hand, Franklin rejected securing a patent for his improved stove, arguing that it would hinder its widespread use (Campbell 1999).

4. Spencer's french contemporary, Emile Durkheim, made much the same argument: Once we understand how morality comes to be, we shall be able to follow its dictates knowingly.

5. Burawoy (1985) correctly argues that Taylor, despite repeated attempts, could in no way fully codify the tacit knowledge, because workers resist such codification.

6. James R. Garfield, secretary of the interior under Theodore Roosevelt, 1907–1909.

7. High membership fees kept smaller farmers out, while financing of local extension agents' salaries by Farm Bureau dues gave a great incentive to agents to keep organizing (Campbell 1962).

8. For an official view of the Industrial party trial, see Prokofyev (1933). For a historical view, see Bailes (1974).

9. It should be remembered that Lysenko's position appeared quite plausible in the context of Lamarckian biology. See Lewontin (1976).

Reprinted with permission of the Special Collections Division, Michigan State University.

3

THE STATE OF THE STATE

The conquerors of our day, peoples or princes, want their empire to possess a unified surface over which the superb eye of power can wander without encountering any inequality which hurts or limits its view. The same code of law, the same measures, the same rules, and if we could gradually get there, the same language; that is what is proclaimed as the perfection of the social organization. . . . The great slogan of the day is uniformity.

—James Scott, Seeing Like a State: How Certain Schemes to Improve the Human Condition Have Failed

"Pay no attention to that man behind the curtain. The great Oz has spoken."

—The Wizard, in L. Frank Baum, The Wizard of Oz

The nation-state has been around for a long time. It is hard for most of us even to imagine a world without nation-states, yet such was the case through most of human history. But what is this thing that we call a state? Many conventional definitions borrow from Max Weber ([1922] 1978) and argue that states are defined by their monopoly on coercive force. I shall make a somewhat different case. Specifically, I shall argue that there are two aspects of nation-states that are of relevance here: enclosure and enrollment. Simply put, states are forms of social networks that enroll by enclosing. Let me explain.

Modern nation-states have their origins in the enclosures of the fourteenth century in Europe. Members of the aristocracy began to realize that they could improve their material conditions—now measured in money—substantially by enclosing the commons land that peasants had used according to customary practice in the past. As Barrington Moore (1966) has noted, the enclosures marked a shift from asking what was the best way to support people on the land to asking how best to invest capital in the land. But at the same time as the landed aristocracy was enclosing the commons, another sort of enclosure was taking place as well. Cities were emerging as relatively autonomous entities with their own laws, guilds, markets, and fairs. The walls of the city were both the literal and figurative enclosure within which commerce took place.

At the same time, enclosure meant enrollment. Those who stayed within the enclosure were enrolled in the activities that took place within the now well-defined space. This was certainly the case for those who now managed the newly enclosed estates. Their choices were defined by the new system of fenced fields and animal agriculture. But it was equally true for the newcomers to the cities, perhaps pushed off the land by the aristocracy, but now enrolled in the activities of the cities as apprentices, journeymen, masters, or simply as unskilled laborers or beggars. In short, enclosures define the range of choices that one can make. They define how one becomes enrolled. As Robert Merton (1957) observed some years ago, they even define how one rebels.

The *system* of nation-states has its origins in the Treaty of Westphalia (1648)—just three years before Hobbes wrote *Leviathan*—by which the European powers created a new system for carving up large spaces. Henceforth, the rough edges of linguistic and ethnic communities, typical of the entire European continent, would be replaced by neat boundaries drawn on maps. Within those boundaries, one would be a subject—later citizen—of a given nation-state irrespective of the language one spoke or the ethnic group to which one belonged. Those who resided outside the state's boundaries would be deemed foreigners, strangers, perhaps enemies, even if they spoke the same language as that of the rulers. Many of the problems so manifest today in the Balkans are the result of problems brought on by enclosure.

In this chapter I shall attempt to examine the state in a new way. Through several cases of enrollment and enclosure I shall show how the state has become an unquestioned entity—unquestioned, paradoxically, even by those who seek to escape its reach. Let me begin by briefly discussing the largest and most successful state expansion ever attempted: the colonial project.

THE COLONIAL PROJECT

When Columbus sailed across the Atlantic in 1492 and claimed the small island of Guanahaní for the Spanish crown, he saw nothing problematic in what he was doing. It most certainly never occurred to him to consult with the native population before staking his claim. In the succeeding five centuries, hundreds of European explorers, merchants, soldiers, scientists, and missionaries embarked on what they perceived to be the great civilizing task of European civilization. Undoubtedly some believed fervently in what they did, while others were more cynical. Some were open to the strange practices of foreign cultures, while others were convinced of the superiority of European culture. Moreover, the lines between these diverse occupations were themselves blurred. Soldiers might be merchants; explorers might be soldiers; missionaries might be scientists (see, e.g., Whiteman, 1983). But one thing is clear: If that civilizing task appeared to require the blessings of the pope in the sixteenth century, by the eighteenth century the project had become a largely secular affair requiring only a modicum of religious trappings.

This marks the first great attempt to extend the boundaries of the modern nation-state, to enclose huge areas of the earth's surface so as enroll those who lived there in the construction of the "mother country." Several different types of colonies were formed, depending on the nature of the place to be colonized. In general, settler colonies were formed in the sparsely populated temperate zones such as those in North and South America, Australia, the Kenyan highlands, and southern Africa. Here, Europeans wrested the lands from the indigenous population through war, disease,[1] famine, and banishment to the areas that were of little interest to the European settlers. Here they created what Crosby (1986) has called "neo-Europes."

In those tropical and subtropical climates where labor was scarce, or the indigenous population too difficult to subdue, they imported nonindigenous peoples as slaves to work the new plantations. Of course, the local populations were almost never enslaved. They knew the local terrain too well, which made escape easy. Instead, Africans were uprooted from their native lands and shipped around the world to populate the neo-European plantations. This was the case in the southeastern United States, the islands of the Caribbean, parts of Central America, and northeastern Brazil.

Finally, in those nations where indigenous populations were large and climates unfriendly to European settlers, they ruled through the indigenous leaders, whom they controlled by a combination of carrots and sticks. India and most of Africa conformed to this model. European-owned plantations were established on the best land (often consisting of crops that were foreign to the area), while the remaining lands were used to feed the local inhabitants.

Britain, France, Germany, Belgium, Netherlands, Spain, and Portugal all had their colonies. The United States, while only a marginal participant in the colonial conquests, nevertheless had the Philippines as a colony, spheres of influence in China and Japan, the Monroe Doctrine in Latin America, the special relationship with Liberia, the territorial wars with Mexico, and the convenient policy of laying claim to the "unused" lands of North America while pushing the native populations to the side or exterminating them.

Of course, from the viewpoint of the populations conquered, exterminated, or displaced by the Europeans, this was hardly a pleasant experience. What the Europeans saw as the progress of enlightenment, of civilization, of modernization, of Christianization, the conquered saw as the systematic extermination of their brethren and ways of life. The "White Man's Burden," so eloquently described by Rudyard Kipling (1899) was light compared to that imposed on men and women of color.

The colonization of the world generated both critics and sympathizers. Most prominent among the critics of the nineteenth century was Karl Marx—who nevertheless saw the benefits of Western civilization as outweighing the burdens imposed on the colonies. Colonialism was good as long as it hastened the spread of capitalism, which—at least in his more determinist moments—Marx saw as merely a necessary step on the road to a communist utopia. Others less well-known wrote of the excesses of slavery, of the repression of peoples, of the horrors of conquest.

At the same time, there was no shortage of sympathizers. African slave traders were all too happy to profit by selling their brethren to the Europeans. Indian Zamindari were all too eager to become tax collectors for the British. And countless Native Americans became proselytizers for one or another form of Christianity.

From its inception the colonial project was a mixture of state expansionism, market creation, and the spread of Christianity.[2] Nevertheless, statism was the driving force. What was seen by all to be absolutely necessary was the carving out of particular geographic areas for future expansion of the motherland. Without the support of nation-states, and especially their armies, neither markets nor religion would have spread so rapidly.

One widespread feature of colonization was the seemingly endless variety of holocausts that it required, each justified in the name of the state, God, or progress. Consider the Spanish invasion of Latin America. Eighty to ninety percent of native Americans died through war and disease (Cook 1998). The entire Aztec and Inca civilizations were destroyed, their cultures, religions, even languages consigned to the trash heap of history. The British and later the Americans were no less aggressive in their desire to remove the indigenous population from the land. Like the Rocky Mountains, the native Americans were viewed as obstacles to European progress. What started out as praise for the sophisticated societies of North America became utter contempt. Whole ethnic groups were wiped out by the superior weaponry of the Americans as well as by disease. For example, the Cherokee nation was forced to march 116 days, covering a distance of twelve hundred miles, from North Carolina to Oklahoma. The death toll was extraordinary: four thousand people died of hunger, exhaustion, or exposure. It became known as the Trail of Tears (Fleischmann 1971).

At the same time, the revival of slavery uprooted millions of Africans from their homes and sent them to the Americas to work on plantations to feed the ever-increasing European desire for cotton, sugar, and tobacco.

While the indigenous populations could run into the interior and had intimate knowledge of it, the transplanted Africans, torn from family and linguistic ties, lacked such alternatives. They made excellent slaves.

Moreover, the chaos wrought by slavery justified the very treatment that Africans received. Coming from dozens of distinct societies, knowing little about their new surroundings, Africans appeared truly inferior to their white masters. Africans, it was claimed, were incapable of sophisticated learning, of maintaining the kinds of social relations expected of civilized persons, of rising to the level of persons of European origins. To make sure that this remained the case, laws were passed prohibiting the education of slaves, denying them citizenship and basic human rights and otherwise ensuring their "natural" inferiority.

In the United States, it would take a civil war to end slavery, and who knows how many more centuries to resolve what Gunnar Myrdal (1944) once referred to as an "American dilemma." In Brazil, the other large slaveholding state of the Americas, slavery was not abolished until 1888. And, while racism is not as overt in Brazil as it often is the United States, it remains a factor in Brazilian politics.

Of course, a few slaves escaped to form a great diaspora throughout the Americas. Even today on the Nicaraguan and Honduran coasts, one can find villages whose population consists largely of the descendants of former slaves. In only one case, Haiti, were the slaves able to overthrow their masters. Under the leadership of Toussaint L'Ouverture, Haiti was liberated from the French, who at the time were also busy fighting wars in Europe. The first and only African republic was established in the Americas. Later it would come under the direct control of the United States for twenty years (1915–1934). Today, it remains the poorest nation in the western hemisphere, a nation denuded, overpopulated, illiterate, destitute.

Other slaves were returned to Africa. British abolitionists privately founded the city of Freetown for this purpose in 1787. Twenty years later, when Britain abolished slavery, Freetown became part of the new colony of Sierra Leone. Similarly, the American Colonization Society established a settlement of freed slaves on the West African coast in 1821. This later became the first modern African republic, Liberia.

In the densely populated areas of the world, European domination took yet another form. Local rulers were bought off by promises of wealth and power. In northern Nigeria, the policy of "indirect rule" was used to control the nation for the British. Emirates were established with British approval to engage in "native administration." Several uprisings occurred but were quickly squelched. In India, the Zamindari used the caste system to encourage long-term indebtedness and to collect taxes for the British. Here, too, resistance occurred. Only when Gandhi launched a campaign of resistance were the British finally forced to come face to face with the contradictions of colonialism. Even then, it took years of resistance before the British left in 1947.

In French Africa, the hated *corvée*, abolished by the French Revolution in France, was reinstituted. Each subject was to perform a certain number of days of work for the state, building roads, government buildings, or engaged in other work. So confident were the French of their hold on their African colonies that Charles De Gaulle, then president of France, offered them independence in 1958. Only one colony voted for it: Guinea. The French, outraged at the unmitigated gall shown by the Guineans, stormed out of the country, taking with them plans for cities, carburetors from tractors, light switches in offices, and anything else that would—they hoped—make the Guineans come crawling for forgiveness. But it never happened. Two years later, the rest of French Africa disintegrated into separate states.

The Portuguese, perhaps because of their economic weakness at home, felt it necessary to engage in a protracted war to retain many of their colonies. In Portuguese Guinea (now Guinea-Bissau), in Angola, and in Mozambique, they engaged in bloody wars against local guerrillas in a vain attempt to maintain the last vestiges of empire. When they finally left, each nation was in ruins, and in Angola and Mozambique the realpolitik of the cold war took over where the Portuguese left off. Civil war replaced wars of colonial liberation, while the Americans and Soviets found themselves at war by proxy.

In sum, the colonial project was *the* great statist project. It lasted for more than four centuries, bringing in its wake mass migrations, economic chaos, death, and destruction. What began as a quest for order, for a world consisting entirely of nation-states and their colonies, ended in massive disorder. The Hobbesian dream became a nightmare when put into practice—even by nations ostensibly democratic. Those regions that were colonized are still attempting to put their houses in order. Civil war, ethnic rivalry, corruption, massive inequalities, and widespread abject poverty constitute much of the legacy of colonial rule.

But even before the colonial project began to fade, new forms of statism emerged. If colonialism has been with us for several centuries, what is often referred to as the totalitarian state is a relatively recent product. It could not have occurred at an earlier point in history—although earlier centuries certainly had their oppressive regimes—because the technical means for totalitarian states simply did not exist. Totalitarian regimes required relatively well-organized transport and communications infrastructure as well as modern military technologies. Those technologies, combined with the Hobbesian vision of the state, allowed centralization with hitherto undreamed of control in the hands of a few. A totalitarian sovereign could know where his subjects were, with whom they associated, how they conducted themselves in daily life, even what they ate for breakfast. Let us turn now to that form of statism.

THE OPPRESSIVE STATE AND THE STATE OF OPPRESSION

Arguably, the cult of the state reached its zenith in the mid–twentieth century, perhaps as a result of the use of newly developed propaganda mechanisms. At that time, in Hobbesian fashion, leaders of nation-states truly appeared larger than life. Stalin and Hitler may have brought fear to the hearts of many, but they were truly seen as heroes by many more. They would lead the Soviet Union and Germany out of chaos and despair. Mao achieved the same status by leading his armies on the Long March and driving out the Japanese. The Japanese went even further, revering Emperor Hirohito as a god. And Franco, Mussolini, and Salazar built their little empires as well.

I shall not dwell here on the obvious and countless injustices carried out in the name of the state in Germany under Hitler, the Soviet Union under Stalin, or China under Mao. Huge bodies of literature already recount these tragedies of history. But other less powerful nations embraced the personality cult with equal passion. Instead, let us examine some of the lesser known statist tragedies.

Romania

Nicolai Ceauşescu (1918–1989) ruled Romania from 1965 to 1989. During that period he utilized the *Securitate,* or Department of State Security, to keep the nation in a continual state of terror. Moreover, by criticizing the Soviet invasion of Czechoslovakia in 1968, he was able to garner support among Western nations. President Nixon visited Romania in 1969 and President Ford granted it most favored nation status. Both ignored the increasingly miserable record on human rights. Similarly, the British government invited Ceauşescu to Britain in 1978 to bolster exports, conveniently ignoring the draconian measures he had taken at home.

At the same time, Ceauşescu carefully attempted to build nationalism at home. The Soviet invasion of Czechoslovakia was the initial premise for nationalist spirit, but other opportunities presented themselves as well. For example, Transylvania, long regarded as homeland to both Romanians and Hungarians, proved a convenient place to display nationalistic sentiments. Indeed, the Hungarian minority was increasingly deprived of any rights under the Ceauşescu regime. Similarly, Ceauşescu played up the plight of Romanians in Bessarabia, then part of the Soviet Union and now part of the Republic of Moldova.

In the name of modernization, the policy of systematization (*sistemati-zare*) was developed. Small villages were bulldozed as they were deemed inefficient. Urban neighborhoods were destroyed so as to rationalize urban services. Some forty thousand people were forced to move to make way for Ceaușescu's palace, the ornate "House of the People," the second largest building (after the Pentagon) on the planet. But, most importantly, by destroying villages and neighborhoods, Ceaușescu was able to destroy nearly all social networks other than those linking people to the state, thereby further consolidating his power. Householders generally received less than six months' notice of removal and were paid a maximum of about two years' salary for their homes. Moreover, citizens were drafted into destroying their own homes by a tax levied on the costs of razing them. When international protests erupted, official destruction was slowed, while services such as bus transport and food stores were eliminated, making the villages unlivable.

In his attempt to build heavy industry in that nation, Ceaușescu virtually destroyed every remnant of civil society. Dissenters were arrested, subject to continual surveillance, removed from their jobs summarily, sent to forced labor camps, and banished to psychiatric hospitals where they were drugged, beaten, and shocked. Failure to report a conversation with a foreigner was made into a crime. Typewriters had to be registered with the police. In an effort to increase population growth, women of child-bearing age were required to undergo periodic gynecological examinations to ensure that they were not breaking the law by using contraceptives or obtaining illegal abortions. Childless couples over the age of twenty-five saw their taxes increase. Members of the *Securitate* were assigned to maternity wards to prevent abortions. Even those critics of the regime living elsewhere had to fear Ceaușescu's assassination squads (Deletant 1995).

To prop up the increasingly impoverished regime, citizens wishing to emigrate were literally sold to other nations. A secret agreement with West Germany provided four thousand to ten thousand Deutschmarks for each German-speaking Romanian. Nevertheless, by 1981 foreign debt topped $10.2 billion. As a result, Ceaușescu imposed austerity measures "unparalleled even in the bleak history of Eastern European communist regimes" (ibid.:248), vowing to eliminate the debt entirely by 1990.

Electricity was frequently interrupted and rationed by the creation of a "lightbulb police," who spied on everyone to make sure that they were not burning too many lights. Gas pressure was reduced during the day and hot water was limited to one day a week. Winter office temperatures were limited to 14°C (58°F). By 1989 food rations were limited to two pounds of sugar, two pounds of flour, one-half pound of margarine, and five eggs per month. Gasoline was limited to thirty liters per month. In 1989, when Ceaușescu was overthrown and he and his family unceremoniously killed, records revealed that the *Securitate* had 38,682 personnel and 400,000 informants—this in a nation of only twenty-three million inhabitants (ibid.:1995).

Argentina

At the beginning of the twentieth century, Argentina was a prosperous nation with a level of living comparable to that of the United States, Australia, or Canada (Falcoff and Dolkart 1975). But unlike those other nations, Argentina depended excessively on an export-led economy. When the global depression of the 1930s hit Argentina, the economy rapidly declined. The Argentine state responded by increasing import taxes, thereby protecting local manufacturing by making the nation noncompetitive with the rest of the world. Even landowners, represented by the Rural Society, supported tariffs on manufactured goods. They argued that the introduction of foreign farm machinery would put money in the hands of foreigners while reducing domestic employment (Whitaker 1975).

As a result, Argentina—a nation of well-educated people—experienced a virtual collapse of class mobility. Despite a national labor movement, workers were unable to raise wages and were not even ensured the right to strike. The armed forces, active in politics since the nineteenth century, felt it was their duty to intervene to save the nation politically. In a coup d'état in 1943, the army replaced the civilian government. Moreover, with fascism on the rise in Germany, Italy, and Spain—nations with which Argentina had long-standing ties—the generals felt that they were on the crest of a new wave of statism. Juan Domingo Perón (1895–1974) rose rapidly under the leadership of General Pedro Pablo Ramirez, who appointed him director of the national Department of Labor. Perón used that post to forge a strange alliance between part of the military and the labor movement.

As World War II drew to a close it became apparent that fascism would be consigned to the dustbin of history. The military arrested Perón, but his second wife, Eva Duarte—now immortalized in the film *Evita*—managed to organize a labor march on Buenos Aires and threatened a general strike. As a result, Perón was released and restored to power (Sobel 1975). By 1946, in an election rigged by suppression of the opposition, Perón became president of Argentina. Soon afterward, he eliminated opposition in both the judiciary and the universities.

Perón withdrew his support of the Axis powers and developed his own rather obscure philosophy of *Justicialismo*, a "third way" between capitalism and communism. In 1949 the old constitution of 1853 was replaced by a new one, which ostensibly granted liberal rights and a separation of powers. In fact, under the new constitution, power was further concentrated in

Perón's hands. Thus, when opposition newspapers accused the regime of torturing political prisoners, a congressional committee investigated the newspapers that printed the charges (Blanksten 1953).

In 1951 Perón was elected to a six-year term as president, but the elections simply legitimated what was already de facto the case. As one observer noted, "Juan Domingo Perón is the law in that country, and his will dominates all public agencies on all levels of government. Opposition parties, while they still exist, are carefully hemmed in, and only the *Peronista* party, blindly loyal to Perón, is permitted to win elections when they are held" (Blanksten 1953:v). Indeed, Perón was quite effective in getting Congress to pass laws that supported his predilections.

Although Perón was exiled (eventually to Spain) in 1955 by the very military that put him in power, his popularity was such that when elections were held again in 1973, his Peronist party captured the presidency. He returned victorious, abandoned his left-wing supporters and remained in power until his death in 1974. Afterwards, his third wife became president, but was soon driven out by the military. Yet, the military demonstrated its utter inability even to maintain order. The nation soon was transformed into an unmanageable collection of military fiefdoms, each with its own capricious military officers. During the 1970s and 1980s thousands of Argentinians, known later as *los desaparecidos* (the disappeared), died at the hands of the military. And even today the ghost of Perón haunts Argentinian politics; outgoing president Carlos Menem unsuccessfully attempted to corrupt the very democratic politics that brought him to power.

Zaire

Mobutu Sese Seko (1930–1997), brought to power and maintained there largely by American support, managed to transform Africa's richest nation into one of its poorest. Mobutu made no claim to national development as the rulers of some of neighboring nations did. Instead, he was quite content to let most of the national infrastructure—never very well developed—turn to dust. Roads, railways, bridges, hospitals, schools, all lay in shambles at the same time as the infrastructure necessary to mine Zaire's riches was protected. In quiet collusion, the multinational mining companies and the Western nations obsessed by anticommunism looked the other way while Mobutu lined his pockets at the expense of the nation's citizens. By the time he was removed from office, dying of prostate cancer, his fortune was estimated at five billion dollars, most of it safely tucked away in foreign banks (*Mail and Guardian* 1997). Now, in a parody of Hobbes's predictions, Mobutu's successors have plunged the nation into a bloody civil war.

North Korea

Modeling his regime on that of Stalin, Kim Il Sung (1912–1994) ruled North Korea with brutal force, embarking on his own peculiar brand of communism. To date, his son, Kim Jong Il, has pursued the same policies—policies marked by hero worship of an unprecedented sort. Unlike most other communist leaders, Kim Il Sung soon began to build his family into a hereditary elite. Installed in power in 1946 by the Soviets, he soon overcame any remaining opposition. His family history was rewritten to show that his ancestors were all revolutionary heroes of one sort or another. By 1973 he had already begun to plan for succession by his son. The organization established to promote his ideas was renamed the Kim Il Sung and Kim Jong Il Thought Institute in 1985.

Today in North Korea, as in Ceauşescu's Romania, travel is highly restricted. Moreover, the nation is divided into three classes: a revolutionary core group of about 2 million people, the "ambivalent unreliable elements" (about 1.5 million persons) and the counterrevolutionary elements (about 3 million persons) who have no rights. Each group wears badges that proclaim its class status. There is an obsessive interest in building heavy industry; as a result food, housing, and even clothing is rationed. The National Security Agency, under the direct control of the Leader, ensures that dissent is quickly suppressed. In 1996, there were 150,000 political prisoners including entire families. They were forced to grow their own food and denied access to medical care.

The last four years have seen widespread famine. A U.S. Congressional delegation estimated that two million North Koreans have died of hunger or hunger-related illnesses during the last several years. Even the government itself admits that at least 220,000 died (*Boston Globe* 1999). Most of these deaths would have been easily avoided if Western food aid had been accepted rapidly and in sufficient quantities. So miserable is the nation that the last East German ambassador observed that it was an absolutist state disguised as a socialist nation (Chun 1997).

Other States

And there were the tragicomic personalities as well. Ugandan president Idi Amin had himself carried around in a sedan chair by white Ugandans in a reversal of colonial fortunes. But this hardly stopped his armies from brutally slaying thousands of Ugandans. In the impoverished Central African Republic, Jean-Bedel Bokassa had himself crowned emperor and renamed his nation an empire. And, like many emperors of times past, he managed to even further impoverish his subjects by raiding the national treasury. To this list we could add Sadam Hussein, Muammar al Qaddafi,

Alfredo Stroessner Matiauda, Augusto Pinochet, Francisco Franco, and Antonio de Oliveira Salazar, to name but a few.

STATISM WITH A DEMOCRATIC FACE

But statism—the belief in the state and its leaders—is hardly limited to well-known or even highly authoritarian regimes. Even those states that could hardly be considered totalitarian—indeed, those that are, or claim to be, representative democracies—have a sad legacy of oppression of difference. Minorities, women, gays and lesbians, the mentally handicapped, and others who did not fit the mold of correct citizenship have been persecuted, jailed, ostracized, banned, or driven underground. Moreover, the democratic nations have hardly been immune to the personality cult and the associated statism. Franklin D. Roosevelt captivated the American nation for nearly four terms of office. Winston Churchill appeared larger than life in Britain. Charles De Gaulle's height was only surpassed by his stature as a leader of France. Jawaharlal Nehru enjoyed similar status in India.

The United States

Despite textbook accounts that suggest that the United States has been largely free of statist tendencies, statism has been alive and well throughout much of American history. From before the beginning of the American republic, the doctrine of Manifest Destiny was used to justify American conquest of the continent. Writing in 1789, Boston minister Jedediah Morse noted, "It is well known that empire has been traveling from east to west. Probably her last and broadest seat will be America . . . the largest empire that ever existed" (quoted in Van Alstyne 1960:69). Countless Native Americans were displaced by what was euphemistically called westward expansion. In both the war of independence and that of 1812, Americans tried unsuccessfully to annex Canada. Florida was wrenched from Spain with relative ease. Mexico lost much of its territory to American imperial ambitions. President James K. Polk explained: "Foreign powers do not seem to appreciate the true character of our government. . . . To enlarge its limits, is to extend the dominions of peace over additional territories, and increasing millions" (quoted in Williams 1969:84). In addition, most of the nations of the Caribbean and Central America have at one time or another been under direct American control. Indeed, historian Frederick Jackson Turner could well argue in 1893 that expansion was itself an engine of U.S. prosperity and democracy.

But American statism has not been limited to territorial expansion. Consider several other major statist tragedies:

- Many proponents of women's suffrage found themselves jailed on trumped up charges, subjected to all sorts of "special" treatment in prison in a vain effort to make them drop their convictions. President Wilson did his best to ignore them.

- Senator Joseph McCarthy (1908–1957) engaged in a one-man reign of terror beginning in 1950. McCarthy claimed that he had the names of hundreds of officials in the State Department who were communist sympathizers. Later, hundreds of intellectuals, artists, workers, and even bystanders were caught in the headlong rush to judgment. Many found themselves blacklisted, unable to obtain employment again for years. Virtually none of those interrogated were found to have committed any crime. Finally, after four years of interminable hearings, he was formally censured by the U.S. Senate.

- On May 30, 1921, an African-American man accidentally stepped on the toe of a white female elevator operator in a downtown Tulsa building. He was arrested and charged with assault (a charge that was later dropped). Soon white mobs stormed the black section of the city, looting and burning everything in their path. The National Guard was called in but did little to prevent the twenty-five thousand looters from continuing their destruction. When the riots ended probably more than one hundred and fifty people had died, nearly all of them black. Over eleven hundred homes were destroyed as was the entire black business district. More than four thousand people were left homeless. Subsequent grand jury investigations concluded that the problem was the lack of sufficient numbers of white policemen in the black section of Tulsa. Only one person was ever prosecuted for anything connected to the riot—a black man arrested for carrying a concealed weapon (Halliburton 1975). Tragically, the Tulsa riot was only one of many.

- From 1932 until 1972 medical experiments were performed on African-Americans without their knowledge by the U.S. Public Health Service. Specifically, the study consisted of following the etiology of untreated syphilis in African-American males in order to determine whether its natural course was significantly different than in whites. The unsuspecting participants were poor sharecroppers recruited through the Tuskegee Institute Medical Center. Four hundred infected persons were denied treatment; as many as one hundred died of the fully treatable disease (Jones 1981).

- Civil rights leaders of the 1960s found themselves beaten, tortured, jailed, and sometimes killed by both vigilante groups protecting white privilege and by the force of law. Not only small-town sheriffs but even entire states spied on would-be organizers, black-balled them from jobs, and looked the other way when they were the victims of illegal actions on the part of white supremacist groups or other organs of the state. The

Mississippi Sovereignty Commission was particularly infamous in this respect. Shielded by the cold war suspicion of anything labeled communist, from 1956 to 1973 it spied on civil rights activists and gave their names to employers and the Ku Klux Klan, often resulting in firing, beating, and even death (Cloud 1998).

- Nor have governmental agencies been particularly concerned about using highway construction as a means for both destroying African-Americans' homes and businesses and keeping the poorer segment of the population (read "black") out of areas reserved for whites. For example, planners and city officials used the construction of Interstate Highway 95 as an excuse to bulldoze the predominantly black Miami neighborhood of Overtown. Moreover, abandoning a 1955 plan that would have bypassed most of the area, city officials insisted on cutting right through the central business district of Overtown. The once vibrant neighborhood of forty thousand people was soon reduced to fewer than ten thousand (Nathaniel-Isaacs 1994). Similarly, New York City planner Robert Moses managed to keep the poor away from Long Island beaches by building highways with overpasses so low as to prohibit the passage of buses, their major means of transport (Winner 1986).

- With few exceptions the American state has sided with employers against workers. For example, in the 1870s several U.S. railroads decided to cut wages dramatically while increasing the dividends to shareholders. Workers protested by stopping trains, diverting them from their intended destinations, refusing to work, and in several cases, burning engines and railway buildings. State militiamen and federal troops were brought in to squelch the protests. Several dozen unarmed workers and citizens were killed in the melee, much to the chagrin not only of workers but to generally sympathetic townspeople (Laurie 1989).

Similarly, as the panic of 1873 increased substantially their numbers, unemployed workers gathered for a peaceful rally in New York's Tompkins Square. Unbeknownst to most of the crowd, their police permit for the rally had been canceled. Police charged into the mob swinging their billy clubs and injured many of the participants. The *New York Times* concluded that the demonstration was wholly the work of radical foreigners, ignoring the dire circumstances in which the workers found themselves (Dulles and Dubofsky 1993).

The 1890s brought even more violence. As workers struck in protest against a wage cut at the Carnegie Steel Company in Homestead, Pennsylvania, three hundred armed Pinkerton guards were dispatched to the scene, resulting in the deaths of seven persons. Soon after, eight thousand state militiamen protected the factory while nonunion workers were hired to take the jobs of the strikers. Similar events took place in the company town of Pullman, Illinois (ibid.). Compiling a list of similar events would itself fill a volume far larger than this one.

While the New Deal of the 1930s did improve the lot of labor by providing certain legal guarantees to workers, many of these have been eroded in recent years. State legislatures have passed so-called right-to-work laws making union shops all but impossible to form. Companies, too, have eroded workers' rights by moving to nonunion states or overseas and by campaigning successfully against unions using the twin ideological tools of American individualism and the threat of communism (Bernstein 1999; Moberg 1992).

Even today, opponents of organized labor will leave no stone unturned. In addition to hiring consulting firms that specialize in union busting, right-wing politicians have introduced legislation in several states—unsuccessfully to date—that would require unions to obtain permission annually to use members' dues for political purposes. Of course, no such requirement would apply to the $1.26 billion in shareholders' money used for corporate lobbying each year (Center for Responsive Politics 1998). Moreover, even in those companies and industries with strong unions, legislators and the courts have denied workers input into much more than wages, benefits, and associated working conditions. Rarely have they been able to penetrate the hierarchical form of the modern corporation.

- Those deemed sexually deviant have also found themselves subject to constant harassment. Some of this consists of privately funded harassment by religious groups that claim to have direct knowledge of God's intentions with respect to sex, while other harassment comes from those unfortunate individuals who are so unsure of their (usually male) gender that they feel it necessary to strike out at those who are different— gays, lesbians, transgendered, etc. But of far greater import is the often direct state support for efforts to discriminate against such persons, especially in smaller communities where anonymity is difficult to maintain. Indeed, in one of its more infamous decisions, in 1986 the U.S. Supreme Court (478 US 186) upheld a Georgia statute banning homosexual relations in private between consenting adults. Ironically, the statute was recently struck down by the Georgia courts as a violation of the state constitution (1998 Ga. LEXIS 1148; 98 Fulton County DR 3952).
- For the most part, the phrase written in 1883 by Emma Lazarus and immortalized on the base of the Statue of Liberty is only half true. It should read, "Give us your tired, your poor, your huddled masses yearning to breathe free . . . as long as they are white and preferably from Western Europe." Before World War I, immigration to the United States was essentially restricted to white Europeans. One exception was Chinese la-

borers, who were permitted to migrate so as to provide cheap labor for railway construction until further immigration was prohibited by the Chinese Exclusion Act of 1882 (ch. 126, 22 Stat. 58). While Western Europe had been the main immigrant source prior to the advent of inexpensive steamship travel, Eastern Europeans were added in significant numbers in the late nineteenth and early twentieth centuries. Then, in an ironic move for a nation made up largely of immigrants, the Immigration Act of 1924 (ch. 190, 43 Stat. 153) restricted immigration based on national origin. Britain, Ireland, and Germany received 70 percent of the national quota, a proportion that was never filled. The system was liberalized in 1965 and finally abolished in 1968. It was replaced by a first-come, first-served system, which shifted immigration flows to Latin America and Asia.

• As Morton Horwitz (1977) has shown, much to the chagrin of some of his colleagues who seem to believe that law school faculty should never criticize the law, American courts have consistently ruled in favor of development interests since the 1850s. In the eighteenth century, domestic use of land always took precedence over industrial use. But already by the late eighteenth century, this view of land was being attacked.

For example, the Massachusetts Mill Act of 1795 permitted millowners to flood others' land as long as due compensation was paid. By the late nineteenth century there was a flurry of court decisions that spelled out new rights for developers. Horwitz quotes a New York Supreme Court decision in 1873 as an example:

> The general rules that I may have the exclusive and undisturbed use and possession of my real estate, and that I must so use my real estate as not to injure my neighbor, are much modified by the exigencies of the social state. We must have factories, machinery, dams, canals and railroads. They are demanded by the manifold wants of mankind, and lay at the basis of all our civilization. (ibid.:71)

Moreover, the municipal corporations of the eighteenth century, at least in theory designed to promote the public good, were transformed into the private corporations of the nineteenth century, in which profits for stockholders were deemed tantamount to the public good.

In an effort to conceal the changes that were made by the judiciary, the doctrine of legal formalism was invented. Under this doctrine law was seen to be fully separate from politics. Furthermore, with the growth of status of science, new grounds for justifying legal change could be created: "A scientific, objective, professional, and apolitical conception of law, once primarily a rhetorical monopoly of a status-hungry elite of legal thinkers, now comes to extend its domain and to infiltrate into the every day [*sic*] categories of adjudication" (ibid.:266).

• Both the United States and Canada engaged in the active internment of entire families of Japanese origin—citizens and noncitizens alike—during the Second World War. On February 19, 1942, President Franklin D. Roosevelt signed an executive order that allowed (and encouraged) the secretary of war to authorize making certain areas of the nation into military areas and to exclude any persons considered a potential threat to national security from them.[3]

A month later the U.S. Congress enacted PL 503, which made it a crime to disobey the military concerning restriction on residence in those areas. Stemming from these two events, all persons of Japanese ancestry were summarily removed from coastal California, Washington, Oregon, and parts of Arizona. Of the 110,000 persons relocated, 70,000 were U.S. citizens. The relocation camps were surrounded by barbed wire and patrolled by armed guards. Those inside were forbidden to leave without permission. They were clearly concentration camps in everything but name.

Moreover, in two cases brought before the Supreme Court in 1943 and 1944, respectively, the Court affirmed the government position. In short, despite the separation of powers, each of the three branches of the government capitulated to military and racist pressures. As Charles McClain put it:

> The net effect of this series of decisions was to legitimize the most extraordinary exercise of power by military authorities over civilians in American history. More importantly, it affirmed the principle that the military or any other arm of government could use membership in an ethnic group—and that alone—as the basis for depriving individuals of some of their most basic civil liberties. (1994:xi)

At the time, in the United States, Japanese immigrants, like all Asians, were barred from obtaining citizenship. However, by virtue of the fourteenth amendment to the U.S. constitution, anyone born within the nation was entitled to citizenship. Thus, the majority of Japanese who were interned were second-generation Americans, often still children.[4]

> Although the internments were justified on grounds of national security, no similar actions occurred in places where security issues were far greater. For example, in Hawaii, where there were far more Japanese immigrants, those few suspected of subversive activity were merely placed under surveillance. They were only arrested if they were believed to pose a security threat. And, even more telling was that Britain and France, al-

though far closer to the action of the war, interned far fewer people than
did the United States (Rostow [1945] 1994).

Of course, a few persons did resist. As noted above, several brave
Japanese-Americans brought suit unsuccessfully in federal court. A few
law professors and government officials protested that the action was
unjust (e.g., Rostow [1945] 1994), but to no avail. And, while reparations
to the victims were ultimately and belatedly paid, they hardly com-
pensated for the damage done to families and communities of innocent
people.
• Even today, the U.S. National Security Agency, which runs the top-se-
cret Echelon eavesdropping system, uses satellites to intercept and elec-
tronically read all electronic communications that cross international
borders. Anytime that you or I place an international call or send an international E-mail, Echelon is listening (Port and Resch 1999). Other nations have their equivalent systems in place as well.

Sweden

Social democratic Sweden, too, has had its statist troubles. A 1934 law
permitted sterilization of those persons found in some way to be unfit. Initially, the law was applied only to the mentally retarded, but later it was
widely used to sterilize women in difficult circumstances. Only in 1976 did
the sterilizations stop, in large part due to protests from women's groups
and victims. Over sixty thousand persons were sterilized as a result of
widespread agreement among the medical, scientific, and political communities. Yet, during most of the period the law was in effect, most Swedes
were unaware of it (Butler 1997; Freedland 1997).

Norway

Even Norway, itself dominated by Denmark and by Sweden at various
times in its history, managed to attempt to suppress its major ethnic minority. By the late eighteenth century, the Norwegian state had begun a
campaign to increase the efficiency of use of private land. The Sami (Lapp)
peoples, among the last nomads on the European continent, saw their economic status decline as a result. By mid–nineteenth century, a royal decree
was issued that provided funds for teaching the Sami the Norwegian language. In 1862, new national guidelines made Norwegian the language of
instruction in any school where more than half the children were native
Norwegian speakers. Moreover, all instruction at the secondary level was
to be conducted in Norwegian.

But suppression of Sami culture reached its height during a reorganiza-
tion of the schools that began in 1879. From 1881 onward, it was decreed

that only Norwegian was to be used in school. Teachers were even instructed to insist that Sami-speaking children use Norwegian after school hours. A policy of "Norwegianization" was instituted as well, whereby Samis were encouraged to settle down and to become farmers. "Nationalism had evolved into an ideology of conformity that was unable to accommodate any culture other than the Norwegian" (Solbakk 1990:124). Social Darwinist and racist views were encouraged despite opposition from some Norwegian officials and scientists.

After the end of the Second World War, Norwegian views of the Sami began to change, in part as a result of the increased politicization of the Sami population. Textbooks began to be distributed in both Sami and Norwegian, although the Norwegianization policies were not rescinded until 1959. Only in 1988 was the Norwegian constitution amended to require the government to recognize the distinct Sami culture. One year later, a Sami Parliament was formed.

* * * * *

Alas, one could easily go documenting injustices wrought by nation-states—both those with totalitarian ambitions and those with far more democratic beliefs. In each case people were enrolled through enclosure, the choices provided by the state limiting people's actions to a prescribed set of alternatives. Apparently democratic states have hardly been exceptions.

Most discussions of state-sponsored injustice stop at this point. In so doing they ignore the private states, the large corporations that have come to dominate the world over the last several centuries. These corporate states have been equally successful in enrolling through enclosure. It is to those private states that I now turn.

THE RISE OF THE PRIVATE STATE

Conventional theories of the state make a sharp distinction between nation-states and corporations. I submit that this distinction is erroneous. If a defining characteristic of a state is that it has a monopoly over the means of coercion, then corporations are without a doubt forms of states even as they are creatures of particular nation-states. Michael Burawoy (1979) has argued for what he calls the "internal state," the set of rights and institutions developed within the firm. Burawoy is certainly correct in noting that such things as grievance procedures, corporate manuals, organizational charts, and union contracts are the functional equivalent of rights, laws, and responsibilities in the context of the nation-state. Corporations, like nation-states, have the power to enroll and enclose. In large measure they can set the conditions of work. They can eject or otherwise punish those who do not follow corporate rules. They can control the movement of persons on their premises. But Burawoy does not go far enough in his analysis.

Today's modern corporation is the last bastion of autocracy. Unlike national autocracies, which have largely lost their legitimacy, corporate autocracy remains legitimate. Corporate CEOs still are permitted to wield enormous power over those who work in the corporation. Indeed, many corporations have even developed their own civil religions. For example, each hotel room in the Hilton chain contains a copy of a hagiographic biography of Conrad Hilton, founder of the company. It is usually placed in the same drawer as the bible. Other corporations maintain oil paintings of the founder and corporate relics of various kinds. Nearly all use corporate logos as a means of making them instantly identifiable. CEOs are also frequently described in heroic terms in the national press. Witness Lee Iacocca, who apparently single-handedly "saved" the Chrysler Corporation by convincing Congress to provide $1.5 billion in loan guarantees. In addition, corporate CEOs are grossly overpaid (especially in the United States) and enjoy many of the privileges previously reserved for heads of state and royalty.

In 1998, CEOs did fabulously well. The average CEO of a large company "earned" $10.6 million in that year. But salary is less and less an accurate measure of CEO pay. For example, Michael Eisner, CEO of the Disney Corporation, received a 1998 total pay package (including stock options and other benefits) of $575.6 million, to become the highest paid CEO in the United States. Moreover, during 1998, executive pay went up 36 percent over the previous year. In contrast, white-collar wages went up 3.9 percent and blue-collar wages went up a mere 2.7 percent. The average American CEO now earns an astonishing 419 times as much as an average blue-collar worker (Reingold and Grover 1999).

Similarly, outside members of corporate boards of directors are often paid equally exorbitant sums. One study of 968 of the largest U.S. companies noted that directors averaged $44,000 per year in pay plus stock options, all for a few days' work. One of the most egregious cases was a Minnesota-based HMO, United Healthcare Corporation, whose directors were paid $368,000 each (Byrne 1996).

These outrageous and utterly unjustifiable salaries for CEOs and directors have been accompanied by both downsizing and wage reductions for ordinary workers. While CEOs have gained handsome increases in salaries, production workers and even middle-level managers have seen their wages decline or their jobs eliminated over the last several decades.

Furthermore, even in nominally democratic societies, one leaves most rights at the corporate door. Freedom of speech, freedom from search and seizure, freedom of movement, freedom of information, and expectations of due process are all restricted or eliminated inside the corporate walls.

Corporations commonly spy on their employees using all the latest available technologies to help them gather intelligence. Corporations employ armed guards to keep out those without the proper credentials and to maintain order within the corporate enclosure. Indeed, in the United States there are 704,000 police officers, but there are 955,000 security guards (Bureau of Labor Statistics 1999).

Consider how the freedom of speech of employees is abridged. Employees are often prohibited from discussing company policies outside the plant. They are spied upon by the monitoring of interoffice memos, electronic mail and internet usage. Even conversations in the toilet may be recorded. For example, a 1997 survey by the American Management Association found that 35.3 percent of the 906 employers surveyed engaged in one or more forms of surveillance. This included taping of phone conversations, taping of voice mail, storage and review of computer files and / or electronic messages, and videotaping of employee performance. In general, the larger the corporation, the more likely it was to engage in surveillance (American Management Association 1997). Big Brother is perhaps more likely to be lurking in the workplace these days than he is in governmental offices.

Employees who are vocal critics of their employers are often subject to firing. Court decisions have upheld such abridgements of free speech as necessary for the course of business. Furthermore, in some nonunion plants, petitioning for redress of grievances may be tantamount to asking to be dismissed.

Employees may also find their persons and personal effects arbitrarily searched by corporate officials at any moment. They may be required to take drug or personality tests, submit to lie detectors, engage in counseling sessions, or otherwise modify their behavior in order to conform to corporate norms. (Disney discovered several years ago that its restrictive dress codes, designed to make all employees look like all-American boys and girls, actually violated French law, which prohibited employers from dictating hair styles or forbidding mustaches and beards.) Such due process rules as exist are limited in scope.

When accused of engaging in activities not sanctioned by the corporation, employees rarely have an opportunity to confront their accusers. Corporations rarely grant employees access to their own personnel records. Most corporations have no judicial system but rely instead on the ability to fire. Moreover, in cases where dismissal is made difficult, it is always relatively easy to make life so miserable for the employee in question that quitting appears a desirable resolution of the problem. In short, the kinds of rights normally expected in democratic societies, such as those embodied in the U.S. Bill of Rights, are frequently abridged or denied in the corporate world.

One of the more imaginative strategies applied by corporations since the 1970s is compulsory arbitration. Unionized employees have used this approach for some time, but applying it to nonunion employees is novel. New hirees are required to sign away their rights to sue the company, submitting to arbitration instead. This is equivalent to signing away a right in order to obtain employment (Ware 1996).

In addition to monitoring employee behavior at work, many corporations attempt to restrict the private behavior of employees as well. This kind of activity is certainly not new. The mills in eighteenth-century Lowell, Massachusetts, had strict rules of behavior for single women employed there. The Pullman Company attempted to regulate the political affairs of workers in its company-owned town (Walzer 1983). The Ford Motor Company had a "sociological department" that inquired into workers' sexual and drinking behavior among other things. More recently, workers have been fired for marrying (based on antinepotism rules), for engaging in extramarital affairs, for smoking, for drinking, for riding a motorcycle, and for numerous other fully legal activities off the job. As Dworkin (1997) notes, the less traditional the relationship, the less protection it is afforded under the law. Thus, an employee fired for engaging in homosexual activity outside the workplace is less likely to be reinstated than one fired for marrying a coworker. Of course, some such situations are complicated by other public goods: in certain settings one might reasonably prohibit workers from having sexual relations with subordinates in order to protect against sexual harassment. However, employers often go far beyond such complex cases in an attempt to enforce their particular version of acceptable behavior outside the workplace.

Of course, corporations are incorporated under laws of nation-states. In that sense they are creatures of the state. Yet, if the welfare state for individuals and families is crumbling, it is alive and well for corporations. A good example, is the Archer Daniels Midland Company, one of the world's largest grain trading and processing companies. ADM was recently fined one hundred million dollars for price fixing. Several of its top executives are now in prison. Yet, ADM continues to generously donate to both the Republican and Democratic parties. This has ensured it continued subsidies for ethanol, a fuel made from corn. In principle, ethanol is supposed to reduce U.S. dependence on foreign oil; in practice it may require as much energy to produce ethanol as the product itself contains. ADM controls 70 percent of the domestic ethanol market. Similarly, quotas on sugar imports protect the market for corn sweetener, another ADM product. One newspaper account names General Electric, Boeing, Pillsbury, AT&T, and McDonald's as among the biggest companies pleading for federal welfare. It also cites a Cato Institute report estimating total corporate welfare at seventy-five billion dollars per year (Chapman 1996).

Furthermore, especially in the case of multinational and transnational corporations, the laws of particular nation-states are often easily ignored. For example, taxes may be avoided by incorporating in several nations and organizing the accounting system such that the taxable income is always highest in the nation with the lowest tax rates. If that does not work, it is always possible to use corporate influence to modify the laws, either by legal lobbying or by illegal bribes.

But what is most astounding about the modern corporation is that it is largely unchallenged. Even in democratic societies, we have all come to take it as natural and normal that we should abandon our rights at the corporate door. And, while the gurus of the free market complain about state interference in the market and in our private lives, they ignore the far more insidious, far less visible, and far heavier arm of the large corporation.

THE STATE AND THE INDIVIDUAL

But perhaps the most pernicious act of the state has been the undermining of individuality. Most obviously, the widespread use of uniforms, common since the eighteenth century, has been effectively employed to depersonalize military and police forces. When combined with drill, marching, and other group-think activities, it has often successfully created soldiers and police officers who follow directions blindly.

But beyond that, nation-states have used everything from architecture to clothing to reduce individuals to "masses." For example, in the 1950s and 1960s China effectively used clothing styles as a way to present the image of uniformity, of sameness, of submersion of the individual in the mass. The Western press repeatedly used images of "armies" of Chinese peasants and workers all dressed the same to impress the public with the need for vigilance against the "red tide."

Buildings have been used worldwide to convey the power of the state, and conversely the powerlessness of the individual. One need only look at the rows of identical housing blocks in Moscow or the public housing in Chicago to confirm this. The same applies to government buildings in Washington, especially those constructed during the 1930s. Buildings like the Pentagon, the south building of USDA, and nameless others on Pennsylvania Avenue are massive blocks of brick and stone, virtually lacking in ornamentation other than some vague pseudocolumns that adorn their exterior walls. They portray faceless power and size, whether such was intended by their designers or not.

Entire cities or neighborhoods have been designed to the same effect. Consider Washington, where the central mall, lined by massive public buildings on each side, with the Capitol at one end on a hill, gives the visitor the unmistakable impression of power. Similarly, the even larger central mall in Brasilia has identical Bauhaus-style government buildings on each side, high-rise monuments to giantism. Traversing the mall on foot in its shorter dimension takes ten to fifteen minutes. Tiananmen Square, in central Beijing, provides much the same imagery. Endless paving stones under one's feet, monumental buildings on each side, and a huge picture of Chairman Mao over the entry to the Forbidden City complete the picture. To this we could easily add Ceaușescu's palace in central Bucharest, and countless other monuments to the state. How, one is clearly supposed to ask, could a single person—or even a small group—succeed in a confrontation with an institution capable of creating and maintaining public places and spaces of such proportions?

Such monuments to scale, such deification of the state, have the concomitant effect of atomizing each person. This, of course, is not the individualism of free expression, of creativity, but the individual shorn of familial and other social ties and plunged into the anomic sea known as the masses. Yet, of course, such monuments, housing blocks and clothing styles are reminiscent of the palace in *Dorothy and the Wizard in Oz* (Baum [1907] 1979). Much like the wizard's palace, such imagery is designed to give the impression of unstoppable power, of the forward march of History with a capital H, of the Great Leader who is larger than life, of the triumphant entry into the predesigned future. This is the statist solution to the passions that worried Bacon, Hobbes, Smith, and their contemporaries. The passions of the masses will be controlled by their very isolation. Even as they stand in close proximity, they will feel their terrible isolation. Who am I to challenge the apparent solidarity of the masses? Who am I to challenge the state? How can something so large, so powerful, so dynamic possibly be wrong? Let us march into the future together . . .

CONCLUSIONS

The legacy of the last several centuries is one of mass murder, famine, torture, imprisonment, and alienation on an unprecedented scale (in part with the aid of modern technologies of warfare, torture, and genocide), all justified in the name of the state. While totalitarian states have certainly managed to develop oppression to a fine art, even liberal democratic states have been far too willing to engage in similar unconscionable activities. Virtually no place on earth, no civilization, no village, no family has been unaffected by statist actions. No volume could hope even to note all the major cases. Moreover, no volume could portray the horror and inhumanity carried out in the name of the state. Instead of producing the moral order that Hobbes envisioned, states have spun out of control, taking millions of people down with them.

Nor is the era of statism at an end. The people of far too many nations still find themselves in the thrall of the state. Even in ostensibly democratic nations, statism persists. Consider the attempt to conceal mad cow disease (bovine spongiform encephalopathy) from the public in Britain. Similarly, in the United States, it appears that the Federal Bureau of Investigation may well have concealed the use of incendiary gas in its attempts to end the standoff with the Branch Davidian cult at Waco.

In sum, the Hobbesian myth of state-induced order lives on, often shorn of its nuances and logic. The self-appointed Leviathans continue to spring up, creating disorder by the very ordering they so desperately seek. Might the market be different?

NOTES

1. European explorers brought to the Americas a wide range of European diseases to which the indigenous population had little or no resistance. As historian Alfred W. Crosby puts it: "It was their germs, not these imperialists themselves, for all their brutality and callousness, that were chiefly responsible for sweeping aside indigenes and opening the Neo-Europes to demographic takeover" (1986:196).

2. The Japanese, ever the masters at adapting Western ideas to their own ends, also participated in the colonial project, colonizing Korea, Taiwan, and that section of the Chinese mainland they dubbed Manchuria. In so doing, they brought their own forms of statism, markets, and religion.

3. In Canada, Prime Minister William Lyon Mackenzie issued an Order in Council five days later to the same effect. Indeed, it appears that the two governments had secretly discussed the matter between them as early as August 1940 (Daniels 1994).

4. In Canada the situation was strikingly similar. People of Japanese origin were sent to camps in the interior of British Columbia, where geography accomplished what barbed wire did in the United States. Able-bodied males were put to work on road crews in the Canadian Rockies. The property of Japanese-Canadians was liquidated as well. For an eyewitness account of the Canadian camps, see Nakano and Nakano (1980).

THE

THEORY

OF

MORAL SENTIMENTS.

By ADAM SMITH,
PROFESSOR of MORAL PHILOSOPHY in the
Univerſity of GLASGOW.

LONDON:

Printed for A. MILLAR, in the STRAND;
And A. KINCAID and J. BELL, in EDINBURGH.
M DCC LIX.

4

SELLING THE MARKET

I respect not his labors, his farm where everything has its price, who would carry the landscape, who would carry his God, to market, if he could get anything for him; who goes to market for his god as it is; on whose farm nothing grows free, whose fields bear no crops, whose meadows no flowers, whose trees no fruits, but dollars.

—*Henry David Thoreau*, Walden

Market competition is the only form of organization which can afford a large measure of freedom to the individual, as consumer or as producer.

—*Frank Hyneman Knight*, Freedom and Reform: Essays in Economics and Social Philosophy

If the twentieth century began with the virtual worship of technology and faded into statism by mid-century, then the latter part of the century has surely been a time of belief in the power of the market. The collapse of the East Bloc, in particular, has let loose the pundits of the free market. Socialism is dead; long live the free market! With socialism defeated, undoubtedly the free market would reassert itself as the natural way to organize an economy. The West had won!

Initially the self-appointed experts rushed to eastern Europe to provide advice on how to instantly transform state socialist regimes into burgeoning market economies. As anthropologist Janine Wedel put it, "Prescriptions offered in Bolivia were repeated in Poland and later in Russia, with little modification for country-specific conditions" (1998:187). With a national monetary regime, private banks, credit, a stock market, new property laws, and sale of the state-owned factories, capitalism would spring forth in all its glory. For example, Harvard economist Jeffrey Sachs rushed to Eastern Europe to advocate the use of what became known as "shock therapy." The basic idea was to privatize or close state enterprises, allow prices to float, make the currency convertible, and set up market institutions. The approach the self-appointed experts advocated was a mirror image of the vanguardism advocated by Lenin earlier in the century. As Joseph Stiglitz, vice president of the World Bank, noted, "With the right textbooks in their briefcases, the 'market Bolsheviks' would be able to fly into the post-socialist countries and use a peaceful version of Lenin's methods to make the opposite transition" (1999:22). Already, by mid-1993, patience was wearing thin in many of those nations (Gebert 1993). Yet, Sachs, writing in the same year, argued that "it is surely not true that the poor and vulnerable have been left out in the cold in Poland's reform" (1993:95).

While in some nations gross domestic product did begin to rise, income inequalities continued to widen as well. Furthermore, unemployment remains endemic and the social protections found in the West are often weak or nonexistent. The decades of communist rule could hardly be erased by a few months of shock therapy. By the time that the damage was done, the experts were long gone, perhaps off to give similar advice somewhere else.

Indeed, the world turned out to be far more complex than advocates of the market could possibly have imagined. Even the Germans, who thought that they could simply absorb the east into a unified state, have found that merely eliminating state socialism does not a free market make. Today, ten years after the Berlin wall came tumbling down and after billions of marks of new investment, eastern Germany remains in a shambles. Unemployment remains high despite a mass exodus toward western Germany, people grumble about being colonized by western Germany, and much infrastructure remains to be developed. Even in Leipzig, one of the brighter spots in the east, one cannot help but be struck by the invasion of foreign and western German chain stores with all their accompanying glitter and the virtual lack of local entrepreneurship. Meanwhile, hundreds of factory buildings remain empty, vacant reminders of the collapse of industry after reunification.

The Russians have fared far worse. Mafia capitalism rules in large sections of the country. The class of nouveau riche Russian capitalists looks a great deal like the old class of commissars, but without the least need for discretion in displaying their newfound wealth. Moreover, although the state planning apparatus has collapsed, it has yet to be replaced by any sort of coherent marketing system. As a result, many factories sit idle, their workers unpaid, their raw materials undelivered, their products unpurchased. One study notes that GDP declined 18 percent in 1992, 12 percent in 1993, 15 percent in 1994, and 4 percent in 1995. By 1996, the Russian economy had shrunk to 60 percent of its size just four years earlier (Gerber and Hout 1998). Unemployment is common; incomes for all but the top 10 percent have fallen. The gender gap in wages has increased in size. Russia's fragile, nominally democratic government is on the brink of collapse. Worse still, the constant changing of the rules of the game has wreaked havoc among the small entrepreneurs who have barely begun to develop their businesses. As a result, despite the "market reforms," less than 2 percent of Russians are self-employed.

In a perverse replay of the Great Depression, the West now appears to be enjoying an economic boom, while the East remains economically depressed. In the United States, in particular, unemployment has reached record lows. With the collapse of the Soviet Union, whatever credibility might have been given the Left has evaporated. Instead, the worship of the free market has infected virtually every aspect of American society. Families are to be given school vouchers, so that they may choose the school they like best for their children. Hospitals are to be turned over to the private sector, so that they can pursue profits and better health care simultaneously. State-sponsored welfare has been dramatically slashed, as we are told that it merely encourages dependency on the state. But at the same time, private charity is lauded as the solution to social ills: Remember George Bush's thousand points of light? Indeed, the new wave of gurus now tells us—as they have for several centuries—that the market can solve virtually all of society's problems. However, unlike Adam Smith, who understood the artificiality of the market society, the new champions of the market see it as the natural, normal state of things. And they increasingly have the means whereby they can involve not just a few nations, but the entire world, in a never ending upward spiral of prosperity, economic growth, and peace. At least that is the story we are told . . .

In this chapter I examine several examples of the free market in action. First, I look at the Irish potato famine of the mid–nineteenth century, a famine caused not so much by crop failure as by belief in the efficacy of the market. Then, I examine one recent attempt to extend the market into locations from which it was previously weak or absent: intellectual property rights. Next, I examine the attempt to destroy public education and social security in the name of the market. Finally, I examine the impact of what is commonly referred to as globalization, the opening of virtually the entire world to free trade under the auspices of the World Trade Organization.

THE IRISH POTATO FAMINE

Potatoes are a New World crop. They were first introduced into Spain ca. 1570 and England ca. 1590 (Hawkes 1994). Nearly three hundred years later, they had become the mainstay in the Irish diet, largely because of their extraordinarily high yields—far higher than any cereal crop. The switch to potatoes as a staple crop took place not so much as a result of increasing population in Ireland as due to the exceedingly unequal ownership of land. Smallholders, especially the rural poor, found that only potatoes would yield sufficiently on a small plot of land to get them through the year.

By the 1840s, half the Irish population depended on potatoes grown on 2.1 million acres and supplemented by dairy products, oatmeal, and, in some regions, fish and eggs. But unlike grains, potatoes could not be stored more than one season. In addition, their bulk made them difficult to transport over long distances. Thus, they offered little insurance against the occasional poor harvest or against regional differences in production. Furthermore, only a small portion of the wide range of potatoes was available in Europe. Modern geneticists would say that at the time the genetic base for Irish potatoes was very narrow. Indeed, since potatoes are multiplied by vegetative propagation, each potato was a clone of every other one. This was a disaster waiting to happen.

In 1845, the fungus late blight (*Phytophthora infestans*) arrived from North America. The blight, combined with unusually cool and damp weather, rapidly rotted both the leaves and tubers of a significant portion of the crop. Moreover, as the etiology of the disease was not well understood, contaminated potatoes were planted in the following years. The crops of 1846 to 1849 were nearly total failures. But this in itself would not have been enough to cause a famine.

Indeed, it was the staunch belief in the principles of the free market that was the major cause of the famine. Echoing the position taken fifty years earlier by Edmund Burke (see Chapter 1), the Liberal British prime minister Lord John Russell insisted that interfering in the marketplace would only make matters worse. So convinced was he of the rightness of his actions that one observer has argued, "It is not entirely fair to judge Russell's actions other than against the accepted economic tenets of his day. That private enterprise was sacrosanct was an opinion held with all the conviction of religious dogma" (Bourke 1993:179).

Hence, landlords were called on to deal with the problem of hunger through local poor relief. However, the landlords' ability to provide relief depended in large part on income produced by the very peasants whose crops had failed. Lacking rents, even many sympathetic landlords soon found themselves out of funds with which to provide food for their tenants.

British aid consisted largely of employment of some of the poor and hungry in public works projects. However, this in no way was sufficient to meet the demand for food. Ironically, during the entire period of the famine, Ireland continued to export grain, meat, and other more expensive foodstuffs—in quantities that would have been more than ample to alleviate the famine. The contrast between Ireland and Belgium and Scotland, areas also severely affected by the blight, is instructive. "The Belgian government, in spite of its aversion to intervening directly by food purchases, departed from its principles and bought large amounts of food, provided free transportation for food shipments, organized public works, and like

Britain removed all tariff barriers on food imports" (Mokyr 1985:277). In addition, local governments aided the hungry. In Scotland, landlords had a greater ability to provide for their hungry tenants than did their Irish contemporaries.

Throughout, the British government claimed that famine relief was beyond its means, yet only a few years later (1853–1856), the British spent £69.3 million on an ill-conceived war in the Crimea, a sum vastly greater than what was spent on the famine (ibid.). In the end, stubborn adherence to marketism led to the death of over one million people by starvation or disease. An even larger number were forced to migrate, mainly to North America.

THE EXPANSION OF INTELLECTUAL PROPERTY RIGHTS

Inventors and creative artists (e.g., authors, artists, musicians) have long benefited from patent and copyright laws, respectively. Such laws, usually defined broadly as Intellectual Property Rights (IPR), were developed in order to promote invention and creative endeavors. So important were such rights considered by the founders of the American republic that they are the only ones specifically mentioned in the original constitution. The legal argument behind such laws, at least in capitalist societies, is that neither inventors nor artists would have any incentive to engage in these activities were there not some way of guaranteeing a return on their investment. Thus, one might well consider patent and copyright laws as a kind of bargain made between society as a whole and the patent or copyright holder. Society gains new knowledge or creative works, which are made known publicly in the form of a patent or copyright application.[1] In return, the patent or copyright holder has a legal monopoly on the ownership and use of the patented or copyrighted material for a fixed period of time. After that, the material becomes public property.

Ordinary property rights confer ownership on a particular object—an automobile, a piece of land, a house—for as long as the owner may wish to keep that object. In contrast, intellectual property rights confer ownership on an idea and its embodiment(s) for a specific period of time. Whereas my ownership and free use of my car generally make it inconvenient and sometimes impossible for you to use it as well, this is not true for intellectual property. Many people may use Einstein's theory of relativity, an improved wheat variety, a novel by Hemingway, by virtue of their theoretically infinite replicability. Thus, intellectual property rights are quite different from rights in ordinary property in both their nature and their consequences. Moreover, whereas ordinary property laws apply equally to all sorts of property, intellectual property laws cannot apply equally to all things intellectual. For example, I cannot claim sole ownership of the word "history," the phrase "good morning," or the discovery of a new planet, while I can claim ownership of a novel I write, a new machine that I develop, or a painting that I produce.

Until not too long ago, each nation had its own intellectual property regime. Some nations had relatively well-codified laws, with strong enforcement mechanisms, while others had weak laws and/or limited enforcement. Indeed, even the notion that copying intellectual property was in any sense problematic was and remains lacking in many cultures. In recent years, however, major changes have occurred, in large part pushed by proponents of market solutions to social problems. On the one hand, the scope of intellectual property has expanded. Things never before patented are now patentable. Plants and animals are now included under U.S. patent laws. Computer software enjoys both copyright and patent protection. On the other hand, the length of copyright has been extended several times due to heavy industry lobbying. Let us examine each of these in turn.

Databases

For many years, scholars, scientists, and businesses have benefited from a wide range of compilations of data. These include bibliographic indexes, statistical tracts, and lists of various things such as telephone numbers. Lawyers could consult legal databases, biologists could consult biology databases, art historians could consult art databases. Anyone could consult a telephone directory, a dictionary, an encyclopedia. These databases were and are protected by conventional copyright laws.

About thirty years ago, with the rise in use of mainframe computers, many of these printed documents began to be replaced or complemented by computer databases. Scholars and scientists have benefited from access to these ever-growing databases as have a wide range of businesses. Today, it is possible to purchase the entire telephone directory for the United States for the price of a good book. For larger sums of money, one may purchase more arcane databases. Even more commonly, one purchases *the right to use* a given database where searching is done through the Internet or on a CD-ROM.

However, most data in databases are not subject to copyright since they usually consist of such things as bibliographic references, statistical data collected by governmental bodies, or names and addresses of households —data often if not usually available to anyone taking the time to compile them. Moreover, there is nothing creative or inventive in bibliographic references or telephone numbers.

Database owners claim that they have incurred substantial losses as a result of data theft. Yet they have not produced any evidence to support that claim. In fact, database owners continue to invest large sums in their endeavors. Owners have found it easy to protect the work they have invested in establishing databases by licensing users. The license usually contains wording that prohibits wholesale copying of the database. In addition, owners may employ various encryption schemes to avoid unauthorized use. Finally, at least some owners may be able to add something creative to their endeavors and thus employ existing copyright law (Sanks 1998).

But in the push to expand the scope of intellectual property rights in what is now a twenty-eight-billion dollar per year industry, owners have been lobbying Congress to grant copyright-like protection to databases.[2] The U.S. House of Representatives is currently debating a bill, the "Collections of Information Antipiracy Act" (H.R. 354), that would significantly increase the rights of owners of such databases. Database owners argue that such protection is necessary to prevent wholesale theft of compilations for which they have invested considerable time and money—theft that is becoming increasingly easy, given the advances in computer technology.

The bill, as currently written, provides a fifteen-year protection for such compilations of data. Both criminal and civil penalties apply to those who violate the law by extracting a substantial portion of the database for commercial use. Although scientists, educational and nonprofit organizations, and individuals are permitted to use such information, they still remain liable if they do harm to an "actual or potential market" for the data. Moreover, it is unclear just what constitutes a database. Some have argued that a work of fiction could be considered a database under the current bill (Maurer and Scotchmer 1999).

Scientific organizations, generally opposed to the bill, have argued that such a law would unnecessarily restrict access to published data long permitted under "fair use" provisions of copyright law. Libraries and electronic freedom organizations have also argued against this and other similar bills on the grounds that they unnecessarily restrict legitimate access to what is otherwise public information. The publisher of *Science*, the official journal of the American Association for the Advancement of Science, argues that further restrictions on data in such databases would raise the cost of scientific research or pose demands that scientists would not be able to meet (*Science* 1998a).

Indeed, the proposed law differs from copyright law in three important ways: (1) It extends intellectual property rights to things lacking in originality. (2) Although it contains a fifteen-year limit on protection, in fact, databases are continually updated. Thus, every year's update extends the database protection for another fifteen years, making it *perpetual* in practice. (3) The act would shift the goal of copyright from the promotion of invention and creativity to the protection of investment (Gardner and Rosenbaum 1998). Thus, the traditional bargain—monopoly for some period of time, in return for disclosure—does not apply. Intellectual property protection for databases merely creates a new place where some people can make money at everyone else's expense.

Shrink-Wrap Licensing

There is also a move afoot to extend greater protection to computer software. Although most consumers probably presume that they are purchasing software when they pay for it, the legalese inside each package claims that the buyer is purchasing a license to use the software and not the software itself. As there is no standard form for these licenses, avid computer users soon find themselves party to dozens of obtuse contracts they never read or signed.

Apparently, the shrink-wrap license was developed by Micropro CEO Seymour Rubinstein in the 1970s (Dvorak 1998). It was designed to avoid selling the computer source code (the instructions that constitute the program) to the purchaser, who could then develop a competing product. However, such licenses have grown larger and more complex over the years, putting more and more restrictions on licensees. In addition, licenses are now found on websites, where they claim to govern the use of the various items on the web. Currently, the legality of these licenses is ambiguous (Einhorn 1998). Under the proposed law, licenses could be extended to almost any good, thereby nullifying any notion of consumer protection. Stephen Fraser (1998) notes that one might buy a pair of boots only to find a license inside that noted that the makers were not liable for any damage caused to the boots or to you by walking in them! They could also contain clauses that violate other expectations of rights of users. For example, Charles Mann (1998) notes that the license for Microsoft Agent, a program that makes small animated figures, contains a clause prohibiting the use of the program to disparage Microsoft. Even more outrageous is the license for PhoneDisc, a telephone database, that prohibits users from using its directories "in any way or form."

Furthermore, previous changes in copyright laws have eliminated the need for licenses. Today, copyright law permits purchasers to copy software for their own use and forbids use of object and source codes to develop competing software. In fact, one observer notes:

> The irony is that North American courts have, so far, interpreted shrink-wrap licenses under the law of contracts as applied to the sale of goods. Thus, software publishers claim contract protection as if they had sold instead of merely licensed a copy of their software. What this ignores is that the limitations to the copyright protection of computer software were legislated by Con-

gress . . . for the protection of users of programs. Without the limitations, it is conceivable that every use of a program that makes a copy of the software in one's computer, a step which is necessary to use a program, would constitute copyright infringement. (Fraser 1998:201)

The software industry is now attempting to "resolve" this problem by amending Article 2B of the U.S. Uniform Commercial Code, the first major update to the code since 1950. To date, some two hundred seminars and public meetings have been held, but the participants have not included those outside the traditional intellectual property community. The result is a draft that would bar *access* to source code—thereby working around the goal of the intellectual property clause in the constitution—and that is ambiguous with respect to treatment of other forms of intellectual property (Montgomery and Maisashvili 1998).

Seeds

Yet another area in which intellectual property has expanded in recent years is that of seeds. In the past, plant improvement was a relatively unprofitable business. As sociologist Frederick Buttel (Buttel and Belsky 1987) noted some years ago, three barriers to profitability in the seed industry existed. First, farmers could plant seeds from the previous year's crop, thereby avoiding purchase. Second, public research supported varietal improvement issuing hundreds of new varieties each year. Finally, other seed companies could easily appropriate any improved variety and sell it as their own. As a result, the seed business consisted of small companies, each selling seed at prices just slightly higher than that of any given crop.

Since the 1930s, however, the seed industry has been transformed. First, in 1930, as a result of lobbying by representatives of the flower and fruit industries, including Luther Burbank, the U.S. Congress passed the Plant Patent Act (35 U.S.C. §§161–164), which permitted the patenting of vegetatively propagated plants (i.e., plants reproduced from cuttings or tubers). At about the same time, hybrid corn was developed. Its proponents claimed that it increased yields markedly by virtue of the creation of hybrid vigor, although recent scholarship challenges those claims (Berlan and Lewontin 1986a). Of greater importance, perhaps, is the fact that seed from the harvest of a hybrid cannot be used to plant a crop the following year as yield will be poor. As a consequence, farmers who plant hybrids must repurchase seed annually. The development of hybrid corn rapidly altered the structure of the seed industry, giving several large companies dominance in corn seed (Fitzgerald 1990).

For the next thirty odd years little changed. Then, in 1970, under the misleading rubric of "Plant Breeders' Rights,"[3] Congress passed the Plant Variety Protection Act (PVPA) (7 U.S.C. §2321 et seq.). In so doing, it ratified an agreement among the industrialized nations that extended property protection to varieties of plants produced from seed. Unlike patent law, the PVPA did not extend to research. However, it did extend the scope of intellectual property protection available to producers of improved plants. Soon after the passage of the new law, seed companies became lucrative investments for agrichemical companies, a trend that has not abated to date.

Property rights in plants were extended still further in a series of court decisions beginning with Diamond v. Chakrabarty (447 U.S. 303) in 1980. The end result was that, with no input from Congress or the general public, living organisms including both plants and animals were made subject to utility patent law—this despite the impossibility of describing how to produce an organism and the lack of novelty in plant and animal breeding.

Thus, over less than a century intellectual property protection was markedly extended to cover the entire living world. What had been the common heritage of humankind was now to be privately held (Berlan and Lewontin 1986b). Living nature, seen once as outside the sphere of commodities, is now fully enrolled in the market economy.

Protecting Mickey Mouse

But perhaps the most egregious violation of the principles of intellectual property protection is the extension of the copyright law in order to make the Disney corporation happy. Although Walt Disney is long dead and therefore cannot be provided with any incentives by any change in the length of copyright protection, the law was recently extended to permit copyrights of up to ninety-five years *after* the death of the author for pre-1978 works and to seventy years for other works [17 U.S.C. sec. 2589(a)]. This ensures that the early Mickey Mouse cartoons will not enter the public domain for some time to come. Clearly, the bargain between copyright holders and the public—monopoly rights as encouragement for creativity—cannot be served by extending the law far beyond the normal lifespan of any author. But that is exactly the situation for current copyright law. All such laws do is to make the rest of us pay to make someone else (or in the case of Disney, a corporation) wealthy.

Extending Intellectual Property Rights
to Federal Grants

Finally, let us consider the extension of intellectual property rights to universities. Under the Bayh-Dole Act of 1980 [35 U.S.C. 200-212 (1988 & Supp. V 1993)], universities are permitted to patent inventions made as a result of federal grants they receive. As a consequence, most of the major research universities have established intellectual property offices and have staffed them with lawyers. In addition, several universities have sought and signed agreements with large corporations by which they receive significant sums of money for research in return for first rights of refusal of intellectual property rights on inventions emerging from the research. Ironically, only a handful of universities have actually benefited from these changes; most have lost money as patents do not automatically lead to royalties. Indeed, most patents never produce any return, but university patent lawyers are only too happy to find patentable objects in professors' labs.

In addition, the desire for patents has led to increased secrecy on university campuses. Graduate students may find that the data they are working on is no longer freely available to them. Professors may need to wait before submitting articles for publication so as to afford ample opportunity to file patent applications. And we shall probably never know the degree to which the opinions of university researchers have been altered by virtue of the potential or actual revenue derived from patents.

The list above is far from complete. For example, U.S. pharmaceutical companies are trying a variety of techniques to delay competition from generic equivalents. With millions at stake over a year or two, company lawyers are filing new types of suits, lobbying Congress and lobbying states to pass laws that make switching to generics more difficult (Barrett 1998). In addition, Congress has passed legislation to protect electronic controls over copyrighted works. Moreover, recently attempts have been made to patent business methods, financial innovations, and even medical procedures.

In sum, from computer programs to plants, from databases to Mickey Mouse, intellectual property rights are being and have been expanded, strengthened, and lengthened, although there is little or no evidence that any public good is thereby furthered. In fact, the strengthening of intellectual property rights is in most cases an example of a virtually mystical faith in the market rather than the result of careful deliberation.

Importantly, despite several centuries of intellectual property protection, there is little evidence to support the central thesis that incentives are actually necessary to spur the production of creative and inventive works. There is even less evidence that would suggest that strengthening those rights would encourage more innovation. In manufacturing, designing around the patent is a well-known and commonly used technique that deprives patents of much of their usefulness. In pharmaceuticals and software design, it appears possible to arrive at similar products by several routes, also reducing the claimed value of patents in spurring innovation. Moreover, having intellectual property rights means little unless one has the monetary resources to triumph in what are often protracted court battles. What appears to be of far greater import is the speed by which others can learn to do what the inventor or copyright holder has done. Furthermore, the appearance of free, open-source software (the code is available to all users) suggests that at least some proportion of inventors reject the very idea that monetary incentives are needed at all (Hellweg 1998). One particular piece of free software, Linux, is now in use on over 750,000 servers (computers that provide access to the Internet)—17 percent of the market—and has Microsoft worried about its proprietary operating system, Windows (Foust and Drew 1999; Lindquist 1999).

EDUCATION

Unbridled belief in the power of markets has also affected the public schools. American schools are constantly compared to those in other nations as if, for example, national average scores on mathematics tests were the equivalent to batting averages in baseball. Of course, such comparisons assume that the knowledge displayed on the tests is universally relevant to good citizenship, individual well-being, and prosperity. Moreover, the comparisons gloss over the enormous methodological problems that make such comparisons difficult if not impossible.

Markets are also deemed better in providing education to elementary and secondary students. School voucher plans, private for-profit schools, and so-called charter schools are touted in an effort to transform pubic education. Such institutions, supporters argue, will provide competition for conventional public schools, forcing lethargic educators and school boards to transform themselves or die for lack of students. For example, economist Milton Friedman sees the only solution as the privatization of the entire school system. According to Friedman (1998):

> Choice and competition will help break the control over the vast financial resources devoted to government education, estimated to exceed $250 billion annually, which is exercised by educational bureaucrats and unions. This will enable educators to find creative solutions to education problems, free of the encumbrances of a bureaucratic and political system whose principal purpose is to protect the vested interests of the education establishment, not the interests of our children.

Friedman claims that for-profit schools will resolve these problems and do so at lower cost, in part through the use of new technologies that will revolutionize teaching. Yet all of this ignores the fact that public schools in wealthy suburbs are well-funded and usually provide a first-class education, while those in inner cities and poor rural counties often fail miserably to prepare students for a better life. Indeed, no other government service is so dependent on where one happens to live. For example, in 1992–1993 $5,237 was spent on each student in districts with median household incomes under $20,000, while $6,661 was spent on each student in districts with household incomes of $35,000 or more (National Center for Education Statistics 1997). Of course, money alone is not the entire story. There are examples of poor schools in wealthy communities and good schools in poor communities, but they are few and far between.

The voucher approach also glosses over the fact that there are no consumers of public education. Parents and all of the rest of us pay taxes, which are to be used to help all children become educated *citizens*. Voucher proponents are silent as to how poorly educated, low-income parents would be able to discern which school would be best for their children. They are equally silent as to how they will provide the transportation necessary to get their children to school. They say nothing about the fact that the public schools do not and cannot turn away students who are in some way inferior (Bromley 1997). What vouchers are far more likely to do is to allow those who can to opt out of the civic responsibility of ensuring that everyone's children receive a good education, leading to still greater inequalities and inequities.

SOCIAL SECURITY

Market enthusiasts have also begun an assault on Social Security, one of the few social programs that has worked well for most of its sixty-five years. The underlying idea behind Social Security is to provide for families in their old age. Unlike private retirement programs, Social Security supports current recipients from funds generated by those still working. While the sums disbursed are hardly large, Social Security means the difference between poverty and a decent old age for many Americans.

However, as the baby boom generation ages, the proportion of the population collecting benefits will rise, while the proportion of the population working declines. Estimates suggest that the program will have inadequate funds in about thirty years. This problem might be handled by increasing the payroll tax (a highly regressive tax), by increasing the taxation of benefits for wealthy retirees, by raising the ceiling on the amount of income on which taxes are paid, by incorporating state and local government workers into the system thereby expanding the income pool, by paying the shortfall out of general tax revenues, by changing the retirement age, or by some combination of the above.

But market advocates insist that the solution is to privatize the system. Presumably each citizen who contributes would have all or a portion of

that payment available for investment in equities. Given the fact that the
stock market has risen at a rate far exceeding that of Social Security benefits, all would come out ahead. On the surface, this appears a reasonable
argument, but it conceals several fatal flaws. First, the stock market does
not always go up; it occasionally declines precipitously. Thus, Social Security recipients would be at the mercy of swings in the stock market. Second, while wealthier Americans may have the knowledge to make wise
investments, most poorer Americans do not. Thus, precisely the persons
for whom Social Security was designed would be at greatest risk under a
privatized program. Finally, Social Security is first and foremost a *social*
program. It is about how we as a nation take care of our elderly. As jour-
nalist Peter Coy puts it, "The beauty of Social Security is that it represents
a shared commitment of society as a whole to meet a need that isn't well
met by families on their own. The bottom line on Social Security: If it's not
social, it's not security" (1998:35).

THE RETURN OF THE STATE

It is ironic that the insistence on the virtues of the free market leads to
the very central planning so (rightly) detested by free market advocates.
Indeed, since the 1950s there has been widespread agreement that one role
of government is to promote economic prosperity and stability. Keynesian
liberals and neoclassical conservatives have been in full agreement on this
point, even as they have argued for radically different policies. Thus, in the
United States the Federal Reserve Board regulates interest rates and the
money supply so as to minimize inflation and keep the economy on an
even keel. The German Bundesbank and other central banks of Europe
have attempted to do the same in their respective nations. (What is often
ignored is that they often do it by keeping unemployment high.) Moreover,
what constitutes a free market approach is entirely unclear. For example,
Ronald Reagan, a staunch advocate of the free market and supply side
economics, (unofficially) adopted Keynesian polices, fueling economic
growth by massive Pentagon spending and a rapid rise in government
debt. Under both Democratic and Republican presidents trade missions
and export subsidies have been accepted government policies.

In addition, stock markets, currency markets, and commodity exchanges require close monitoring to ensure that traders do not use inside
information to cheat others. As economist Ronald H. Coase has argued:

> It is not without significance that these exchanges, often used by economists
> as examples of a perfect market and perfect competition, are markets in
> which transactions are highly regulated (and this quite apart from any gov-

ernment regulation there may be). It suggests, I think correctly, that for anything approaching perfect competition to exist, an intricate system of rules and regulations would normally be needed. (1988:9)

In short, despite the rhetoric about the natural and self-regulating character of markets, rather substantial bureaucracies are necessary to sustain, protect, regulate, and police what are often held up as the epitome of free markets. As these markets become larger and become connected to the day-to-day affairs of more people, the need for monitoring increases. A small shift in the stock or currency markets can bring an entire economy to its knees. Yet it is precisely these markets that are peculiarly vulnerable to wide swings and speculation. And precisely because such changes are impossible to predict, they bode ill for other institutions. Thus, the market society requires a wide variety of nonmarket institutions to ensure its continued functioning.

Furthermore, as global trade increases, the local, regional, and national differences in goods and services become visible not as acceptable, perhaps even celebratory, differences but as higher transactions costs. Everything from ingredient labeling to copyright law, from the size of pallets and shipping containers to the rules for investment, from pesticide use to accounting procedures, becomes the subject of international treaties, intergovernmental organizations, faceless bureaucracies. The World Bank, the International Monetary Fund, the World Trade Organization, the World Intellectual Property Organization, and other such unelected, complex, and often impenetrable bureaucracies dictate to all thousands of details of international commerce. A recent editorial in *Business Week* summed up the situation as follows: "The biggest problem with the WTO is the hearing process—more the 16th century Star Chamber than a body that was created by democratic governments in the late 20th century. Hearings are held in secret, outside attorneys are excluded, and amicus briefs often aren't considered" (Leonhardt 1998:35). But merely opening the process a bit will hardly resolve what is the major issue. Such international rules, no matter how well-written, no matter how clear in their application, tend to be biased in favor of multinational corporations and the major trading powers. This is the case because they are the key actors, sometimes behind the scenes and sometimes overtly, that lobby for or even dictate international policies and practices.

To understand the scope of the problem, one only need consider the case of the Codex Alimentarius Commission, the international organization formed in 1963 to facilitate trade in food and food products. While nearly all the nations of the world are members, the Codex meetings tend to be dominated by Western nations and large corporations. A study of the 1989–1991 Codex meetings is indicative. At that time 55 percent of the attendees were from Western nations, while 25 percent represented corporate food interests. Public interest groups represented a mere 1 percent of the participants. The U.S. delegation of 243 persons dwarfed the entire African delegation of 142. The Nestlé corporation alone sent 38 representatives to the meetings (Avery, Drake, and Land 1993). When one considers the range of issues considered by international bodies—from environmental pollution to fishing rights—the magnitude of the institutional challenge and the lack of public debate becomes apparent.

Furthermore, the large corporations themselves act all too similarly to centralized, autocratic states. They downsize their workforce in the service of the god of profit—or at least that of management. They "tax" shareholders and workers alike to pay their CEOs salaries that can never be justified. They move from communities in search of higher profits, leaving behind thousands of unemployed workers with unsalable homes and devastated communities. All this is done in the name of good corporate planning. Are workers consulted? Are communities consulted? Certainly not. Instead, they are often blackmailed by extracting tax breaks, special public services, low-interest loans, and other favors.

The same applies to attracting large industry to a given state or city. As long ago as 1973, Leonard Wheat (1973) demonstrated that tax and other incentives had little or no effect on regional economic development. They merely determined whether a given corporation would locate in a particular town or one a short distance away. At the same time, such incentives often proved costly to cities and states. More recent data suggest that if anything the situation has worsened. Today, cities and states often feel under great pressure to do anything that will attract jobs and stem population decline. In many cases, the result is merely that a given business moves from one city to another with no net increase in employment. This was the case when the catalogue merchant, Spiegel, moved from Chicago to Columbus. Even worse, the cost of obtaining some jobs far exceeds any presumed advantages they might bring. The Mercedes-Benz plant recently opened in Alabama cost that state between $150,000 and $200,000 per job in lost revenues and other development costs (Corporation for Enterprise Development 1998). Moreover, such public largesse never goes to small, locally owned businesses, putting them at a considerable disadvantage. Furthermore, small businesses usually don't move, are involved in local communities, and pay their fair share of taxes.

As corporations continue to grow in size, their failure becomes unthinkable. Chrysler cannot fail. Bank of America cannot fail. WalMart cannot fail. Too much is at stake. A recent example was the hedge fund Long Term Capital Management (LTCM). Having lost two billion of its four billion dollars by fall of 1998, it was facing liquidation. But one of the partners called the Federal Reserve Bank of New York. The Federal Reserve in turn pressured a consortium of major banks to put up $3.5 billion in new capital to prevent the fund's failure so as not to "spook the market" (Spiro 1998). (I suggest that the reader consider whether the same might be done were you to face bankruptcy!) If the fund were to fail, it was argued, economic recession or even depression might ensue. Its very size guaranteed that government would intervene to ensure its continued existence. Thus, the central feature of free competition, the creative destruction that is claimed to be the hallmark of free market capitalism, is undermined by the very success of these behemoths.

This is in stark contrast to small, local businesses. They frequently fail and hardly anyone notices when they do so—except their owners, who may have lost their life's savings. They usually have a strong stake in the community, such that they are both unable and unwilling to move. They receive few tax breaks. They pay market rates for investment capital and public services. They frequently know their customers well, often by name. They provide most of the jobs in virtually every community. At their best, their owners are concerned about the economic and social health of the community. Believers in the power of the market often ignore the sharp contrast between these two types of firms.

Ironically, many if not most of the owners of small businesses aspire to become the next Microsoft or General Motors. Thus, they identify with precisely those persons who are most likely to put them out of business. And they believe the Horatio Alger–like rags-to-riches tales, tales that are endlessly repeated in the entrepreneurial press.

Finally, the focus on the market opens the door for the central planners who (cloaked in the labels, language, and fervor of the free market) discover inefficiencies, market failures, externalities, and free riders everywhere. Not finding the free markets of the Economics 101 textbooks in the real world, they feel compelled to introduce regulations to make the market work, to internalize the externalities, to make the free riders pay. Moreover, since these "deviations" from textbook theory are defined as technical errors, they can be fine-tuned by brigades of economists and policy analysts who, without any need to consult with the public at large, can proceed to "adjust" economic policy. An agency here, a regulation there, a tax on this, a subsidy for that. Like the now banished planners at Gosplan (or perhaps the Sorcerer's Apprentice), they go on endlessly adjusting reality to conform to the model, never noticing the grotesque relationships they produce.

Perhaps the most popular tool in the economists' toolbox is cost-benefit (or risk-benefit) analysis. Here it appears that the calculus of the market can be applied to public policy decisions. The idea seems straightforward enough: sum up the costs as well as the benefits and see which is greater. If the costs outweigh the benefits, then the project is abandoned; if the benefits outweigh the costs, then continue forward. Yet the usually flawless mathematics conceals deeper problems. Instead of debating the arguments in a democratic fashion, cost-benefit analysis asks how much each position will cost and whom it will benefit. This assumes that the values that people hold are merely casual preferences, much like my preference for chocolate as opposed to vanilla ice cream. As philosopher Mark Sagoff notes, "Cost-benefit analysis does not, because it cannot, judge opinions and beliefs on their merits but asks instead how much might be paid for them, as if a conflict of views could be settled in the same way as a conflict of interests" (1988:38). Beliefs about what *we* should do are confused with notions of what *I* want. For example, I like to drive to work. You cannot convince me otherwise. It is comfortable and convenient to open the garage, get in the car, turn on the radio and perhaps the air conditioning, go to work, and park the car in a lot provided by the university. I like it for the comfort and convenience that it provides. But you might convince me that I should stop driving because it has adverse environmental consequences. Doing that would appeal not to what *I* like but to what *we* ought to do.

Moreover, even on its own terms, cost-benefit analysis is deeply flawed. What is to be included in the list of costs and benefits? How will the costs be measured (especially those that are not monetary or quantifiable in character)? How will varying meanings of things be factored in? How are the costs and benefits to be distributed? Will all share the costs and benefits equally? Or would they be divided based on need or dessert? What would a fair and just distribution of costs and benefits look like? How will future generations be included in the calculus? How will we know that the lowest-cost option is the best one for society? How do we know that this is the option that, given the alternatives, most people would consent to? Cost-benefit analysts are largely silent on these issues as they are contentious. Open discussion of these issues would reveal the bankruptcy of the heroic assumptions on which cost-benefit analysis rests. As economist Daniel Bromley (1998) notes, cost-benefit analysis evaluates the future in terms of the present, whereas public policy must always evaluate the present in terms of the future. In Alice in Wonderland fashion, cost-benefit analysis tries to answer Alice's question, "Would you tell me, please, which way I ought to go from here?" without considering the Cheshire Cat's reply: "That depends a good deal on where you want to get to." Cost-benefit analysis might tell us the least expensive way to get where we want to go, but it cannot tell us where we want to go. It cannot answer Alice's question.

Of course, this is not to deny that things have costs. But one can consider the costs of things without engaging in cost-benefit analysis. When the founders of the American republic decided to revolt against what they considered to be British tyranny, they did not engage in cost-benefit analysis. When the French revolted against the monarchy, they did not engage in cost-benefit analysis. When the United States decided to enter the Second World War, we did not engage in cost-benefit analysis. Yet, everyone was aware that these decisions had very high costs associated with them. There is clearly a place for policy analysis in public decision-making: "The role of good policy analysis and economic assessment is not to determine the goals of society in advance on a priori grounds on the basis of an academic theory. It is rather to inform the political process by which society chooses its own objectives" (Sagoff 1988:217).

CONCLUSIONS

The current fascination with the market threatens to overwhelm all other forms of thought and action. All decisions, whether individual preferences or matters of great social importance are to be subjected to the calculus of the market, a calculus that proponents see as incontrovertible, as undeniable. All institutions are to be governed by the laws of the market, laws that are not made by humans but are inscribed into the very nature of the world itself. All functions of government, from prison management (see Schlosser 1998) to the post office, are to be handed to the private sector so as to increase their efficiency.

Yet, in one of the great ironies of history, unbending faith in the market poses many of the same problems as unbending faith in science or the state. Indeed, each of the stories told above could have been told as stories of science, state, or market. Each brooks no tolerance for opposing views. Each permits no alternative visions of the future. Each creates what sociologist John Law (1994) has called "hideous orderings." Can we escape from their seemingly flawless and ubiquitous logic? Are there alternatives to the three Leviathans? Or are we doomed forever to cling to one or more of them? It is to these questions that I now turn.

NOTES

1.   Such a bargain makes no provision for the possibility that the creative endeavor or invention might actually be harmful to society. Most European patent laws prohibit patenting objects deemed harmful or immoral.
2.   The European Union has already passed such a law through Council Directive No. 96/9/EC, O.J. L77/20 (1996). The EU directive provides no boundaries as to what constitutes a database. Nor does it explain what a "substantial modification" might be. The World Intellectual Property Organization (WIPO)

has developed a proposal for a world treaty on the subject with similar deficiencies (see Sanks 1998).

3.   By the time of the passage of the law, most breeders were no longer independent. Instead, they worked for large seed companies or public plant breeding bodies. Hence, the "rights" conferred were for companies rather than breeders.

5

BEYOND THE LEVIATHANS

The idea of a natural individual in his isolation possessed of full-fledged wants, of energies to be expended according to his own volition, and of a ready-made faculty of foresight and prudent calculation is as much a fiction in psychology as the doctrine of the individual in possession of antecedent political rights is one in politics.

—*John Dewey*, The Public and Its Problems

While proponents of scientism, of statism, and of marketism see themselves as providing (at the very least) solutions to the problem of order, their very "solutions" contain the seeds of their own destruction. As John Law (1994) has suggested, there is a belief that if only everything were so ordered, then all would be right with the world. Yet, every attempt to make the entire world conform fully any particular ordering principle creates a reaction in direct proportion to the effort expended in defending the principle.

SCIENTISM

Scientism leads not to the rational world prescribed by Bacon, but to the resurgence of belief in magic, to new forms of superstition, to the rejection of (at least parts of the) scientistic belief system, and attempts to substitute various alternatives. What had been previously described as side effects, as externalities, as temporary inconveniences on the road to scientific progress, now close in on us, threatening our very lives. The air we breathe, the food we eat, the soil we walk on, the water we drink, the very climate we take for granted are now problematic in ways unimagined a century ago. Moreover, the continuous fragmentation of both science and engineering into ever smaller subfields has several paradoxical effects.

Even those who claim to be experts are laypersons in other fields, due to the sheer volume of scientific and technical information. Thus, the geologist who specializes in predicting earthquakes has little to say to the biologist who specializes in the life cycle of *Salmonella*. The computer sci-

117

entist who generates an algorithm for resolving a puzzling problem in computational mathematics is a novice when confronted with the chemistry of fatty acids. Even within the biological sciences, the molecular biologist who is searching for a gene that codes for a particular trait—at home amidst various pieces of laboratory equipment—often looks with incomprehension at the field ecologist who attempts to analyze the interactions among flora, fauna, and climate in the Amazon rain forest. Thus, the expert society is—by definition—also the society of increasingly ignorant laypersons.

This proliferation of scientific fields and subfields conceals the contradictions, the impossibilities, the antithetical assumptions that grow unnoticed at the interstices between the sciences. Thus, we often find that, when confronted with actual problems in the world, scientists from different fields are at odds with each other. Molecular biologists tell us that modified organisms may be released into the environment with impunity, while ecologists tell us that ecological disasters are sure to happen. Chemists tell us that certain compounds are harmless to humans, while medical researchers tell us to avoid them.

As a result, on the one hand we find the growing iatrogenesis of which Ivan Illich (1976) wrote. The allopathic medical community finds that its quest for the perfect drug leads to all sorts of what are usually called side effects but what are in fact part and parcel of the phenomenon of pharmaceutical use. As much as pharmaceuticals have reduced illness and saved lives, far more people now die from adverse reactions to drugs than from automobile accidents. There is now even a scientific journal that focuses entirely on diseases caused by pharmaceuticals: *Iatrogenics: The Official Journal of the International Society for the Prevention of Iatrogenic Complications.*

In addition, medical science poses new ethical questions for society without the slightest regard for their answers: What sex would you like your children to have? What shall count as a birth defect? a missing limb? a cleft palate? Short stature? How short is short? When should one be allowed to die? How shall death be defined in light of ever-more sophisticated machinery for maintaining bodily functions? Should information about inherited diseases be reported to insurance companies and employers? Should parents be allowed to choose the sex of their children? their eye color, hair, stature?

On the other hand, we find ourselves thinking and acting in terms of what sociologist Ulrich Beck (1992) has called the risk society. Every time we ingest a drug, every time we ride in an automobile, every time we eat a bit of food, everything with which we come into contact everyday, is a potential risk to our health and safety. And for each of these things there is an expert who will tell us how trivial the risk is, as well as another expert who will tell us how grave it is. In sum, "Science is *one of the causes, the medi-*

um of definition, and the source of solutions to risks" (ibid.:155; emphasis in original). No longer can the simplistic notion that science is merely the search for the truth prevail. One must ask, as does philosopher Sandra Harding (1991): Whose questions? Whose truth? Whose knowledge? Whose science? When that is done, science itself becomes part of the problem as well as part of the solution.

Some persons, fleeing the horrifying uncertainty generated by these debates, rush to alternatives far beyond the bounds of mainstream science. Laetrile, the low-sugar diet, and the endless psychobabble that publishers spew forth all written by persons with apparently respectable credentials serve to reinforce the notion that the alternative to the now lost certainty of science is to follow the latest prescription for a beautiful body, a long life, a loving family, a successful business. At the extreme, some find themselves compelled to cling to new forms of superstition, to unexamined beliefs, to antiscience.

STATISM

Like scientism, statism also leads to its opposites. To the extent that the state is held up as the only legitimate institution—the church, the family, the school, the retirement home, the farm all rolled into one—then it, too, tends to create precisely the contradictions that its advocates claimed it would eliminate. Bureaucracies proliferate, each taking its share of the social product. The world becomes filled with Kafkaesque bureaucrats who oversee each aspect of one's life at the very same time as they themselves are caught in the webs generated by other bureaucrats. The very attempt at rationalization through central planning leads to such complex plans as to make conformity with the plan impossible, absurd, or both. Since the bureaucracy that oversees the plan must also create measures of performance, people begin to work to the measures. Production measures based on weight lead to ever heavier products. Trains run empty so as to fulfill the distance measures foreseen by the plan. Forms to be completed require ever more signatures, and each signature gives yet another bureaucrat an opportunity to sabotage the very plans the forms are designed to serve.

Illicit markets for goods and services spring up to furnish what the state cannot provide. If currency is unavailable, then any other object will do as well. For example, in Ceauşescu's Romania, Kent cigarettes substituted for cash. Citizens carried them in the hopes of finding scarce goods, not intending to actually smoke them. Of course, those engaging in such activities risked both being caught by the *Securitate* and being robbed by others in the market. They were far less safe and secure than citizens of any mixed society.

But statism is hardly confined to regimes such as that of Ceauşescu. One only need look at the contemporary U.S. government. Prior to 1960 the U.S. government had relatively few rules governing the behavior of government officials. This had the effect of giving bureaucrats significant discretion in carrying out their duties. However, several law professors and influential politicians concluded that such discretion was undesirable as it permitted those with connections to circumvent the law. By making the law more precise, more scientific, they would protect Americans from the inevitably power-hungry bureaucrat. They successfully argued for the expansion of administrative code—detailed rules to guide bureaucratic behavior. This, they claimed, would limit bureaucratic power and protect us from its abuse. As lawyer Philip K. Howard put it, according to the proponents of modern legal theory, "The words of law will tell us exactly what to do. Judgment is foreclosed not simply by the language of the words. It is also foreclosed by the belief that judgment has no place in the application of law" (1994:18).

But the result of this shift from simple laws, in which a few rules would suffice, to detailed laws, in which each option is to be spelled out in its entirety, has been not at all what its proponents intended. The *Federal Register*, the depository of administrative code for the federal government, grew from fifteen thousand pages in the last year of the Kennedy administration to seventy thousand pages in the last year of the Bush administration. At the same time, business agreements that were just a few pages expanded to several hundred pages (ibid.).

As the law became more complex, fewer persons could even begin to comprehend it. Rather than limiting the power of bureaucrats, the very complexity of the law enhanced their power. Bureaucrats could now pick and choose among hundreds, perhaps thousands, of often conflicting rules. Moreover, whereas in the past there were just a few rules to be followed and interpreted, now each of the myriad rules required its own interpretation. Worse still, the rules were to be applied everywhere in the same way, without regard to the circumstances of a particular case. As a result, even the most well-meaning bureaucrats find themselves hemmed in by rules that prevent them from doing what is obviously the most appropriate and sensible thing to do. Finally, rather than making decisions and being responsible for those decisions, bureaucrats can now hide behind the endless complexity of the law.

Consider a hypothetical case in point. The biblical commandment against murder simply says, "Thou shalt not kill." But there have always been exceptions to this rule. In contemporary American society, one may kill in self-defense. One may kill in the midst of war. One may plead not guilty by reason of insanity. One might kill by accident and without malicious intent. For centuries common law took care of these exceptions by examining not only the killing but also the circumstances in which the killing took place. However, if one were to apply the same approach now used to delineate much U.S. law to this particular problem, one would have to spell out in enormous detail all of the possible ways in which killing might take place. But this would hardly serve to produce justice. Instead, it would usurp the power of judge and jury and place it in the hands of those able to interpret volumes of law independent of the circumstances in which the actual killing took place. As Howard puts it, "Compulsive devotion to uniformity in law can generally be achieved only by infidelity to fairness in life" (ibid.:38).

As a result of this obsession with detail, we are now saddled with a government that is obsessed by process. This government puts such high requirements on new housing that low-income housing is all but impossible to construct. The Environmental Protection Agency is hopelessly bogged down in the testing of pesticide compounds in a vain effort to produce the last word on the subject. We have developed procedures for avoiding corruption in public works that are so complex as to invite the very corruption that we desire to prevent. We have a Food and Drug Administration that is so cautious in approving drugs that it fails to note the lives lost during the approval process. We have an Occupational Health and Safety Administration that is sometimes more concerned about following rules than promoting workplace safety. We have a military that has spent thousands of dollars for what should be inexpensive off-the-shelf hardware and that has spent more money processing travel vouchers than the cost of the travel itself.

Nor is the statism of the large corporation any better. It generates equally byzantine bureaucracies, shielded from accountability and caught in the very webs they weave. To appreciate the scope of the problem, one only need watch what happens when unionized employees of a large corporation work to the rules. Suddenly, production is delayed, forms are rejected because they lack proper authorization, "just-in-time" becomes a nightmare to management.

Rulers of large corporations now often believe that information technologies will cut through the Gordian knot of bureaucratic control. In the short run, they are no doubt correct. But, alas, information technologies used on a grand scale bring with them their own order-induced chaos and waste. Entire corporations grind to a halt over errors in programming. Customers are caught in endless loops of recorded telephone messages: "For more information, press 1." The coming of the millennium brings with it the year 2000 or Y2K problem. Whether real or imagined, the cost of reprogramming thousands of computers is staggering. One only need note the popularity of the comic strip character Dilbert to appreciate how common such information technology-induced bureaucracy is.

MARKETISM

Nor is marketism an exception to the rule. It, too, generates its contra-dictions, its opposites. Proponents of free markets would have us believe that they produce a just and fair distribution of corporate and personal in-come and wealth. They would have us believe that the salaries or profits we earn are always just rewards for hard work or careful investment. Were that only the case. Consider some of the many things that make free mar-keters' claims weak at best, absurd at worst:

1. Quite obviously we do not enter the world of the market as equal par-ticipants. Some of us come from wealthy families, others from poor ones. Some of us can afford higher education, while others cannot. Thus, in the great casino of the market society, some begin with far more chips than oth-ers. The claim of equal opportunity is more myth than reality—myth main-tained by the occasional Horatio Alger story. The freedom to choose heralded by the proponents of the free market is useless to those lacking the financial means to participate in it.

2. Monetary policy appears to us as a purely technical issue. Alan Greenspan, current chair of the Federal Reserve Bank, and his contempo-raries in other nations set the prime rate so as to keep inflation under con-trol. But, in point of fact, low inflation increases unemployment. Even now, in times of relatively low unemployment, Federal Reserve policies contin-ue to sacrifice jobs for low inflation. Thus, those at the bottom of the in-come ladder are sacrificed so that banks and other lenders may protect their earnings.

3. In the name of promoting U.S. agricultural products, the United States provides a variety of export subsidies through the Foreign Market Devel-opment Cooperator Program ($27 million in 1997) and the Market Access Program ($90 million). In principle, such subsidies are meant to encourage consumption of U.S.-made goods abroad (Foreign Agricultural Service 1998). Of course, only companies that export benefit from such subsidies. Among the beneficiaries of this policy has been McDonald's, a company known at least as much for its low wages and poor working conditions as for its hamburgers (Moore and Stansel 1995).

4. Despite the creation of the World Trade Organization, U.S. import tar-iffs and quotas continue to persist on a number of products. For example, clothing, shipping, broadcasting, steel, and various agricultural products are the subject of tariffs, quotas, or both. Such protectionism costs domes-tic consumers of these products more than seventy billion dollars per year, while depriving foreign producers of potential markets (Cox 1999). Con-sider the case of sugar: U.S. sugar producers are protected from sugar pro-duced in poor, tropical nations. This means that you and I pay more for

sugar and that the profits of domestic sugar producers are inflated. In addition, until recently, Florida cane sugar producers benefited from cheap labor brought from Jamaica on special visas to harvest the crop by hand. For nearly a half-century, the sugar companies were constantly in court fighting continuing allegations of violating labor laws and providing inadequate housing. Finally, in the mid-1990s, the companies replaced the laborers with harvesting machines (Vick 1993). In short, import tariffs and quotas restructure prices and wages so as to allow some to increase their profits at others' expense.

5. Current U.S. law permits companies that engage in research and development (R&D) to gain significant tax advantages. R&D is broadly defined to include not only complex new technologies but fairly pedestrian innovations. Ostensibly, these tax breaks allow U.S. industry to compete more effectively in world markets. They may do that, but they also shift income from labor to capital as most of the innovations developed are designed to reduce labor costs. Moreover, they favor those industries that are already capital-intensive and where major R&D investments may be made.

6. U.S. tax laws permit homeowners to deduct the property taxes and interest payments on their mortgages on their tax returns. Wealthy homeowners with a vacation home may claim an interest and tax deduction on that home as well. Those who live in rental units, including most of those at the bottom of the income ladder, are thereby penalized in favor of the middle class and the wealthy.

7. Perhaps the most egregious violation of the free market model is the huge property tax breaks granted to large corporations in efforts to induce them to locate in particular communities. Clearly, no small businesses benefit from such extortion from states, cities, and towns as they do not wield the necessary clout. Again, small businesses and everyone else who pays taxes subsidize the handful of large corporations that hardly need such support.

8. In often subtle ways, health and safety regulations subsidize large firms at the expense of small ones. For example, early in the twentieth century large food canners quickly embraced sanitary codes, knowing that their enforcement would put their smaller competitors out of business (Levenstein 1988). More recently, new meat and fish processing regulations have imposed considerable new paperwork burdens on small food processors while requiring few changes in the operation of their larger competitors. Whether or not it was intended by the drafters of the new laws, their effect has been to shift profits from small firms to large ones.

9. As noted above, patent and copyright laws have been expanded in scope and length of period of protection. Regardless of their specifics, such laws confer monopoly privileges on certain companies and individuals, allowing them to increase their profits and incomes at the expense of the rest

of us. Yet, without some sort of intellectual property laws, those who invested would have no way of recouping their investment. The market is incapable of telling us how much protection patent and copyright holders should receive; that can only be decided outside the market, preferably based on some notion of fairness and justice.

10. Labor laws—whether requiring closed shops or so-called right-to-work laws—shift the distribution of income. Workers in union shops often enjoy higher wages than those in nonunion shops, reducing the share of income returned to capital. Right-to-work laws make union organizing difficult, thereby keeping wages down while increasing corporate profits. Both change the distribution of income.

11. Workplace safety and environmental protection laws reduce corporate profits, at least in those cases where corporations must compete with other corporations that are in other jurisdictions. If all firms are required to have safer or more environmentally sound workplaces, then the costs of safety are passed on to consumers of the products of those firms. Either way, income and profits are redistributed.

12. Transport infrastructure redistributes income in subtle but profound ways. New interstate highways have destroyed countless small businesses—motels, gas stations, convenience stores—in the small towns of America. In most cases, they have been replaced by the large national chains that are now commonly found at nearly every highway interchange. Similarly, the Washington, D.C., metro system radically altered property values around metro stations, spurred apartment and retail development, and doubtless made other locations less attractive. In both cases, highways and subways, incomes and profits are rearranged. In addition, good highways subsidize the auto industry and all who own vehicles (who benefit from fewer repairs). Conversely, investments in subways reduce the incomes and profits of those who produce and own vehicles, while reducing costs for those who would prefer to use mass transportation.

13. Zoning limits the uses to which property can be put, thereby redistributing the value of land. The land zoned for single-family housing will never be as valuable as that zoned for high-rise housing. The laws that prohibit me from building a cement factory next to your home reduce the income I can earn from the use of my land. Zoning laws that require large lots necessarily increase the costs of providing public services. Laws that require space in front of buildings restrict property owners' incomes in favor of public spaces. But the elimination of zoning also redistributes value: my cement factory can make your home unsalable and perhaps unlivable.

14. In the market society that Adam Smith described, there were only small firms. But the unbridled market leads to ever larger corporations that, as noted above, all have their own internal planning agencies, that all

do whatever is necessary to avoid the perils of price competition. Today's large multinational and transnational corporations are not the price takers that Smith described. They are often price *makers*. They watch each other even while they carve the world into separate market segments. They copy each other's behavior—if Pepsi does it, so must Coke; if General Motors, then surely Chrysler; if Kellogg's, then certainly Post—in a manner reminiscent of the way in which imperial nation-states keep a wary eye on potential enemy activity even as they divide the world geographically.

They eschew price competition as much as possible, preferring to focus instead on style, taste, and symbolic value. Such firms set the price that they believe the market will bear. Consider the fact that larger banks charge more for the use of automatic teller machines (ATMs) than do smaller ones. Consider the way the airlines watch each others' pricing, often raising prices in reaction to other airlines' decisions to do so. Since large firms are price makers, they shift the distribution of income and wealth in their favor.

At the same time the megacorporations find it easier and easier to engage in price-fixing. According to Assistant Attorney-General for Anti-Trust Joel I. Klein, international price-fixing is on the rise. In 1998 a record twenty-five grand juries were investigating charges of price-fixing, although not all nations are willing to cooperate in such investigations (Garland and Thorton 1998). But not all nations have the same antitrust laws as the United States.[1] Even Great Britain, where Thatcherists preached the virtues of the free market for years, suffers from considerable, and mostly legal, price-rigging (Kuttner 1998).

Moreover, as firms get larger, they become more and more difficult to control. Indeed, even the dean of the Yale School of Management has worried in print over whether private power is becoming so gigantic that it is no longer controllable by governments (Garten 1999). Yet, driven by stiff competition from other large firms, mergers and buyouts continue apace.

Market enthusiasts will be quick to point out that monopolies and oligopolies frequently collapse when market structure changes—witness IBM's demotion with the shift from mainframe to personal computers. But such arguments ignore the fact that for long periods of time such oligopolies dominate the market. Furthermore, they do so by using all the means at their disposal—advertising, product differentiation, packaging (and occasionally collusion)—to avoid price competition. In the rare instances when they do fail, they are soon replaced by others. This is hardly the open competition based on prices that free market advocates claim is just around the corner.

15. Also, consider that while capital freely flows across national borders, labor is subject to all kinds of elaborate controls. As a large investor, I can decide to invest my money where it will earn the highest return—perhaps

in a manufacturing plant in Argentina. But, if I am a barber or a physician or a plumber or even a university professor, I cannot simply move to the place where wages are highest. All sorts of laws, rules, and regulations restrict my ability to maximize my income. Thus, those few persons who have large sums of money to invest—already the most privileged members of all nations—are able to gain far greater returns on their investments than are those of us who only have our own labor to invest. The obvious result is that the free movement of capital combined with the restricted movement of labor leads to greater and greater inequalities of wealth and income.

16. Finally, all governments, not least that of this nation, provide lucrative contracts for furnishing the government with goods, especially for defense. All governments are significant sources of employment for substantial numbers of people, providing them with income and wealth that might not otherwise be available to them. Most governments award licenses for the use of the airwaves, for taxi operation, for the use of government lands for mining, logging, or grazing. They provide postal services at sometimes subsidized rates. All governments generate statistics—numbers upon which individual and corporate actions are based. Most governments provide transfer payments—social security, welfare, subsidized health care and education, veterans' benefits—to a large portion of the population. This "interference in the market" rearranges the distribution of wealth and income in complex and often invisible ways.

Proponents of free markets, and perhaps especially libertarians, will balk at my list. They will assert that all of the points I raise here are *obstacles* to the truly free market. Indeed, the examples described above are the result of political intrusion into the marketplace. Export subsidies and import tariffs are particularly clear examples of political actions. Free market advocates naively think that economics and politics can be separated. But to do so would require draconian measures that no free society would tolerate. As Michael Walzer argues, "A radically laissez-faire economy would be like a totalitarian state, invading every other sphere, dominating every other distributive process" (1983:119).

Beyond that, issues of workers' rights, safety, environmental protection, public health and safety, health care for the indigent, social security, zoning, and transportation infrastructure are places where state intervention is necessary—perhaps obligatory. One need only read a Dickens novel to understand why our forebears fought long and hard to place these issues on the public agenda, to remove them from the realm of the market.

One might also argue, as many neoclassical economists do, that the existing markets resemble those of theory sufficiently closely that the models are adequate, that they have what statisticians call "robustness." Yet, econometrician Paul Ormerod (1994), in a lengthy review of the technical literature, notes that once the rigid (and heroic) assumptions of the neo-classical model are relaxed even slightly, the models literally fall apart. Furthermore, despite considerable sums of money spent on developing macroeconomic models, their performance is quite poor. Thus, even on its own terms, despite the appropriation of terms like "rationality" and the mathematical sophistication of its models, neoclassical economics tells us little about how real markets operate.

Indeed, it is worth noting the sharp disparities between the markets of neoclassical economics and those of marketing and management. In the neoclassical model, numerous small firms compete in markets with ho-mogeneous commodities the prices of which are determined by the "laws" of supply and demand. As every student of introductory economics learns, given a certain level of demand, the price of a given commodity rises when supplies are scarce and declines when that same commodity is in abun-dance. Conversely, given a fixed supply, prices rise when demand rises and fall when demand falls. There is little reason to quibble with the theory as this much seems virtually self-evident, although one might wonder where profits would come from if actual markets worked as smoothly as those in the model (Ormerod 1994).

But all this assumes that things for sale in the real world have nearly the same characteristics as the commodities described by the theory. Some things surely do. Adam Smith's pins are a likely candidate. But the entire marketing literature and the actual practices of most firms are at odds with the theory. Marketing experts generally share the atomistic individualism favored by economists (Kover 1967), but they counsel their clients to avoid the perils of undifferentiated commodity production at all costs. Product differentiation is designed to make it difficult or impossible for consumers to compare prices. Is a Ford Taurus a better buy than a Chevrolet Lumina? Are Rice Crispies a better value than Cheerios? Brand names are also used to differentiate among what are otherwise nearly identical products, there-by avoiding the perils of the marketplace. And, advertising—itself a multi-billion dollar industry—touts the real or imagined, concrete or symbolic advantages of owning one or another product. A cheap brandless watch will provide the time nearly as well as a Rolex, but by buying a Rolex one buys watch, company reputation for quality, and—perhaps most impor-tantly—status.

One might argue that all that advertising is merely wasted money. But if that is true, then the CEOs and top management of the world's largest corporations must all be wrong. Yet, "of the top twenty brands in Ameri-ca in 1925, almost seventy years later no fewer than eighteen of them are still the best-selling products in their categories" (Ormerod 1994:55). Indeed, it is ironic that even while CEOs and managers embrace the free market in public, they privately plan the next campaign to thwart it.

Furthermore, in order to translate the theorems of neoclassical economics into practice, the world must be remade in the mold provided by the neoclassicists. Here the similarities and differences with the natural sciences need to be made clear. Physicists will tell you that a pound of feathers falls to the ground as fast as a pound of lead *in a vacuum*. But everyone knows that in everyday situations where there are no vacuums, lead falls faster than feathers. To make the physics true in practice one must change the world to permit the existence of something akin to a perfect vacuum. This logic has been extraordinarily successful in developing and improving a wide range of technologies by changing the everyday world to more nearly resemble that of physical theory. Thus, waterwheels were made more efficient, electricity was produced, refrigerants were developed, and radio signals were made commercially viable by rearranging the everyday world to resemble conditions once found only in the laboratory.

To instantiate the free market, something quite similar must be done: the social world must be remade to resemble that of the theory. As sociologist Michel Callon argues, "Economics, in the broad sense of the term, performs, shapes and formats the economy, rather than observing how it functions" (1998:2). And just as the creation of a vacuum requires elaborate equipment to control the surrounding context—to prevent the entry of air or other "impurities"—so the creation of a market society requires control of the surrounding context. But whereas physicists never suggest that the entire world should be remade as a vacuum in order to prove the validity of their theory, market enthusiasts demand just that. All aspects of collective, social action must be eliminated, stamped out, uprooted, invalidated (Bourdieu 1998). Labor must be made more flexible, less secure. Firms must be downsized to conform to market dictates. Jobs must conform to the logic of the market with respect to working hours, wages, benefits, tasks. Ideally, there should be no trade unions, no families, no friendships, no voluntary associations. The security of the welfare state must be discredited because it promotes social solidarity, because it is about us as citizens rather than about me as consumer. As Smith quite clearly understood, and as his descendants apparently do not, the atomized individuals of the marketplace must be made, for they are surely not born.

Indeed, behind the gloss of mathematics, as sociologist Pierre Bourdieu puts it, "economism removes responsibility and demobilizes by annulling politics and imposing an entire series of undiscussed ends, maximum growth, competitiveness, productivity" (1998:56). The certainties of neoclassical economics appear as a set of untested assumptions—assumptions so opaque as to be invisible even to many of the proponents of neoclassical economics themselves. These assumptions must remain unchallenged, undiscussed, self-evident, if the neoclassical edifice is to be built, for if they were ever brought to public debate, they would be rejected out of hand. Who would want to live in a world of isolated individuals, each attempting to maximize his or her preferences? Who would want an omnipresent state suppressing all relations that might be found to be in restraint of trade? Who would want to calculate each action so as to amass as much capital as possible? Certainly no religion, no culture in history ever lived this way or suggested that it would be desirable to do so. The eminent Chinese sociologist Fei Shaotong ([1948] 1992) noted that traditional Chinese villages rarely contained markets, precisely because of their potential inhumanity. In the village, only gift exchange was considered acceptable. Markets were held in open fields some distance from the village, where trading with strangers "without human feelings" (*wuqing*) could occur.

Moreover, as markets are freed from constraints and large corporations are permitted to get even larger, nations are put at risk. The U.S. savings and loan debacle of the 1980s is a case in point: It took six years and $125 billion in tax money to reorganize the industry. Now, Japan faces a similar crisis as its banks sit on at least $230 billion in bad debts. But it is not the banks that will resolve the problem; it is the Japanese state that is now in the process of trying to rectify the situation and put the economy back on track (Bremner 1998). Similarly, at the regional level trading blocs have emerged—NAFTA, the European Union, Mercosur—each with its own quasi-governmental powers, but each formed in the name of free trade. Each requires its own adjudication procedures, its own trading rules, its own bureaucrats to fill the world's hotels and conference centers.

Under the rubric of structural adjustment, the International Monetary Fund tells errant nations how to act so as to maintain their place in the global market society. If food riots occur, if governments topple, if government services deteriorate, so be it. That is the necessary price to pay for being part of the New World Order.

The World Bank only loans money to those who open their economies to the market (although as the Japanese have become more important participants, the bank has tempered its rhetoric and perhaps its practices). As such, the bank wields enormous power, especially with the poorer nations of the world, which have no other options available.

One of the great ironies of decreased tariffs is the worldwide rise in what are known as nontariff trade barriers. Unlike tariffs, which are visible and therefore easy to monitor, nontariff trade barriers come in a multitude of shapes and sizes. A nation can require that imports meet health, safety, environmental, labeling, or any of a host of other criteria. Furthermore, by making the criteria obscure enough it becomes possible to delay shipments or reject them at the port of entry. Of course, there are quite legitimate reasons for having such requirements. In general, nations want their consumers to have safe food. They do not want products on the market that are potentially injurious to purchasers. They often do not want their environment fouled by imported goods. But how is one to judge what is injurious to health, safety, or the environment and what is merely a trade barrier? The answers to such questions are often far less than clear.

The current solution is to create an organization to oversee world trade. As such, the rapidly growing bureaucracy of the World Trade Organization dictates to nations what products they must allow within their borders. How strong should auto bumpers be? Must tuna fishing be dolphin-safe? Can governments insist that the wood they purchase be harvested in an environmentally friendly manner? May children be employed in rug manufacture? Should all cheese be pasteurized? Should cattle be treated with hormones to increase their rate of growth? Should the Danes be allowed to export apples that are smaller than the official size allowed? How should genetically modified organisms be labeled, or should they be labeled at all? Is barring their importation a violation of the rules of free trade? The WTO must now use its claimed Solomonic wisdom to settle such questions.

Moreover, the smooth flow of international commerce requires more central banks and more coordination among them. Each bank must have greater powers to stabilize currencies, to ensure that currency and stock markets remain free of insider trading, collusion, bribery, and fraud. And this is no simple task when each day $1.5 trillion in foreign exchange is traded electronically. In contrast, global exports of goods and services is a mere $25 billion per day (Clinton 1999).

This movement of vast amounts of capital each day is driven by what has come to be known in financial circles as "securitization," the issuance of high-quality stocks and bonds. Proponents argue that nations should focus on increasing the number of companies listed on their stock markets so as to attract investors. This, in turn, will drive up the value of stock shares, attracting still more investors. Moreover, global capital markets discipline corporate CEOs since fund managers have little interest in poorly performing companies. One enthusiastic proponent of securitization even argues that "an economic policy that aims to achieve growth by wealth creation therefore does not attempt to increase the production of goods and services, except as a secondary objective" (Edmunds 1996:119).

Of course, this enthusiasm glosses over five major problems: (1) Only those at the top of the economic ladder have money to invest in securities. (2) Downsizing may play well with stockholders but it hardly does so for workers and their communities. (3) The gap between those who have the wherewithal to invest and those who do not is widening, leading to social unrest in some nations. (4) Goods and services must still be produced; image is not everything. (5) Securitization creates enormous economic volatility as has been shown dramatically by the collapse of stock prices in several Asian nations. To date, international financial institutions have been able to contain such crises (although not without considerable pain for those at the bottom of the economic ladder). Whether they will be able to do so in the future remains to be seen.

Marketism also demands international standards for everything traded and tradable—and there can hardly be anything that is not in some way implicated in world trade. So woe be it to someone who attempts to sell internationally a tomato that is too small or a steel bar that is not of the proper dimensions. Hundreds of international bodies are created, each sheltered (necessarily) from the hustle and bustle of daily life, each consuming reams of paper defining and redefining products, processes, services, tests.

Of course, this new central planning is not that of Gosplan, the central planning agency of the former Soviet Union. It is not all under the control of some single allegedly rational central planning mechanism. Instead, it is a labyrinthine collection of international, governmental, nongovernmental, and quasi-governmental agencies, with enforcement powers or without them, with governmental observers or without, with wide participation of various interests or with none. And no one has more than an inkling of how all this works, for to question it is to question the very faith in the power of the market that called these bodies into existence in the first place. Thus, the quest for the market society leads not to a stateless world but to a world in which the state becomes all-pervasive, yet nearly invisible.

At the same time, marketism inserts market relations everywhere. All human activity, all altruistic behavior is reinterpreted in terms of rational calculation. Even the value of beautiful landscapes is monetized by economists in a vain effort to force everything into the box provided by the market. In the market, one distributive rule applies: Whosoever has the money to purchase a good may buy it. (Its corollary is that anything can be produced for which there are willing purchasers.) But clearly there are certain things that are not to be bought: votes, judges, juries, people, freedom of speech, love, parts of the national heritage—to name but a few. Even a market society must guard against these dangers or risk dissolving into chaos.

Beyond that, there are at least two other legitimate distributive rules, each of which has its established place in all societies: dessert and need (Walzer 1983). One may deserve to be rewarded for bravery, duty to country, risking one's life to save that of a drowning child, producing a magnificent work of art, or winning the Grand Prix. Similarly, one may deserve to be punished for murder, kidnaping, or even parking in a no-parking zone. In contrast, one may distribute goods based on the rule of need. Individuals, organizations, or governments may give aid to those who are hungry, disabled, very young, very old, in need of education, a heart transplant, a pair of shoes. These rules of distribution—dessert and need—are incompatible with the market. They necessarily violate the central distributive rule of the market. They do not distribute according to ability to pay. But ignoring dessert and need leads to the collapse of the social order.

Proponents of the market consistently emphasize choice. But many of the choices of the market prove to be illusory, trivial, or both. How many brands, sizes, bottle shapes, and types of ketchup do I really need? Thanks to the magic of the market, the average U.S. supermarket today contains thirty thousand separate items (Food Marketing Institute 1998). Do we eat better as a result? Are our meals more nutritious? If so, how does one account for the virtual epidemic of obesity in the United States today? And what is missing from the myriad choices of the market cornucopia? I can buy Israeli tomatoes, Dutch peppers, Norwegian sardines, Spanish palm hearts, Jamaican mangoes, California tomatoes, Chinese tea, Brazilian coffee, Chilean grapes, and Florida oranges at my local supermarket, but I can't find very much local produce there because it doesn't fit the annual contractual arrangements of the supermarket chains. I might also ask: Where can I purchase a train ticket to the next town? Why can I not find most foreign films in the local video store? Is my life better because I can purchase fifty brands of salad dressing? Is our society more loving? More just?

Of course, in principle, the market does treat everyone in the same way: as anonymous individuals who have a desire or need to buy something that the market provides. (In practice, racism, sexism, and other prejudices are still common in the marketplace.) But this "individualization means market dependency in all dimensions of living" (Beck 1992:132). Those who do not have the means to purchase goods in the market simply do not exist. They are no more than another form of waste that the market society generates. We move to the suburbs to escape them altogether.

This means that the poor and homeless in the United States and, to a lesser extent, in Western Europe have become more and more invisible. They have not only been disenfranchised politically, but in the marketplace as well. We slink past them on the street, hoping they will not ask us for money. We fear them even as we try to deny their existence.

The same is true internationally. Whole nations, especially in Africa, have been written off. Their incomes are so low that they hardly purchase anything from the rest of the world. Moreover, they have little that the world wants. Some regions and even entire nations have been allowed to sink into anarchy, genocide, and warlordism. As Jean-Christophe Rufin (1991) has suggested, with the cold war over and the market uninterested in their goods, they now resemble nothing so much as those areas defined in ancient times as being outside the Roman Empire.

And beyond the market, in the world of social goods, there is more and more a wasteland. In the United States, highway infrastructure is in poor condition. Public schools in inner cities are literally falling down. Health care is only available for those who can afford it. Homelessness is unchecked despite record high official levels of employment. Illicit drug use remains a massive problem despite throwing billions of dollars at it. Indeed, the market works well here, too. The more public funds are spent on drug enforcement, the scarcer the drugs and the more lucrative dealing drugs becomes. How can poor, inner-city kids resist the temptation to earn six hundred dollars per hour selling drugs versus six dollars per hour flipping hamburgers—if they can find a job. Meanwhile, drug treatment centers and needle exchanges remain understaffed, underfunded, and undersupported.

In sum, while markets surely distribute wealth, income, and other goods, they in no way do so automatically in a just and equitable manner. They only do so as the rules of the market dictate—rules necessarily complex and multifaceted—but always necessarily the result of political decisions. Thus, who participates in those decisions is at least as important as who participates in the market itself.

FUNDAMENTALISM: A SOLUTION?

I would be remiss if I simply ignored the strong words and action generated by those who call themselves (or are called by others) fundamentalists.[2] Whether of Christian, Muslim, Jewish, Buddhist, or even Hindu origin, such groups share certain features. In some ways, members of such groups share the concerns put forth above that scientism, statism, or marketism is undermining moral values. Perhaps it is the new forms of technology that are restructuring social life in ways that erode its meaning. Perhaps it is the secularism of the state that is seen as the threat. Perhaps it is the insidious invasion of market values that is defined as the culprit. Perhaps it is some autocrat who is imposing his will on the people. In each case, fundamentalisms are responses to the upheavals of the modern era *and* proposed resolutions for them (Barber 1996).

Whatever the particulars, fundamentalisms all share the notion of a return to fundaments, to foundations. In nearly all cases, such foundations are located in a particular and often innovative reading of one or another holy text. Marty and Appleby explain:

Feeling this identity to be at risk in the contemporary era, these believers fortify it by a selective retrieval of doctrines, beliefs, and practices from a sacred past. These retrieved "fundamentals" are refined, modified, and sanctioned in a spirit of pragmatism: they are to serve as a bulwark against the en-

croachment of outsiders who threaten to draw the believers into a syncre-
tistic, areligious, or irreligious cultural milieu. Moreover, fundamentalists
present the retrieved fundamentals alongside unprecedented claims and
doctrinal innovations. These innovations and supporting doctrines lend the
retrieved and updated fundamentals an urgency and charismatic intensity
reminiscent of the religious experiences that originally forged communal
identity. (1993:3)

Fundamentalists mark off their terrain (literally or figuratively) from
others while proclaiming a new religious and social order. They seek to create community by excluding those who do not belong. They actively seek
converts and in some societies actually take control of the state as in pre-
sent-day Iran and Afghanistan. In some nations, such as Egypt and Pak-
istan, they have considerable political power. In others, such as China,
they are of considerable concern to the government. Many fundamentalist
groups are particularly apprehensive about the emancipation of women,
an action they find to be in contradiction to holy texts. Yet, even if they wish
to withdraw from the everyday world, their very success forces them
to cope with problems of economics, politics, and technology—areas in
which sacred texts are usually silent. This generally forces them to compromise, but may also generate considerable violence.

American fundamentalist movements, most of which are Protestant,
tend to be fragmented. This is due in part to the Protestant notion of reading the Bible for oneself. Every new reading, each new "orthodox" interpretation, risks further fragmenting the tradition even as it revives it. For
example, most of those *who call themselves fundamentalists* in the United
States favor a literal interpretation of the Bible, believe that miracles ended when the Bible was completed, and advocate separation from all other
groups who do not share their view. In contrast, Pentacostals believe that
miracles still occur today. Evangelicals wish to separate themselves from
both of these groups (Woodberry and Smith 1998).

Fundamentalists are caught between withdrawing from the world by
developing total institutions that promote that withdrawal and interacting
with others, thereby engaging new ideas and losing the very orthodoxy
that they seek to promote. The total institution may work for awhile but it
is likely to lead to long-term decline or marginalization. In contrast, interaction with others is likely to lead to confrontations with new ethical
concerns and new political conundrums for which there are no simple answers.

Fundamentalisms are also marked by two other characteristics that they
share with scientism, statism, and marketism. First, fundamentalisms prescribe a particular form of order as the only possible one. As such, like scientism, statism, and marketism, they also (and equally ironically) relieve

individuals of moral responsibility even as they express moral outrage. One is exhorted (or coerced) into doing what the text says is right and good, even if multiple readings of the text are possible and the world has changed markedly since it was first written. Second, they discourage independent judgment, critical thinking, and exposure to alternative views. As sociologist Anthony Giddens suggests, "Fundamentalism may be understood as an assertion of formulaic truth without regard to consequences" (1994:100). Yet, as he also notes, in the modern world traditions only continue to exist if they can be justified through discourse. Put differently, fundamentalisms tend to terminate discussion, but the world today demands that traditions be justified through debate and dialogue.

Thus, fundamentalisms are as problematic in grappling with moral dilemmas as are science, state, and market. They offer order at the expense of individual autonomy, peace at the expense of suppressing dissent, morality at the expense of moral competence. Their proponents may succeed in capturing the state, but even (or perhaps especially) then, they are unable to deliver the religious utopia for which they strive. As Benjamin Franklin wisely observed several centuries ago, "Vital Religion has always suffer'd, when Orthodoxy is more regarded than Virtue" (quoted in Campbell 1999:122).

BEYOND SCIENTISM, STATISM, AND MARKETISM

Lest the reader misunderstand, let me reiterate that it is not my intent to suggest that we could somehow get along without science, without the state, without markets, or without religion. To the contrary, each is a necessary part of our contemporary world. The book in front of you is the product of computers, typesetting and printing equipment, international copyright law, markets in which publishers can sell to booksellers who, in turn, can sell to the public. The content of the book draws on notions of morality that must be rooted in faith. There is simply no way to do away with science, state, market, or religion. They are here to stay. But what can be done away with is the absurd belief that science, state, market, or religion can produce the perfectly ordered society, the place where we no longer need to engage in politics, where we will all know what to do and how to live, where human needs and desires will be effortlessly fulfilled by the inexorable workings of the well-oiled machine, the rational-bureaucratic state, or the invisible hand of the market. Indeed, if we do not do away with those beliefs, we are far more likely to create a global prison than a global utopia.

But where to start? How can we solve the problem of order without yet another all-pervasive ordering? Is there a way to vanquish the three

Leviathans we have so carefully built and enthusiastically embraced without raising yet another one? I believe so. Simply put, we must build a democratic society. But to do so, we must first look to the past, for the three Leviathans will only fade away if their foundations—indeed, the very idea of foundations—are undermined.

OF CHICKENS AND EGGS

In medieval times, it was widely believed that the social order was preordained by God. Each person was born into a particular place in that social order. Thus, serfs did not hope to become knights (although they might have envied them). What upward mobility did exist was confined to the church. In principle, if rarely in practice, a rural priest could aspire to become a bishop, a poor nun could aspire to become a mother superior. Kings ruled by virtue of their direct link to God, so their overthrow was virtually unthinkable.

By the sixteenth century this view of the world was largely in shambles. Luther's famous ninety-five theses had provoked a flood of religious reform, but they had also proven useful to German princes eager to escape control of the church, to peasants desirous of eliminating medieval ties to the land, and to the merchants in the newly rising towns, who wished greater freedom from both church and state. But if the medieval order was no longer seen as God-given, then something had to replace it. Society had to be invented. The preferred solution came to be the appeal to a presocial time in history, before society was founded. Hobbes, and later John Locke (1632–1683) and Jean-Jacques Rousseau (1712–1778), found this approach to understanding how society was possible to be both plausible and politically desirable.

But the entire problem of order is widely misunderstood. There was no presocial time in human history. To be human is to be social to the very core of one's body and soul. It is to have an identity that is derived socially, through interaction with others. Consider the situation: We are each born into a world that is preconstituted, already in existence, before we arrive on the scene. That world is the taken-for-granted world of everyday life. As infants we must learn the limits of the world. We must learn where we end and all else in the world begins. Only after we have accepted the world naively can we begin to critique it. As Michael Walzer puts it, "My place in the economy, my standing in the political order, my reputation among my fellows, my material holdings: all these come to me from other men and women" (1983:3).

Thus, the language I use, the opinions I have, the religion I practice, the choices I make, the clothes I wear, the gestures I use, my very thoughts, are in an important sense given to me. My opinions are not somehow inherent in my genetic makeup. Nor are they the result of some process of personal introspection. Rather, they are literally given to me by my parents, friends, acquaintances, teachers, the books and magazines I read, the experiences I have, the enemies I make. I can only have an opinion to the extent that I interact (either directly or indirectly) with others, for it is through that interaction that I discern what *my* opinions are, what I hold dear.

The social character of human beings is also evident in the punishments handed out to people over the centuries. Banishment, exile, shunning, excommunication, and solitary confinement were designed to make persons endure the suffering of being alone. So great is this need for human companionship that religious cults are often able to "reprogram" those who join. This on occasion has led to bizarre tragedies such as those at the People's Temple in Jonestown, Guyana, where in 1978 nearly one thousand people died of self-inflicted cyanide poisoning and at Heaven's Gate in Rancho Santa Fe, California, where in 1997 thirty-nine people committed suicide together, convinced that they were going to another planet. Similarly, victims often come to identify positively with kidnappers. Brainwashing of political prisoners is all too effective. What happens in each of these cases is not merely changes in behavior as a result of fear, but virtual personality transformations as cult members, kidnaping victims, and prisoners come to believe what those around them say.

Similarly, the choices I have are not mine. They are given to me by society, even as it is I who make the choice. Thus, I cannot decide to be pharaoh, to open the Northwest Passage, to be emperor of China, to serve in Hannibal's army. These are choices denied to me by virtue of where I am situated historically. Furthermore, I cannot decide to be queen of Holland, a girl scout, an African peasant, a drag queen, or a member of the British peerage. Gender, sexual orientation, race, class, and nationality (themselves having no existence other than as social relations) block those options. Of course, it is always possible for one to go off Don Quixote–like tilting at windmills, but in doing so one risks ridicule at best, physical violence or even death at worst.

But at the same time gender, race, class, and nationality open choices to me—as a white, heterosexual, American male—that are not open to others. When I go to the store, I need not worry that the store detective will see me as a potential thief. When I apply for a job, my whiteness and maleness are not a cause for concern for me or for most others. When I buy a home, I can buy it in a neighborhood I like and I can be reasonably confident that the neighbors will not be hostile toward me. If I am pulled over by a traffic cop, I know it is not a case of racial harassment. When I stand up in a public meeting to make a comment, I know that what I say will not be put down as the rantings of a "mere" housewife. When I read the newspaper or watch television, I know that people like me will be depicted in positive terms. Perhaps most importantly, I need not worry about the effect of my race, my maleness, or my heterosexuality on others (see McIntosh 1995). Similarly, when I work in poor nations, I am often whisked through customs. I get better service in some shops. I can almost always find someone who speaks (at least a rudimentary amount of) my language. I do not ask for any of these things nor have I done anything to deserve them; they are the privileges that come with being a white American male. And, quite obviously, these privileges come at the expense of others.

Even notions of self-reliance are the product of social relations. Stephanie Coontz explains:

> Self-reliance and independence worked for *men* because *women* took care of dependence and obligation. In other words, the liberal theory of human nature and political citizenship did not merely leave women out: It worked precisely because it was applied exclusively to half the population. Emotion and compassion could be disregarded in the political and economic realms only if women were assigned these traits in the personal realm. Thus the use of the term *individualistic* to describe men's nature became acceptable only in the same time periods, social classes, and geographic areas that established the cult of domesticity for women. The cult of the Self-Made Man required the cult of the True Woman. (1992:53; emphasis in original)

In sum, the only way that men could appear as isolated individuals, as Great Men, as characters in Horatio Alger stories, as the sole movers and shakers of history was by virtue of those who literally took care of all the other aspects of life that required tending. Those others included women, servants, slaves, teachers, and children, who helped to maintain the image of the solitary individual who did it all himself. Similarly, as John Dewey suggested in a somewhat different context, "the notion that intelligence is a personal endowment or personal attainment is the great conceit of the intellectual class, as that of the commercial class is that wealth is something which they personally have wrought and possess" (1927:211).

The same applies to the American pioneers who—myth would have it—conquered the continent single-handedly. They did not arrive on American shores as Robinson Crusoe–like isolates. They arrived in groups, with a variety of skills and abilities. In addition, historian Alfred Crosby (1986) notes that those first European settlers in North America who survived did so only by virtue of receiving a helping hand from the Native American population and because the animals they brought with them (e.g., cows, hogs, goats, sheep) rapidly created a renewable food source that was suited to European tastes, culinary practices, and notions of what constituted food. Over time, by planting European crops and raising European animals, they developed what he calls "Neo-Europes" both in

North America and elsewhere. In contrast, tropical climates, where such crops and animals would not easily survive, proved far less hospitable to Europeans.

During the eighteenth and nineteenth centuries other ethnic groups migrated to what became the United States. They did not distribute themselves randomly over the landscape. It is no accident that the Appalachians are inhabited largely by descendants of Irish and Scottish immigrants, the upper Midwest by descendants of Scandinavian immigrants, and so on. In each case, immigrants looked for others like them with whom they could rapidly form social networks. In addition, land grants, farm programs, canals, publicly financed railroads, military maneuvers (usually to annihilate or remove Native Americans), and government-sponsored wars with Mexico eased the way for settlement.

Today, the self-made American rides down a freeway paid for by government, lives in a home serviced by water, sewer, electricity, gas, cable television, and telephone. Such persons buy virtually all their food in supermarkets, growing only a small portion of it themselves. The cornucopia of goods from around the world in supermarkets and shopping malls conceals from virtually everyone the complex social organization necessary to bring those goods together. Moreover, the endless array of choices—which soap to buy, which television program to watch, which food to eat—gives everyone the illusion of individualism precisely as it creates conformity. In the short run the new boom box or pair of shoes or automobile or child's toy may seem to fulfill desires, but the newness rapidly wears off and what was novel and exciting soon becomes old, dull, commonplace.

This is not to suggest that we are somehow fully socialized, like honey bees. They appear to have no choices at all. Their lives appear to be largely governed by chemical signals that are nearly invariant. In contrast, we do have choices, but they are very clearly circumscribed by society. Thus, the problem is not how to get autonomous individuals to come together in society so as to prevent the "war of each against all," but rather how to create a society in which individual autonomy is respected even as we maintain our sociality. As sociologist Emile Durkheim ([1893] 1964) observed more than a century ago, individualism is itself a social institution.

Contemporary social theory as well as contemporary public discourse tend to oscillate between a radical individualism (e.g., Coleman 1990; Friedman 1962; Homans 1950) and an equally radical structuralism (e.g., Althusser 1997; Wallerstein 1974). In the former, there are only individuals. One cannot see the forest for the trees. In the obverse view, all is determined by social structures that inexorably change the world. The actions of individuals are merely epiphenomena. One cannot see the trees for the forest. But these apparently opposite views have a great deal in common. In particular, both views stand outside any real, experienced world. They claim to reveal a world that is only available to the initiated. Yet, anyone who lives in a contemporary society has felt the anonymous power of the state at one time or another. Conversely, we have all felt the elation that comes with creating something ourselves.

The antimony between individual and society, agency and structure, is itself absurd. It is as if (because?) the Calvinist doctrine of predestination had been accepted in secularized form. We all are to know God individually, yet what we do has already been predetermined by forces beyond our control. We appear forced to choose sides: Are we for individuals? for society?

But there is a third way. I am talking here not of some sort of halfway point between the two, in which individuals and society, structure and agency come together. Instead, the third way that I wish to argue for decenters (ah, yes, a postmodern term here!) the entire antinomy. We are, as David Rasmussen (1973) once put it, "between autonomy and sociality." We are each free to choose, but only within the range of choices offered to us by society. Conversely, we are determined by society, but only to the extent that our lives are shared. Thus, we may create societies in which there is great individuality or others in which individuals are submerged in the collectivity.

Consider the case of individualist theories. Economist André Orléan (1994), in his critique of economic theories that focus entirely on the market, notes that the entire approach collapses when one considers the virtual impossibility of leaving everything to the market. The example he provides is that of deciding on which side of the road to drive. In any given locale, the rule must be that one keeps to the right or to the left. Advocates of the market, if they were true to their position, would suggest that the way to determine which side of the road to drive on is to let people try either side until eventually they learn by virtue of accidents to do it one way or the other. Yet, only by leaving the road and engaging in another activity—discussion, debate, negotiation, compromise—can one efficiently determine even something as apparently trivial as which side of the road on which to drive.

But what of cases when something more is at stake. In those cases, discussion and debate is even more important, not merely to achieve a calculated compromise among persons with fixed preferences, but because debate can and often does cause people to *change* their preferences and even their convictions. They may change for any number of reasons: a realization that their position is illogical, a discomfort with the implications of their position, and, perhaps most commonly, a realization that the position they had taken was ill thought-out.

The famous and widely used and accepted rhetorical case known as the Prisoner's Dilemma is a classic example of the problem of individual decision-making. A common form of the dilemma is posed as follows: Two persons are arrested and questioned separately by the police. Both persons know that if they both refuse to cooperate, the police will have a weak case. As such, each of them will only have to spend two years in prison. They also know that if they both help the police, the case will be much stronger, leading to perhaps six years each in prison. However, the police offer to make a deal. If one of them helps in the investigation, he will go free, while the other person (now charged with all the crimes) will spend ten years in jail. The dilemma faced by the prisoner is whether to talk and risk the possibility that the other prisoner will have talked as well, or to say nothing in hopes that the other prisoner will do the same.

Note that what is important here, what constitutes the dilemma, is that the prisoners barely know each other and are unable to talk to each other. Put differently, the prisoners have no history of any relationship; they are in a situation where they have been "set up," where they are forced to rely solely on their own wits. Commitment to others, trust, and cooperation are ruled out by the very nature of the situation—not only for the prisoners but for the prosecutor (about whose motivations we know nothing) as well. Indeed, none of the participants in the Prisoner's Dilemma have any social relations that extend beyond the dilemma itself. In this situation it is hardly surprising that the prisoners act as atomized individuals (Gilbert 1996). Were they able to converse, to argue, to debate as social beings, were they to have a history, they would be able to come up with the most desirable solution fairly easily.[3] Indeed, if one assumes cooperation to be the norm, the Prisoner's Dilemma is hardly a dilemma at all (Moore 1994).

Doubtless there are cases in which the Prisoner's Dilemma really applies. Indeed, there are perhaps cases in which it should apply. But in most cases, dialogue can take place, in which (some level of) trust, cooperation, and commitment to others are the rule. If this is not the case, then perhaps the solution is to introduce it. Each prisoner in the Prisoner's Dilemma has only two options: confess or do not confess. But in actual situations, we are far more creative. If I am the prisoner, I may try to contact my fellow prisoner (whom I may know well). I may tap on the wall in code, for example. Alternatively, I might overpower the guard, steal his gun, and escape. I might convince the guard that what he is doing is immoral. I might also try to negotiate with my captors. Perhaps I might create a disturbance by setting the bed on fire, thereby escaping in the mayhem. In short, in real situations, it is often possible to transcend the prisoner's dilemma creatively through social interaction.

Public choice (or rational choice) theory also accepts the peculiar view of humanity found in the Prisoner's Dilemma. Consider Kenneth Arrow's ([1951] 1963) classic volume, *Social Choice and Individual Values*. Arrow would have us believe that values are purely individual and that social choices are merely the sum of individual choices (Moore 1994). In fact, I would argue that Arrow's book would have been far better named *Individual Choice and Social Values*. Arrow begins by informing the reader that in capitalist democracies there are two forms of social decision-making: voting and markets. He then goes on to note that the difference between the two is ignored in his study as both are special cases of the more general category of collective social choice.[4] Furthermore, a few pages later he informs the reader that he will assume that individual values are fixed and unalterable by the decision-making process.

But this works neither in the case of legislative voting nor in many markets. In legislative voting, bills are debated. Debaters (in both legislative and other arenas) *discover* their values through the debate. What are vague opinions or ill-formed tastes become solidified, modified, confirmed, or rejected by virtue of the debating process. Similarly, in many markets, buyers and sellers do not merely confront each other with a fixed price. They negotiate the qualities of the product being exchanged. This contrasts sharply with the process of voting for candidates and of making a purchase in a discount store. In both of these cases, the choice is between a discrete set of options that cannot be altered and over which no debate or negotiation takes place. I cannot tell a candidate that I will vote for her if she in turn votes in a certain way on a certain issue. Similarly, I cannot tell the discount store that I will buy what is not for sale there or that I would purchase a given item if the price were a bit lower or the quality better. I either vote for the candidate or not. I either buy the item in the store or not. The *social* character of the relationship is minimized in both cases (cf. Bromley 1997).

The rational choice modelers will go to rather extreme lengths to push their particular view of the world. Perhaps the most egregious example of misuse of the approach was a recent article by two economists in the prestigious *American Political Science Review*. They argued, based on a rather elaborate mathematical model, that the unanimity rule in jury verdicts was frequently likely to convict the innocent and let the guilty go free. The mathematics is impeccable. However, in the authors' own words, they make the following assumption in their model: "Since we do not model the effect of jury deliberations, determining their effect from a theoretical standpoint is beyond the scope of this article" (Feddersen and Pesendorfer 1998:24). In other words, the authors assume that the members of the jury do not deliberate.

Rational choice theorists would have us believe that people nearly always and *always easily and quickly* make rational choices. They assume that the rational person is one who has fixed preferences that cannot be swayed by argument, who cannot learn that he or she is mistaken, and who merely bargains with his contemporaries so as to get his way as frequently as possible, as if politics and all of social life were at best merely a peculiar form of dickering to buy a used car. Thus, the actor in rational choice theory is best described as a pig-headed, ignorant, though calculating, boor. Starting from this absurd position, rational choice theorists build elegant models that show us the utter poverty of democratic decision-making when such "rational" persons are involved. And, to compound the irony, many of the proponents of rational choice theory are themselves well-read, thoughtful academics who heatedly debate which of the many versions of rational choice theory is the right one and to whom the theory would most certainly not apply! But were rational choice theory correct, then surely there would be no debates among rational choice theorists themselves. They would have already made the most rational choice among the alternatives.

Ronald Reagan apparently shared the rational choice view, noting in 1986, "Private values must be at the heart of public politics" (quoted in Coontz 1992:99). Yet as observers from Adam Smith ([1759] 1982) to George Herbert Mead (1962) have noted, our preferences, our values, our convictions, our arguments, and the very language we use to express ourselves are given to us through social interaction. Rationality does not inhere in persons, but is the product of discourse (Habermas 1998). This is not to argue that we all have the same set of values, that we somehow share them as we might share a loaf of bread. No, as Alfred Schutz (1970) pointed out, "if I were you . . ." never applies. That is to say, each person has a unique biography. We share values in the sense that we learn them through the process of interaction. Moreover, as Paul Ricoeur (1967) notes, we can only express ourselves through the "deposited and available meanings" that are provided by our language. Thus, we do not say what we mean, but rather we are meant.

Now consider a structuralist alternative. Sociologist Immanuel Wallerstein (1974) has written at great length on what he calls the "modern world system." By this he means the world economy that arose from about 1450 to 1640. In this world economy some states are at the core, some at the periphery, and some in between—at what he calls the semiperiphery. Over time, the location of the core has shifted, while some states have moved closer and others further away from that core. Without doubt, we are the inheritors of the world system of which Wallerstein writes.

In some ways Wallerstein's work is clearly a masterpiece of historical sociology. The scope of his work is breathtaking. Yet, it is precisely because of its aerial view that it is flawed. There are no people in Wallerstein's accounts. There are no actors, no shakers and movers. Instead, the reader is led to believe that changes in the social world are the result of changes in structures, much as the earthquakes of California apparently are caused by huge tectonic plates crashing into one another. Indeed, the very notion of the modern world system harkens back to debates about planetary motion, to Galileo's *Dialogue Concerning the Two Chief World Systems—Ptolemaic and Copernican*. One finds the same lack of actors in Louis Althusser's (1997) Marxism. There, too, history is revealed as the working out of the clashes between inexorable forces. The result is that politics is rendered impossible. Nothing that any individual or even a small group might do would be sufficient to modify the system.

Perhaps the strangest field of all is that of international relations. Here, we find the Hobbesian perspective realized. Indeed, international relations is the intellectual equivalent of (American) football. It is the quintessential masculine game in which tough decisions are made in light of the "real" issues in that state of nature in which nations face each other. As J. Ann Tickner (1992) has noted, women comprise only 5 percent of the top ranks of the U.S. foreign service. Furthermore, decisions regarding international relations are considered too dangerous for ordinary people. Better to leave it to a carefully trained elite who understand the state of nature that prevails among nations. For "realists" such as George Kennan and Henry Kissinger, only the accumulation of military power will protect us and our allies from the evil forces that lurk out there in the rest of the world. Hence, the United States continues to spend far more than any other nation on arms and arms research. According to the U.S. Arms Control and Disarmament Agency (1999), the world spent $120 billion between 1996 and 1998 on arms sales; 56 percent was supplied by the United States. The result is what President Eisenhower warned us about: the military-industrial complex. The military sponsors research to develop new weapons. The new weapons are sold to our "friends" but ultimately fall into the hands of those who are not so friendly. This requires research to develop even more sophisticated weapons and the process is repeated all over again.

What the realists ignore is that the very arms that are supposed to protect us from our enemies are often used to oppress other peoples and to make the world a far more dangerous place. For example, the Chilean military was well-supported by U.S. arms before it toppled a democratically elected government and installed a military dictatorship. And during Augusto Pinochet's dictatorship thousands of civilians were killed merely for voicing their views. Similarly, American arms bolstered the Shah of Iran, eventually leading to the Islamic revolution that overthrew him and cast the United States in the role of the Great Satan. Again and again, American "realism" has created the very problems it claimed to prevent.

During the cold war, in particular, all domestic violence was viewed as instigated by relations between the Soviets and the West. Even anticolonial battles, such as the war in Angola, were described in the rhetoric of the cold war. Now that the cold war has ended, political scientist Samuel P. Huntington (1996), in his recent book *The Clash of Civilizations*, has taken up the

Hobbesian banner once more. Criticizing the realists for looking only at nation-states, Huntington would have us believe that the world is inexorably divided into opposing civilizations. For Huntington, "Human history is the history of civilizations. It is impossible to think of the development of humanity in any other terms" (ibid.:40). Yet, with a little imagination one might think of human history as a succession of biographies (e.g., Durant 1939), as changes in everyday life (e.g., Braudel 1973), or as the rise of the west (e.g., McNeill 1963). Historians have interpreted history in these ways among others.

Huntington correctly notes that the simple two-sided world of the cold war has given way to a far more complex world in which there are multiple sources of potential conflict. However, although he provides scant data, Huntington sees these new conflicts through the lens of civilizations. On an ominous map, Western, Latin American, African, Islamic, Sinic, Hindu, Orthodox, Buddhist, and Japanese civilizations are portrayed as all too homogeneous and unified groups of nations that view outsiders with more or less suspicion. Somehow the reader is to believe that intracivilizational conflicts pale in comparison to intercivilizational conflicts. Conflicts within nations are hardly worthy of mention.

More importantly, it is precisely the belief in the rightness of Huntington's view of the world that would make it a self-fulfilling prophecy. We Westerners need to stick together against the heathen hordes who might at any time pose a threat. We need to arm ourselves to the teeth. We need to wipe out any notions of multiculturalism, which just might make us appear weak. The Leviathan is dead; long live the Leviathan.

CONCLUSIONS

But if the Leviathans have failed us, what options remain open to us? If we are neither fully social nor fully autonomous, then what sort of means might be employed that would recognize our individuality, our cultural diversity, and our common humanity? I believe that the answer is right there before us. It is already apparent in the myriad spontaneously created organizations that are found throughout the world. We need only seize it and use it to our collective advantage. It is known as democracy. It is to that subject that I now turn.

NOTES

1. It should be noted that U.S. antitrust laws hardly have kept large corporations from forming and even prospering. However, they have shifted their

strategies from dominating a single industry to vertical integration and con-glomeration. For a critical view, see Arnold (1937).

2.   Scholars are divided as to how to classify religious movements. Marty and Appleby (1993) lump all religious movements that seek to preserve the identi-ty of a group in the face of social change under the category of "fundamental-ist." In contrast others make finer distinctions. For example, Woodberry and Smith (1998), in an examination of American Protestant denominations, distin-guish between fundamentalists, evangelicals, and charismatics. In this text I will use Marty's broader definition.

3.   Economist Gordon Tullock (1985) argues that in market situations, the very need to engage in future exchange tends to reduce the likelihood of the prison-er's dilemma and to encourage cooperation.

4.   He also informs the reader that "the present study is concerned only with the formal aspects of the above question" (Arrow [1951] 1963:2). But as soon as he says this, he adds in a footnote, "It may be added that the method of decision sketched above is essentially that used in deliberative bodies, where a whole range of alternatives usually comes up for decision in the form of pair-wise com-parisons" (ibid.:3, n. 3). In short, Arrow has his cake and eats it, too. On the one hand, he tells us that the exercise is a merely formal one. But at the same time he alludes to processes in the real world. Presumably, the formal exercise will tell us something about that world. This appears to be precisely the sleight of hand that Latour (1996) describes as a central feature of much modern theoriz-ing: theory and practice are at once split and united.

6

NETWORKS OF DEMOCRACY

The personal development that some writers attribute to citizenship in a democratic order is in large part **moral** *development: gaining a more mature sense of responsibility for one's actions, a broader awareness of the others affected by one's actions, a greater willingness to reflect on and take into account the consequences of one's actions for others, and so on.*
(emphasis in original)

—*Robert A. Dahl*, Democracy and Its Critics

Nothing is beyond politics. In an evolving human world of plural values, where there cannot be an undisputed list of goods, where there is no reason to expect harmony, and in which all ends are potentially subject to criticism and revision, democracy is the most attractive available foundational political commitment.

—*Ian Shapiro*, Democracy's Place

Politics does not rest on justice and freedom; it is what makes them possible.

—*Benjamin R. Barber*, Strong Democracy

Americans tend to think of the ultimate goals of a good life as matters of personal choice.

—*Robert Bellah et al.*, Habits of the Heart: Individualism and Commitment in American Life

Democracy is in some sense a well-worn term. For the ancient Greeks, it was participatory and direct, but it included only male citizens; foreigners, women, tradespeople, and slaves were excluded. For the founders of the American republic, democracy was to be avoided. Better to have senators elected by state legislatures, better to have the president elected by the members of an electoral college, better to divide power in a variety of ways so as to ensure that the majority would always be somewhat frustrated in its rule. And, for Americans, like their Greek and (especially) Roman forbears, the landless, slaves, and women were to be excluded from having a say in the republic. In more recent times, the term "democratic" has been interpreted in a rather peculiar way. The Deutsche Democratische Republik, the People's Republic of Korea, and other countries with similar

147

labels belied the fact that these nations were hardly democratic and rarely for more than a few of the people.

But why have democracy at all? How does democracy respond to the challenges of scientism, statism, marketism, or to any of the hundreds of fundamentalisms? Simply put, democracy is the only system of personal and collective self-determination that permits—indeed, encourages—the discovery of moral values. In its ideal form, democracy permits each citizen, each member of the collectivity, to discover what is moral, what is virtuous, what is right. This is done not through the act of voting, but through the debate, dialogue, deliberation, and action that are essential to democratic practice. As Benjamin Franklin put it, "By the Collision of different Sentiments, Sparks of Truth are struck out, and political Light is obtained. The different Factions, which at present divide us, aim all at the Publick Good; the Differences are only about the various Modes of promoting it" (quoted in Campbell 1999:205). And, as Benjamin Barber suggests in the epigraph above, it is through democratic participation that justice and freedom become possible.

If we were fully socialized from birth, as are apparently social insects, we would have no need of moral values. We would simply assume our roles in the social order and keep them until death. If we were truly autonomous individuals of the sort that Hobbes described, we would either pay little attention to each other[1] or we would be in need of some Leviathan to tell us what to do, thereby preventing the war of each against all. But as we are between autonomy and sociality, we must discover what is moral, what is right, and what is virtuous through interaction with others. We can only do this if we are free to participate in democratic debate. Such debates have as their objective not the negotiating among fixed preferences derived from *individual* values, as Kenneth Arrow ([1951] 1963) suggested, but the joint discovery of what our values are.

Put differently, there are no inalienable rights (despite the American Declaration of Independence). There is no one scientific method by which the True Nature of the world may be revealed. There are no isolated individuals capable of rationally calculating what is in their best interests. There is no innate propensity to truck and barter. There is no one True Religion that will ensure that we live moral lives. Only by making the world together, only by discovering what is right and what is wrong through discourse and action can we build knowledge, wisdom, and a just society.

Of course, no amount of debate, discussion, or dialogue will ensure that our conclusions and subsequent actions are right and just. No single form of democracy, whether representative or participatory, will guarantee our future. As fallible beings, we have made and surely always will continue to make mistakes. Put differently, such debates are learning experiences. Over the centuries we have learned together that murder, torture, slavery, racism, and the subjection of women are wrong. We have learned the importance of equality before the law, of justice for those accused of crimes, and of the importance of due process. Yet, violations of these simple principles are all too common. Furthermore, there are undoubtedly many common practices that today we regard as right or morally innocuous that our descendants will look upon with horror—if we expand, rather than reduce, the scope of democracy.

Political scientist Robert A. Dahl (1989) suggests that there are two major alternatives to democracy: guardianship and anarchism. Advocates of guardianship from Plato to the present claim that some small group—the vanguard party, the bureaucrats, the scientifically or technically trained, the clergy, the literati, the philosopher-kings—are the sole persons who have the necessary wisdom and moral competence to rule. They apply that wisdom by enacting laws that tell others what to do. But even as an ideal guardianship has at least two major flaws: First, guardianship keeps the vast majority of the population in a state of lifelong childhood. We (must) tell our young children what is right or wrong rather than reasoning or debating with them. Guardianship extends that parent-child relationship indefinitely thereby depriving adults of one of the defining features of adulthood: moral competence. Second, guardianship suggests that my interests are best determined by someone else. In certain instances this may well be true, for as Marx, Freud, and Nietzsche noted in their own distinct ways, we do not have complete knowledge of our own motivations and interests (Ricoeur 1974). That is part of being a social being. However, this can hardly justify the claim that others know best *most of the time*.

Scientism, statism, and marketism are all forms of guardianship. Their advocates claim that we must yield to the superior moral wisdom of science, the state, or the market. That claim to wisdom, of course, is not simply floating around in space somewhere. It is manifested in a set of practices by scientists, government officials, or those who organize and control the market. There is little doubt that some such persons have superior *technical* knowledge, but their claims to superior *moral* knowledge are naive at best, self-serving and fraudulent at worst. Essayist Wendell Berry has eloquently explained the problem:

> The specialist puts himself in charge of one possibility. By leaving out all other possibilities, he enfranchises his little fiction of total control. Leaving out all the "nonfunctional" or otherwise undesirable possibilities, he makes a rigid, exclusive boundary within which absolute control becomes, if not possible, at least conceivable. (1977:70–71)

We may well live in a society comprised of specialists, but for any given issue we are all laypersons. As laypersons the questions we pose of the specialist may be technically naive, but they often if not always incorporate the situation within which technical knowledge is desired. When I hire a plumber to fix a leak, I specify the situation within which the leak exists, even as I acknowledge the plumber's superior knowledge of plumbing. I do not hire a plumber to poke around and see if anything needs fixing, precisely because I suspect that if I were to do so I might be told that everything needs fixing in order to meet some standard of perfection peculiar to plumbers and plumbing. Similarly, in a truly democratic nation one might request the services of (natural and social) scientists, bureaucrats, and bankers for the technical knowledge that they have acquired, but one must reject any special claims they might make to superior moral competence.

In contrast to various forms of guardianship, democracy does not promise the right answer to all problems. Such promises are always false, whether made by philosopher-kings, vanguard parties, religious zealots, or state bureaucrats. Democrats do not make such promises, but precisely because they lack the arrogance of moral superiority, they are far more likely to succeed in improving social situations. Put differently, "An imperfect democracy is a misfortune for its people, but an imperfect authoritarian regime is an abomination" (Dahl 1989:78).

The other group of critics of democracy are anarchists. Although they come in many stripes and persuasions, anarchists generally argue that we would be better off without any institutionalized means of coercion. But this poses several practical problems: How would one deal with those who engage in criminal activity? How would an anarchist community protect itself from invasion by one state or another? Moreover, beyond these empirical questions, one must ask as Robert Dahl does: Why should noncoercion be valued more than other values such as justice, freedom, equality, and security? Moreover, only in democratic societies can the relative weights to be given to conflicting values be discussed and implemented.

The Greeks, the apparent inventors of democracy, appear closest to the position that I wish to take here. At least for those who could legally participate, democracy was deepest there. Both the rights and obligations of citizens were widely shared with few class differences. Moreover, unlike most contemporary democracies, Greek democracy was direct. Participation in the everyday affairs of the republic was both a right and duty. Even the offices of the republic were rotated among all those eligible, based on drawing of lots.

Although they are more inclusive, today's democracies pale by comparison. In general, most of us get to vote once a year for persons who will claim to represent us at a distant location on myriad issues about which we—and perhaps they—are uninformed. Moreover, the issues that matter most are the ones in which we participate the least. Indeed, they are the ones in which participation is not even seen as legitimate. In the work-

place, education, technology, health care, and the retail store our participation is usually sharply limited. For example, as consumers, our participation is limited to decisions as to whether to purchase or not. Certainly,
the range of goods at our individual disposal has grown logarithmically,
but with few exceptions, we still are left with simple, binary decisions
about them.

As workers, our options are equally limited. We may decide to work for
a particular company or not. Albert O. Hirschman (1970) argued some
years ago that we have three options in institutional life: exit, voice, and
loyalty. We may leave the firm in disgust at policies and practices we deem
unsatisfactory, unethical, or even illegal. We may remain loyal to the firm,
ignoring or enduring the insults to our sense of what is right and just. Or
we may have voice; we may complain about the situation. But this third
choice is by far the most limited. In many cases, we may be summarily fired
for our voice, the precise conditions varying from nation to nation, and
even from firm to firm. We may be disciplined for expressing our views.
We may be subtly or not so subtly eased out as a consequence of making
our views known. And, as Karl Marx ([1867] 1967) noted many years ago,
we live in societies in which employment is not merely a choice, but a requirement for obtaining the means of subsistence.

Although we live in a world of unprecedented technical change, most
of us have little or no control over the technologies that invade our lives.
A cornucopia of new technical changes, from genetically altered foods to
genetic testing for inherited diseases, from telephone marketing to private
electronic spying, from food irradiation to nuclear bombs, pass by us while
we stand agape in wonder or appalled in despair. Economists tell us that
we do participate through the market for these "goods," but they ignore
the way that these technologies transform the lives of even those who reject them.

In education, too, we have few opportunities to participate in the decisions that affect our lives. Much of education consists of rote memorization of countless facts and regurgitation of formulaic recipes for obedience.
In the United States, students numbly recite each morning, "I pledge alle-
giance to the flag . . ." In other nations equally absurd statist rubbish prevails. While elementary education poses unique challenges not present
when educating adults, even our universities remain bastions of autocracy both in their management and in the way in which learning takes place.
And, despite much lip service to lifelong education, formal education is
still seen as something reserved for children and young adults.

In health care, doctors still often maintain a godlike quality. Arrogance
among physicians is legendary. Rarely do patients have the information
they need to make intelligent decisions about medical care. Even if they do,
they tend not to use that information, for fear of offending the physician

upon whom they depend for their health. Moreover, even for those who can afford health care, there is no guarantee that one will not spend one's last days hooked to a maze of tubes and electrodes waiting to die.

Our families, as well, remain largely autocratic. In nuclear families, the husband usually makes most of the crucial decisions, while wife and children submit, with more or less resistance. As in the most autocratic societies, brute force often governs household relations. Spousal abuse and child abuse are all too common.

The arts and media, as well, brook little participation. In our winner-take-all society, only the very best artists, musicians, actors, writers, critics, journalists, poets, and television announcers are rewarded (Frank and Cook 1995). As a result, there is little diversity in the arts and media, little opportunity for even good artists, musicians, actors, writers, critics, journalists, poets, and television announcers to ply their crafts. Only occasionally do we have the opportunity to take the role of participant in the arts or media. Only rarely do we get to engage in developing our own media, our own music, our own arts. If the arts were a fundamental part of ancient Greek life, in our own day they have become a separate reality far removed from our participation.

But none of this need be the case. In every one of the domains described above, and perhaps in others that I have overlooked, democratic means are available. Grassroots organizations exist that challenge the elitist view that only a few have the skills, the money, the intellect to participate in (re)making their own worlds. But even those grassroots organizations appear to be in decline. Americans, who have been known for their civic participation since the days of Tocqueville ([1835–1840] 1956), now participate in few grassroots movements, preferring instead to send money to mass organizations (Putnam 1995). But this hardly needs to be the case. In the remainder of this chapter I examine some of the potentials for networks of democracy that permit or encourage more participation and more responsible citizenship than that which exists at present.

POLITICS WITH A CAPITAL P

Let us begin with the narrowly defined world of Politics: those aspects of daily life that involve government. Clearly, the current system in representative democratic regimes of voting once or twice a year is inadequate. It merely allows me to give my right to make decisions to someone else. If I am unsatisfied with the manner in which that person represented me, I have the option of throwing the rascal out by voting for someone else the next time. This is analogous to my choices in the marketplace. If I buy a car and don't like it, I can always buy another brand next time. Meanwhile, I am out of luck. Of course, this is far better than the situation in numerous dictatorships, military regimes, and other nondemocratic states. In those nations the freedoms essential to anything remotely resembling democracy are often denied.

However, representative democracy can be much improved. Political scientist Douglas J. Amy (1996), among others, has suggested that proportional representation in multimember districts would vastly improve what we have in the United States today. It would replace the winner-take-all approach as follows: In a district in which there were ten seats, a party getting 50 percent of the votes would get five seats. Other parties would get seats in proportion to their share of the vote. This would have the advantage of increasing minor party representation as well as the representation of various minorities.

However, there are other ways to govern that can complement representative democracy. In particular, there is what political scientist Benjamin Barber (1984) has called "strong democracy." As he puts it, "In strong democracy, politics is something done by, not to, citizens" (ibid.:133). Strong democracy does not start with a set of legitimate moral imperatives and proceed to impose them on people; instead, it starts with a dialogue, the outcome of which is a set of moral imperatives that are then translated into action. It does not start with some presupposed, logically deduced, notion of the public good that is then to be put into practice; it uses the dialogue, the debate, the discussion, the deliberation as a means for discovering what the public good might be. It involves compromise without being compromised (Benjamin 1990). This means that the public good might change through time and space, that what was considered good in the past might be rejected now, that what is considered good now might be rejected in the future.

While it is certainly clear that the direct democracy of the small city-states of ancient Greece is no longer an option, there are few reasons why political participation need be limited to voting for representatives. At the local level, forms of direct participation can still work. In small towns this might mean an expansion of the town meeting system, still used in parts of New England. In large cities, neighborhood meetings might serve the same purpose, either alone or together with representational systems. Alternatively, one might rotate membership in a citizens' assembly such that everyone gets to participate occasionally (Barber 1984). Even at the level of the nation-state, direct participation through initiatives and referenda can be effective, especially if combined with face-to-face meetings among small groups of voters. Public schools, libraries, and town halls already have meeting rooms that could, with few obstacles, be adapted to such uses. Nor should we forget the more informal settings that have supported democracy in the past: the pub, the tavern, the café, the tearoom. These are places where politics can be and is discussed, where changes great and small can be planned.

But democracy is not properly understood if it is limited to the achievement of consensus or majority rule. Indeed, consensus may well be merely the silencing of the minority. As Ian Shapiro puts it, "One person's consensus is often another's hegemony" (1996:121). Thus, democracy is and must be as much the position of the opposition as of the majority. Put differently, democracy can be and is coercive; it imposes the will of the majority on the minority. But unlike all other systems of governance, democracy permits the minority to make its case again, to attempt once more to convince the majority of the rightfulness of its position. This is the secret of the stability of democracy: unlike authoritarian systems, democracies give voice to the opposition, making it possible for the opposition to one day become the majority. Stability does not and cannot mean the lack of opposition. That would require either unanimity, usually a utopian situation, or ruthless oppression of the opposition. In short, "Democracy is the ideology of opposition as much as it is one of government. It is about displacing entrenched elites, undermining the powerful, and empowering the powerless" (ibid.:51).

Greater direct citizen participation can also increase the effectiveness of moral suasion in the political arena. Consider the case of environmental conservation. Current policies consist largely of carrots and sticks. We are rewarded for taking certain actions and punished for others. In most cases both reward and punishment are monetary. In the short run, this approach works, but it fails to foster moral responsibility for the conservation of the natural environment in anyone. Moreover, it implies that environmental conservation is an individual problem, whereas it is thoroughly social in character. A two-year-old who is fascinated by an old porcelain vase that has been in the family for generations might be rewarded for not touching it or punished for touching it. Either way, she or he will soon learn to manifest the correct behavior. But an adult family member needs no such behavioral incentives; she or he can learn through discussion that the vase is valued and is to be handled (if at all) with care. The same applies for popular concern for the environment; ultimately moral suasion is more effective for most adults than incentives.

Participation in politics also requires a certain level of economic equality. But, by most measures, the United States has the most unequal distribution of income of the industrialized nations (Atkinson, Rainwater, and Smeedling 1995). Wealth is distributed even more unequally than income. Between 1989 and 1992, 68 percent of the increase in wealth went to the top 1 percent of households. In addition, while in 1979 the richest 1 percent of Americans had a 22 percent share of total wealth, by 1992 that number had nearly doubled, to 42 percent. Moreover, while the middle class has over two-thirds of its wealth locked up in the homes it owns, the top 1 percent have over 80 percent of their wealth in real estate investments, businesses, and various securities (Wolff 1995). One figure should illustrate the magnitude of the problem: Bill Gates's wealth alone is equivalent to that of the 120 million least-affluent Americans, nearly one-half of the population (Kuttner 1999). While complete income equality is neither feasible nor desirable, the current situation makes a mockery of claimed notions of equal opportunity. Who really believes that a child brought up in dire poverty, perhaps even homeless, has the same opportunity to succeed as one raised in an upper-middle-class suburb? How can we expect those near the bottom of the income ladder to participate in politics when they must spend most of their time obtaining the means of subsistence? Without greater equality in the distribution of income, political democracy has a hollow ring to it.

What applies inside nation-states applies equally well in the larger world. In international relations democratic states need to encourage and support democratic movements in other nations. Instead of celebrating our "victory" at the end of the cold war, we need to begin to confront the precarious state of many of the poorest nations of the world. One need only examine the situation in Sierra Leone, Somalia, Angola, or what is left of Yugoslavia to note the anarchy that now reigns in regions once the site of disputes interpreted solely in the light of East-West conflict. These nations are now either abandoned entirely by the West or they are merely places for military intervention (to test new weapons of war?). Instead of grappling with crippling poverty and injustice, overurbanization and environmental degradation by helping to build democratic, economically prosperous states, we have been far too content to ignore these problems unless they directly affect our economic interests. And in those cases we have been far too ready to use force merely to hold back those who appear to be threatening to us.

In contrast, rather than building U.S. foreign policy purely on holding back the "barbarian hordes" and, where possible, extending the market economy, we should be embracing and nurturing fledgling democracies. Russia, in particular, is in danger of falling back into a new form of nationalistic autocracy, in part because Western advice and financial support has focused almost entirely on building markets and has neglected building strong democracies. Indeed, Western advice has often conflated the free market with freedom while ignoring rapidly growing inequalities and corruption.

In contrast, we might better serve our own interests by helping democrats in other nations to build the necessary institutions of a democratic polity and civil society. This is not to suggest that we should impose our own version of democracy on the rest of the world. To a great extent we can do more by example and by addressing our own failings in the domestic and international arenas, than by trying to convince others of the alleged superiority of our system of government.

Finally, I should note that the Internet offers the potential for greater political democracy, both within and across national boundaries. Newsgroups, chat rooms, and other interactive media permit people to engage in debate and discussion in new ways. But the Internet is no panacea. It cannot substitute for face-to-face interaction any more than can the television or the telephone. Internet connectivity is limited and selective. People searching only for persons who are like-minded can easily lead to greater fragmentation rather than cohesion. The Internet offers access to thousands of nongovernmental organizations devoted to hundreds of subjects, but it can also be used to spread messages of hate and intolerance. As with all technologies, the Internet will be what we make of it: either an aid in building more democracy or another detraction from it.

But political democracy is not enough. Most of the decisions affecting our daily lives are no longer made in the political sphere. There is no reason to exclude those affected by decisions from those other spheres. Instead the rule should be: "Everyone affected by the operation of a particular domain of civil society should be presumed to have a say in its governance" (Shapiro 1996:232). Thus, those who are affected need to be included in decisions made in the workplace, in science and technology laboratories, in education, in health care, in the arts, in the media, in the family, and in the enforcement of law. It is to these settings that I now turn.

THE WORKPLACE

Existing liberal democracies are based on a sharp distinction between public and private. As political theorist Carole Pateman suggests, "The structural division of social life within liberal democratic theory, into separate spheres of the private and the political provides a barrier against consideration of the question of organizational democracy" (1975:10). Yet, most of us spend most of our waking hours in the workplace. It is there that we forge our identities. Most of us are no longer independent entrepreneurs or yeoman farmers who can set our own hours and working conditions. Instead, most of us work in large-scale organizations—corporations, government agencies, schools, colleges and universities, or other large bureaucracies. In these organizations most of us are told what to do, how to do it, and when to do it. For the vast majority of persons, the minute division of labor produces alienation in much the way Karl Marx ([1844] 1964) saw it 150 years ago. Yet, ironically, after spending eight or more mind-numbing hours being told what to do, we are then supposed to act as free, thoughtful individuals at the voting booth and in the marketplace.

Furthermore, for those of us fortunate enough to be in positions that allow some responsibilities, the situation is even more contradictory. As André Gorz suggested a quarter of a century ago, "Workers are expected to be versatile but to accept narrow specialization; they are expected to adjust to new situations and to be creative and at the same time to perform dull repetitive work and be submissive to the hierarchy" (1973:23). To this one might add that we are expected to maintain our enthusiasm while understanding that our job might cease to exist tomorrow. In short, we are denied the opportunity to fashion our collective destiny, to determine what is the right thing to do.

Astonishingly, virtually all mainstream economics textbooks and most of the economic literature treats firms as if they were places of social harmony in which all efforts were focused on increasing profitability so as to serve the stockholders. But all large firms and most small ones are places of social conflict. They are contested terrains on which owners, managers, and employees spend much of their time dreaming up ever more effective ways of increasing their share of the pie. While most owners may opt for profitability, managers are usually more concerned with the success of the firm as an organization and about their own pay, benefits, and working conditions. Workers have similar interests although they may be directly in conflict with those of management or owners. Moreover, the salaries of both managers and workers are only marginally connected to the profitability of the firm. Thus, coercion must be used to ensure satisfactory levels of output.

Moreover, owners long ago lost control over the day-to-day operations of most corporations (Berle and Means [1932] 1968). Most investors are far more interested in the return on investment than they are in the daily management of firms. Institutional investors such as banks, insurance companies, personal trusts, pension funds, and mutual funds now control half of all corporate equities in the United States (New York Stock Exchange 1998). They insert yet another layer of bureaucracy between owners and managers. Most institutional investors have neither the inclination nor the time to influence corporate operations. Finally, although some writers talk of shareholder democracy, the very term is an oxymoron. Shareholders do not get equal votes; voting power is dependent on the number of shares owned. In most cases, share ownership does not confer control, which rests firmly in the hands of management (Dahl 1989).

Management itself is often autocratic and capricious. Rather than involving workers in day-to-day decision-making, decisions are often taken in (perhaps no longer) smoke-filled rooms. The consequences of such uninformed decisions are usually obvious to all. One only need read Dilbert to comprehend the resentment this instills in workers. At its worst, management engages in downsizing, cutting jobs in an attempt to reduce costs, but undermining any loyalty to the company that might remain. Indeed, as economist John Kenneth Galbraith (1967) noted some thirty years ago, workers are unlikely to align themselves with corporate goals unless some social goal is fulfilled as well.

Furthermore, there is no particular reason to assume that corporations should exist solely for the purpose of maximizing profits. Robert Kuttner (1996a) has argued that corporations need to become responsible to other stakeholders besides shareholders. Industrial engineer Seymour Melman has noted that there are many possible goals by which to evaluate organizational performance: "These include minimizing business cost, maximizing productivity, full employment, minimizing accidents, minimizing pollution, and minimizing energy use" (1981:325). Doubtless other goals could be added to the list. Indeed, even a brief look at the history of corporations reveals that they were never designed for the sole purpose of accumulating profits.

Corporations were initially established to engage in tasks deemed publicly desirable. Thus, corporations were established to build roads, canals, and railways—public works far too expensive to be undertaken by the state—in return for both limited liability from legal action and the right to collect tolls. The reader will remember from the discussion above that Adam Smith was quite suspicious of such undertakings precisely because he felt that they often strayed from public purpose, lining the pockets of investors at public expense.

But over the last century the public purpose of corporations has been eclipsed by their private purpose. The first blow was the 1888 Supreme Court decision in *Minnesota and St. Louis Railroad v. Beckwith* (129 U.S. 26) that gave corporations rights under the 14th amendment to the U.S. Constitution. In defiance of logic, the Court declared that from that time forward corporations would be treated as natural persons. As Thurman Arnold put it more than sixty years ago, "The ideal that a great corporation is endowed with the rights and prerogatives of a free individual is as essential to the acceptance of corporate rule in temporal affairs as was the ideal of the divine right of kings in an earlier day" (1937:185). Even as late as 1903 corporate charters lasted no longer than twenty to fifty years. Then, Delaware legislators discovered that chartering corporations with few strings attached could generate income for the state. Within a few decades Delaware became the legal home of most corporations and public purpose faded into the background (Rowe 1996).

Nor is there any reason for assuming that ownership should be linked to control. Despite claims to the contrary, ownership is never inviolable, nor is there any reason why it should be. When ownership conflicts with some other public good, we often restrict it. Courts have long upheld the legitimacy of eminent domain, the procedure whereby a government takes property (usually with proper compensation) in order to fulfill some public purpose. In addition, myriad laws restrict the modifications that can be made to historic buildings, prohibit polluting effluents from factories, and zone neighborhoods so as to protect adjacent property owners from uses that depreciate the value of their properties. Still other laws limit the number of hours people may work, prohibit child labor, protect the health and safety of workers by specifying certain physical structures and material changes in workplaces, and restricting the production and sale of dangerous devices, foods, pharmaceuticals, and buildings. While most of us would agree that these laws are imperfect, sometimes failing in their goals and often imposing bureaucratic rules that are only marginally related to their purpose, most of us would also agree that they are necessary and appropriate. Who would want to work in an unsafe building? Who would want dangerous ingredients in their foods? Who would want to live next to a cement factory? In sum, if we are quite willing to restrict property rights for these reasons, then there is certainly no legitimate reason to allow ownership to trump other rights in the workplace.

But what might participation in the workplace mean? The "solution" most often taken throughout the twentieth century has been collective bargaining. Ever since Samuel Gompers established the American Federation of Labor in 1886, it has been the preferred choice of many workers. Yet, rather than giving voice to workers, collective bargaining merely institutionalizes the distinction between those who command and those who obey in exchange for wages and fringe benefits. At least some labor leaders see this as no longer acceptable (Swinney 1998). Moreover, in an economy where corporations can move easily across national boundaries, gains made through unionization are far more vulnerable than they were in the past (Kuttner 1996b). Thus, collective bargaining, although it offers some protections to workers, must be seen not as a form of democracy but as a stalemate.

Is then the solution employee ownership? workers' control? How should such participation be organized? What would its impact be on productivity? How would expertise be recognized? There are no simple answers to these questions, but there are enough cases on record to provide some guidelines as to how to proceed. Worker-owned firms, worker-controlled firms, worker representation on corporate boards of directors, worker participation in shop-floor management, worker cooperatives of various sorts, and even an entire region of worker cooperatives (in Mondragon, Spain) all exist. These experiments show both the promise and the difficulties in creating democracy in the workplace.

One thing is clear: ownership alone is neither necessary nor sufficient. This is amply demonstrated by the continuing conflicts at United Airlines.

Despite the fact that workers own 55 percent of United Airlines, internal procedures have changed little. As a result, union activists were upset when they recently learned that management was distributing a twenty-seven-page handbook that, according to the unions, was designed to thwart an organizing drive among ticket agents (Leonhardt 1998). More recently, the union-owners instituted a new performance-based pay system that links managerial pay to employee satisfaction (Leonhardt 1999). However, the organizational structure remains as authoritarian as it was the day the workers took over. Most Employee Stock Ownership Plans (ESOPs) share that same problem: They provide ownership without control, property without voice.

Sociologist Paul Blumberg noted some thirty years ago that "it is what occurs at the lowest level, on the factory floor, that matters most to the worker" (1968:3). This is hardly surprising since it is on the factory floor (or the equivalent location for service workers) that decisions most directly affecting the world of work are made. In fact, the only comprehensive national study of the subject, a volume produced in 1973 for the secretary of Health, Education and Welfare (Work in America 1973) was quite clear in its results. Workers in repetitive, boring jobs were less likely to participate in political or community life. They were more likely to be dissatisfied in their work as well. In addition, the report noted that "what the workers want most, as more than 100 studies in the past 20 years show, is to become masters of their immediate environments and to feel that their work and they themselves are important—the twin ingredients of self-esteem" (ibid.:13). Furthermore, a thorough review of studies of participation found that no major effort to increase participation led to a decline in productivity; in most cases productivity rose from 5 to 40 percent.

More recently, similar findings have begun to appear in the business press. For example, *Business Week* (Byrne 1995) notes that hundreds of managers are flocking to what it calls "Management Meccas" to learn how participatory management styles have enhanced work productivity while reducing tension between workers and management. In some firms "open book management" allows everyone in the firm to understand the current financial situation. In still other firms "self-managing teams" organize the work collectively. Of course, it would be a mistake to see all these as true democracy in the workplace. Just as some nations have adapted the trappings of democracy to regimes that are in fact quite autocratic, so some companies have tacked participation onto conventional management practices.

In his 1970 *magnum opus*, economist Jaroslav Vanek (1970) developed the mathematical underpinnings of a *General Theory of Labor-Managed Market Economies*. He concluded that worker-managed economies would be as efficient as capitalist economies although they would differ from them in a variety of ways. Much of the literature appears to support his claims. Worker participation appears to increase productivity. Rather than creating endless disputes, worker participation tends to permit dramatic changes that would otherwise be impossible.

However, Henry Hansmann (1990), working from a number of empirical cases, has argued that worker-managed firms pose serious problems of governance that make them less efficient than capitalist firms. Hansmann suggested that there are two kinds of added costs associated with worker-managed firms: those of inefficient decisions and those of the costs of the decision-making process itself. He concludes that participation is the major liability of worker-managed firms since firms managed by others tend to be more efficient than those that are worker-managed. Sociologist Peter Leigh Taylor (1994) laments that even the Mondragon cooperatives have tended to become less democratic in the pursuit of greater efficiency.

But both Vanek and Hansmann miss the crucial point. As Taylor notes, efficiency is not the sole value to be maximized. Indeed, there is no reason to believe that efficiency leads to happiness, the good society, or any other social good (Sagoff 1988).[2] In addition, firms—even capitalist firms—exist for reasons that transcend narrow considerations of efficiency. These considerations include not only what happens in the workplace itself, but how the organization of the workplace affects other societal institutions.

Consider first the impact of an obsession with efficiency on the workplace itself. One form this takes is Taylorism. But the discipline of Taylorism leads to various forms of worker resistance. Much of twentieth-century labor history consists of strikes, slowdowns, working to rule, and other actions designed to thwart Taylorist practices. Even in nonunion plants, workers have developed a variety of means to limit the ambitions of managers and owners. Sabotage of equipment, neglect of quality in the production of manufactured goods, and even outright theft of company property are commonplace activities. One might go so far as to argue that too great a degree of attention to efficiency will itself lead to inefficiency!

In addition, the promotion of efficiency as the paramount value is disastrous to both communities and families. I have already noted the consequences for communities when large firms decide unilaterally to pick up and move. But even when firms stay, the emphasis on efficiency above all else is problematic. Such an approach is most obvious in the company town. There no one except a few top company officers participates in community life. Such communities are notorious for the oppression that they manifest. But even when there are multiple firms, overemphasis on efficiency is detrimental to the community. It leave workers with little time to participate in community affairs and it certainly provides no education as to how that might be done. Thus, efficiency is often the enemy of any sense of community. It creates the conditions of alienation. Workers find themselves isolated, powerless, with little reason to go beyond what has become "the daily grind."

Furthermore, the quest for efficiency in the workplace is harmful to family life (Beck 1992). Long hours, stressful work, and job insecurity wreak havoc on families. Even in times when unemployment is low, the very specter of it underlies and undermines the structure of daily life. At the bottom of the economic ladder, workers move endlessly from job to job without ever advancing. Such workers may even work multiple jobs to make ends meet. Further up on the economic ladder, couples may find that they both can get jobs that pay reasonably well—but in different cities. They may also find that they are expected to work fifty or even sixty hours a week, ignoring all other obligations. One recent report notes that fully 40 percent of Americans now work evenings, nights, and weekends, often on rotating shifts. Night and rotating work, in particular, may lead to sleep disturbances, gastrointestinal problems, and general malaise. Such workers are far more likely to be candidates for divorce as well. And it hardly needs mentioning that nighttime care for children is virtually nonexistent (Presser 1999).

Thus, the democratization of the workplace is desirable not merely because of its effects on the workplace but because it is the key to democratization of all the other institutions of society. Workplace democracy permits and even encourages the negotiating of the relative importance to be accorded to values such as efficiency, individual autonomy, creativity, and self-realization, as well as all activities that stand largely outside the workplace. It even permits workers to raise the now taboo issue of how much work and how much leisure they wish.

SCIENCE AND TECHNOLOGY CHOICE

Science and technology do not merely affect society; they are part and parcel of society. They are ways by which we govern our individual and social behavior, ways by which we monitor ourselves and others, ways by which we make society. In this sense, they are no different than other forms of social action. They are ways by which we (re)make the social world.

Some would argue that there are no choices in science and technology, but they are more likely than not concealing the choices inherent in the design of scientific projects and technological artifacts. For example, auto manufacturers argued for decades that pollution control was impossible for any reasonable price, but when forced by law to reduce emissions, they had little trouble in so doing. This is not to suggest that science and technology are infinitely flexible. It is unlikely that anyone will produce a perpetual motion machine, no matter how much money and expertise they can garner to support the project. However, time and again the history of science and technology has shown that the world is flexible, that (some, though not all) alternative views are equally feasible and plausible.

In a world in which technical change was slow and gradual, there would be little concern about technology choice. But in a world in which technical change is everywhere occurring at breakneck speed, technology choice becomes fundamentally political. Adherents to market views suggest that decisions about technology choice should be left entirely to the market. For many technological choices this is a reasonable approach. In most cases, we can let the market decide whether people will be offered green shirts or blue ones, vanilla or chocolate ice cream, houses with gingerbread trim or postmodern lines. Although these decisions are as social as any others—taste is social, not individual, even though it is individuals who make the decisions—they are not likely to have any significant social consequences.

In contrast, other technological decisions, even though made by individuals in interaction with the market, can have major social and political consequences. For example, genetic testing raises the specter of people being denied jobs and insurance on the basis of their genetic makeup. Individual choices to drive automobiles create traffic jams and pollution, cover vast areas of cities with asphalt, reduce demands for (and hence availability of) public transportation for those not wishing to drive, and (quite literally) pave the way for a reduction of services in city centers as residents decide that suburbia is more attractive. Similarly, seemingly trivial individual decisions to use disposable soft drink containers lead to massive waste disposal problems. Farmers' decisions to use (or refrain from using) certain pesticides have consequences for groundwater pollution, farmworker health, and the safety of our food. Management decisions to use assembly line technology to organize the workplace have consequences for those who work there that go far beyond earning a living. It is hardly an accident that the introduction of assembly line technology into the postal service has given rise to the term "going postal." Nor is it difficult to explain the prevalence of carpal tunnel syndrome among workers in poultry factories. [Philosopher Andrew Feenberg (1995) is certainly right in asking whether assembly line technology would have been so widely embraced in a nation of workers' cooperatives.] Each of these and many other technological decisions show the impossibility of neatly separating private, market-based decisions from issues of politics. Given that technology choice is political, it is clear that excluding it from the realm of democratic debate and decision-making is illegitimate. These technologies affect who we are, how we live, and what we care about.

Less obviously, the same is true for science. While science is generally further removed from use, science and the knowledge it generates is not without a point of view. What Nagel (1986) called the view from nowhere is what Donna Haraway (1995) has more appropriately called "the God trick." Specifically, what scientists do is to reveal (following Bacon) how nature responds when certain things are done to it, when it is "pressed and molded." Thus, physicists tell us that all things fall to earth at 32 feet per second squared when in a perfect vacuum. But perfect vacuums do not exist. More importantly, in our everyday experience different things fall at different rates despite having the same weight. Thus, three problems emerge:

1.   Knowledge is not of equal benefit to all. At least three groups have an interest in scientific knowledge: those who propose a given avenue of research (e.g., scientists), those who benefit by it (e.g., industrialists or the military), and those who use the knowledge gained to pursue further research (e.g., other scientists or engineers) (Fuller 1988). Thus, what knowledge is pursued has consequences (not always knowable in advance) for the distribution of social goods such as prestige, wealth and income.

2.   Despite claims to the contrary, scientists always (must) ask questions from particular points of view. The view from nowhere does not exist. The questions asked and the methods used are fundamentally influenced by who the scientists are and what they care about (Harding 1991).[3]

3.   Scientists are very good at telling us what would happen under ideal conditions and how to approximate those conditions, but they are not particularly good at telling us what happens when conditions cannot be controlled. Thus, for example, despite huge investments in sophisticated measurement and complex mathematical models, weather forecasting beyond several days remains fairly inaccurate.

But most of the dilemmas we face occur precisely in deciding which scientific questions are worth addressing from what points of view and in predicting very complex and uncontrollable events. For example: Should we fund attempts to understand the etiology of and find cures for AIDS or breast cancer? Should we look for cures or focus on prevention? Or perhaps should we attempt to develop vaccines? Similarly, we might ask how much funding to throw at earthquake forecasting versus designing structures that resist earthquakes or removing populations from earthquake-prone areas. The conundrum is even more obvious when we try to decide how to divide the research pie between AIDS research and earthquake prediction.

These questions do not have simple answers. But one thing is clear: scientific credentials are not necessary to decide the answers to the questions (although this is often claimed to be the case). Indeed, the very interested character of scientists makes them very poor judges of the relative value of particular scientific and technological trajectories. Ask an astronomer and you will find that astronomy is the central science and tragically underfunded. Ask a biologist and you will find the same is true of biology.

Moreover, although the arcane details of science and technology are more and more beyond the education and (more arguably) the intelligence of the average citizen, science and technology choice depend little on the knowledge of specific details about the theories of science or the workings of technologies. What knowledge is needed is readily available from the experts in the field. In contrast, it is the moral and ethical issues they raise, their probable effect on everyday life, and hence their desirability that are important in science and technology choice. In that realm, there are no experts.

Consider, for example, the case of biotechnologically altered food. Citizens are legitimately concerned about food safety, impact on the environment, the potential for allergic reactions to such foods, and the authenticity of food itself. Scientists may and often do produce estimates of the risks involved in eating such foods or the risks to the environment from the accidental release of biotechnologically altered crops or animals. They may test for allergic reactions. But ultimately the question is not what the risks are, but whether they are worth taking. Citizens will certainly weigh the risks and benefits in making such decisions. But the decisions are not amenable to some sort of risk-benefit analysis. Such analyses must be based on heroic assumptions about how things are to be valued and it is precisely how things are to be valued that is at issue. Instead, the decision must be far more like the deliberations of a jury.

In fact, it is exactly this approach that was used recently by the French government in deciding whether to proceed with the production and sale of genetically modified foods. Following a procedure similar to one pioneered and used successfully by the Danish government, a diverse group of ordinary citizens was chosen to engage in a dialogue with experts over several weekends. That was followed by a public meeting during which questions were posed to the experts by the citizens. Finally, during a closed session the citizen panel produced a brief final report that was presented to the French government (Sénat 1998). Among other recommendations, the citizen panel proposed a system of labeling, more ecological research, and reform of the expert assessment procedures. The media gave widespread coverage to the issues and stimulated public debate (Premier Ministre 1998).

Of course, not everyone need participate in the making of scientific and technological choices (although one might pay citizens to help make technology choices much as one pays jurors to decide criminal cases). Nor need every choice be given the same scrutiny. As Richard Sclove (1995) suggests, the analogy with law is appropriate. In democratic societies, we do not feel compelled to pass laws to govern every social action. Nor do we feel that every bill must be discussed by Congress for an equal period of time. Indeed, we are willing to delegate passage of certain types of laws to state and local governments, while others are reserved to Congress. The same applies to scientific and technological choice.

Science and technology need to be evaluated based not only on likelihood of success in achieving their stated goals (in theory, in the market, etc.), but also in terms of their potential positive and negative consequences for society (e.g., a less polluted environment, harm to individuals or groups) and their contribution to democracy itself. Thus, for example, one might evaluate human genetic research based on its likelihood of success (both in identifying genes and in preventing disease), its potential for stigmatizing certain individuals as genetically inferior by virtue of their having or lacking certain genes, and by what its impact might be on moral autonomy and community. Only after having deliberated at some length would some kinds of genetic testing be approved or disapproved and then no doubt with some caveats, exceptions, and uncertainties. Dahl (1989) has suggested the formation of a "minipopulus" to discuss issues of this sort. Such a group might consist of one thousand persons chosen randomly who would debate an important issue and guide or even make public decisions about it.

But might not the choices made turn out later to be wrong? What about the unintended or unforeseen consequences of technologies? Of course, no matter how democratic technology choice might be, as fallible beings we may make the wrong decisions. But in this sense, technology choice is no different from any other political choice. The decision to amend the U.S. constitution in 1919 to ban alcoholic beverages was followed by years of violence, flaunting the law, and organized crime. In 1933 the amendment was repealed. Often, far less dramatic changes are made to respond to unintended and unforeseen consequences of legal action. There is no reason why the same logic cannot be applied to technology choice.

But here again, a system for voting for or against given technologies is certainly not sufficient and probably not necessary. What is needed is public deliberation and debate. Recently, in response to increasingly heated debate over medical research and the advice of the Institute of Medicine, the National Institutes of Health have formed a Director's Council of Public Representatives to advise on research priorities. However, while the group contains patients, relatives of patients, and several advocacy group representatives, it does not include the groups that yell most loudly. Moreover, NIH director Harold Varmus wishes to use the group to help to quantify the costs and burdens of various diseases thereby attempting, perhaps unwittingly, to replace debate with a simplistic cost-benefit analysis (Agnew

1998). Whether this new advisory council will succeed or merely serve as a buffer for scientists remains to be seen.

More successful has been the Environmental Protection Agency's *Toxics Release Inventory*. Soon after the 1984 disaster in Bhophal, India, Congress passed the Emergency Planning and Community Right to Know Act (42 U.S.C. §§ 1101–1149). The law mandated that all U.S. manufacturing plants annually report the quantity of toxic compounds they emit. Equally important, the law required that the information be made easily accessible to the public. Thus, EPA has made available an on-line database, printed lists, CD-ROMs, magnetic tape, an annual book, and microfiche. One effect has been to put pressure on large corporations to reduce such emissions. The *Inventory* has had the positive result of creating the basis for face-to-face meetings between citizens' groups and industry officials. Moreover, instead of lengthy and expensive court proceedings, the *Inventory* has encouraged direct action to resolve problems. However, most users of the *Inventory* are the industry officials themselves. In addition, there is the potential that industries will simply move to places where the public pressure to reduce emissions is weakest (see Lynn and Kartez 1994).

Also needed is more direct action by residents of affected communities both to force the end to pollution and to ensure that it does not occur in the first place. Today, all too often it is low-income and minority neighborhoods that are selected as the sites for dumping toxic materials. Yet, environmental justice organizations have arisen to fight such practices. One example is Mothers of East Los Angeles—Santa Isabel (MELASI), a grassroots organization that successfully blocked a medical waste incinerator and an oil pipeline that had been rerouted by twenty miles so as to avoid an affluent neighborhood (Rysavy 1998).

Of course, not all problems are quite so straightforward. Often research is needed to determine the extent of a given problem and to identify possible avenues of resolution. U.S. communities frequently face these problems, but despite huge research expenditures by both government and industry, such problems are rarely addressed. One promising alternative is community-based research, that is, research by, for, and with community groups. In such research, problems are identified by community groups and studied with more or less help from experts. One study of twelve extant groups in the United States found them to result in concrete social change (e.g., improved health care, a clean water supply, reduced environmental pollution) and to be very inexpensive at about ten thousand dollars per project. Some are connected to particular universities while others are independent research institutes (Sclove, Scammell, and Holland 1998). However, there is no governmental program to fund such research in the United States.

In contrast, the Dutch have had what are called science shops since the 1970s. Today there are about a dozen general science shops and about twenty-five specialized ones in the Netherlands (General Secretariat 1999). The shops answer questions posed to them by community groups. Recently, the Canadian government announced it will create science shops following the Dutch model. However, unlike their Dutch counterparts, the Canadian science shops will focus solely on social science research to address community needs (*Science* 1998b). Over the next two years, some sixteen Community University Research Alliances will be established and funded at $160,000 each. Some university administrators are already worried that the new program does not fit easily into the existing scientific reward system (Kondro 1998). However, one might argue that such funding arrangements might be precisely what is needed to change the reward system within universities.

Also worthy of note is the growing movement toward what is known as participatory plant breeding. In a number of nations, scientists are now working directly with poor, often illiterate farmers to develop new, higher yielding varieties of crop plants. Scientists have discovered that their technical knowledge combined with farmers' intimate knowledge of the local environment makes it possible to select improved varieties more quickly, to tailor them better to farmers' needs, and to maintain greater biological diversity (Eyzaguirre and Iwanaga 1996). Surely, if such a participatory approach can work among some of the poorest people on the planet, it can be even more effective among the far better educated and wealthier citizens of the United States.

In sum, scientific and technological decisions can no longer be allowed to remain beyond the realm of democratic debate. Science and technology are no less value-laden activities than art or music. We may yield to the superior knowledge of the scientist or engineer in matters technical, but we have no reason to yield in moral matters. As philosopher Paul Feyerabend noted, "It is time to realize that science, too, is a special tradition and that its predominance must be reversed by an open debate in which all members of the society participate" (1978:86).

EDUCATION

Education has become so associated with formal schooling today that most people are virtually unaware of the distinction between the two. Yet, formal schooling as we now know it is a relatively recent phenomenon dating from the sixteenth century (Aries 1962). Even when classes were initially established, they did not in any way imply age segregation. A far older tradition dating as far back as Plato saw education as fundamentally moral education—preparation for life in society. But where Plato used the Socratic method in which reflexivity was encouraged and applauded, by the early nineteenth century U.S. schools focused on rote memorization of myriad facts and figures so as to learn the three Rs: reading, 'riting, and 'rithmetic.

One reading of the history of U.S. education might be as a contest between proponents of education as preparation for moral competence and those who viewed it far more instrumentally as a means of social control. Proponents of social control soon won the day. One of their key spokespersons was sociologist Edward A. Ross. As he put it in a book by that name in 1915: "Thus can education help in 'breaking in' the colt to the harness" (Ross 1915:166).

Not surprisingly, given that orientation, U.S. public schools have been modeled on the current vogue in industrial relations throughout their history. Monitorial or Lancasterian schools, common in the United States in the nineteenth century, mimicked the organization of the factory at the time: knowledge was chopped into small pieces and passed on to students. In the early twentieth century schools were organized along the principles of scientific management (Spring 1972). Even John Dewey stressed cooperation in his educational writings so that the school could compensate for the isolation found in the larger society. But his focus on cooperation, instead of encouraging democratic values, often served to reinforce conformity with group norms, a useful skill in the factory. As Clarence Karier (1973a:92) put it: "His values respecting order, conflict, and social change were close to those held by members of the National Civic Federation, who supported progressive social legislation in the interest of the new emerging corporate society." Moreover, Dewey ([1916] 1961) conflated freedom and democracy with science and technology. By learning experimental method, claimed Dewey, students would become better citizens of the democratic melting pot.

Furthermore, as schooling became nearly universal, educational leaders felt it necessary to track students to reduce inefficiency in the distribution of what were increasingly termed "human resources." Vocational guidance was introduced to help ensure that each student was placed in the appropriate track. At the same time social programs and sports were introduced to create social cohesion across the class boundaries defined by the various tracks. Student governments were introduced so that students could learn procedures; however, they were virtually never given any significant power to govern.

When issues of moral competence were raised by educators, they were often linked to educational testing. Advocates of eugenics introduced IQ testing into American schools, convinced that virtue and test scores were highly correlated. Conveniently, this permitted them to claim that those

who scored poorly on the tests were not only less intelligent, but genetically defective and socially undesirable. Edward L. Thorndike and his
student, Henry E. Garrett (who later became president of the American
Psychological Association), used testing as an apology for racism as well
(Karier 1973b).

Prior to World War II, colleges were reserved largely for the children of
the upper (and later middle) classes. Therefore, they permitted students
considerably more freedom than high schools. But today's universities are
often large bureaucracies with professional administrators and highly specialized faculty members. The natural sciences have long ago succumbed
to hyperspecialization, so much so that even biologists of different stripes
have difficulty understanding or even appreciating each others' work. Un-
dergraduates are not taught how to do science as much as they are taught
how to replicate well-known experiments and regurgitate mountains of
facts, many of which will be obsolete before they graduate. Graduate students do get to participate in and criticize science in the making, but they
do so within the narrow confines of a subdiscipline. Thus, as the old saw
goes, they learn more and more about less and less until they know everything about nothing. In short, "professionalism discourages independent
evaluation outside one's established field, and . . . it is great for the ego but
takes a toll on integrity" (Wilshire 1990:67).

The social sciences, in their efforts to be "scientific" have tended to
adopt the trappings of the natural sciences by employing similar procedures: sophisticated mathematics, experimental design, hypothesis testing, and formal logic. The results have been less than stellar. As sociologist
Irwin Deutscher (1969) noted thirty years ago, often the newer complex
methods explain less than do the older simpler ones. Similarly, economist
Paul Ormerod (1994) has noted that econometric models of national
economies are less accurate than simple extrapolations. But hardly anyone
seems to have been listening.

The humanities have hardly escaped the hyperspecialization. Historians who have a grasp of world history are few and far between. Far too
many philosophers can engage in endless debates about things only of interest to a handful of similarly minded colleagues. Literary criticism often
consists more of one-upmanship than of shedding light on the human condition.

The result of all this is a university that claims to be universal when, in
fact, it is a potpourri of disparate, disjointed, disabled specialties, the unity of which is merely an untested assumption. It is no wonder that Umberto Eco could note that "nothing more closely resembles a monastery
(lost in the countryside, walled, flanked by alien, barbarian hordes, inhabited by monks who have nothing to do with the world and devote them-

selves to their private researches) than an American university campus" (1983:83).

Of course, there have been attempts to overcome the excessive fragmentation of the university. On the campus where I work, integrative studies have been made a central part of the undergraduate curriculum. Indeed, the natural sciences, social sciences, and arts and humanities all have their own integrative studies units, thereby ensuring the very disintegration that they claim to overcome.

Perhaps the situation is best summed up as follows:

> As a socializing institution with very particular rules and regulations, school fosters in many students—both those who achieve and those who don't—a widespread reluctance to express opinions or question authority. To most who experience it, school contradicts the very principles of liberty, diversity, and freedom of choice that America purportedly values most. As a consequence, many young people leave school with the belief that their actions don't matter, that they can't make a difference. Is it any wonder that both young people and old feel a broad-based disaffection from the very notions of democracy itself? (Trend 1997:129)

But, of course, education need not be so parochial, so narrow, so authoritarian, so oppressive. It can be made far more democratic. It can help people to discover moral values together. Even within the confines of the school or college, learning can be cooperative and collaborative rather than individualized and compartmentalized. It can emphasize learning—an outcome—rather than teaching—an input (Barr and Tagg 1995). It can be made far more integrative and far less specialized.

This is not to suggest that specialized knowledge is irrelevant, but it is to suggest that the existing disciplines no longer make much sense. In the Middle Ages knowledge was divided into the Trivium (grammar, logic, and rhetoric) and Quadrivium (arithmetic, geometry, astronomy, and music). Today these categories appear quaint and outmoded. They connect things we do not normally link while they neglect many realms of what counts for knowledge today (Busch 1996).

The medieval division of knowledge was destroyed and replaced by our modern categories—the natural sciences, the arts and humanities, and, somewhat later, the social sciences—some 350 years ago. But these categories now are equally obsolete. They maintain the artificial division between what German historian Wilhelm Dilthey (1961) called the *Geisteswissenshaften* (the human sciences) and the *Naturwissenschaften* (the natural sciences). Implicit in the categories is the belief that the human sciences employ historical, interpretive understanding (*verstehen*) while the sciences of nature attempt predictive explanation.

But this distinction glosses over what all fields of knowledge share: They tell us something about ourselves. Meteorology tells us not only about the weather; it also shows that we care about the weather. Counting endangered species tells us about their numbers, but it also illustrates our concern for their number. Thus, we need not study human beings to learn about human beings. Virtually any field of study we might imagine will illustrate, demonstrate, validate some aspect of our lives. Put differently, all sciences are *moral* sciences; all knowledge is moral knowledge. It reveals who we are, what our ambitions are, what we care about. The project of democracy will be advanced to the extent that we recognize knowledge as fundamentally moral in character.

Also of importance is the democratic governance of schools and colleges. Most schools and colleges are run in an autocratic manner. In elementary and secondary schools, organizational structures resemble those of factories. Principals are the CEOs, teachers the foremen, and students the line workers. At neatly arranged desks, resembling nothing so much as a sewing factory, students learn how the joy of learning can be made into drudgery.

But schools could be run (with the probable exception of the lower elementary grades) in a far more democratic manner. Students, teachers, parents, and community members could decide together what the curriculum would be as each has a stake in the school. Indeed, part of the process of learning might be helping to decide how to make the school an effective place to learn.

Although arguably less oppressive than elementary and secondary schools, colleges and universities are hardly models of democracy either. Usually, faculty make decisions about curricular activities while administrators make other decisions (although the boundary between administrative and curricular decisions is blurred at best). Often, an appointed (or in some cases elected) board presides over the entire process. Students rarely have much input into it.

But here, too, it is possible to conceive of far more democratic alternatives for governance. Students, in particular, could and should play a much greater role in university governance than they do now. For the university as a whole, students, faculty, staff, and perhaps community members might draw lots to oversee major programs and activities. In the classroom, grading might be eliminated as students focus on building their competencies in various subject areas.

In addition, we need to reconceive education as extending far beyond the boundaries of schooling. There is little reason to assume that all students will benefit from being confined to schools for twelve or sixteen years in a row. While some lip service has been given to lifelong education, far more is needed to open the schools to whoever desires to learn as well as to permit students to interrupt their formal education to engage in other activities.

HEALTH CARE

The provision of health care is perhaps one of the most difficult areas in which to foster participation. Medical care providers (e.g., physicians, nurses) almost always have far greater experience and usually have greater understanding of the scientific basis of various health problems. Thus, relations between patients and providers are usually asymmetrical.

The U.S. medical care system is largely based on pharmaceuticals and expensive machinery (e.g., magnetic resonance imaging). The system is self-perpetuating: The National Institutes of Health (NIH) use most of their multibillion dollar budget to search for cures for various diseases. Cures are sought by developing new classes of pharmaceuticals and ever more sophisticated technological gadgetry. Pharmaceutical and medical equipment companies use the research conducted at NIH to develop ever more expensive, high-profit drugs and equipment. The high cost of testing, usually overseen by government agencies, also adds to the cost of the final product.

At the same time, more than 40 percent of Americans are unable to afford medical insurance. Those who do have insurance face rising premiums, higher deductibles, and higher employer costs. This, in turn, is the result of rising drug and equipment costs as well as enormous administrative costs and outlandish salaries for CEOs of private care companies. As the population ages, this problem can only become worse, since it is the heroic effort to extend the life of the elderly ill by another month, week, or day that is far and away the most costly intervention.

What is ignored in all this is that most of the great advances in the health of the population over the last century are traceable not to pharmaceuticals or medical equipment but to better sanitation, safer food, better nutrition, and elimination of the most serious workplace hazards. At the same time, many of the most serious health problems are traceable to human-produced compounds and practices. A more participatory health care system would have to (1) be fully inclusive of the population, (2) focus more on prevention and healthy living than on expensive and exotic cures for diseases, (3) give greater voice to the public in prioritizing health care expenditures, and (4) give those persons covered by managed care a greater say in their collective care.

But even in the current context, far greater participation and far more democratic alternatives are feasible. One example of an attempt to produce this inclusivity is the Oregon Health Plan. Under the plan, treatments covered by Medicaid are based on a prioritization of 700 diagnoses and treatments. The legislature drew the line at number 587, providing no funds for lower priority treatments. This allowed the state to add some one hundred thousand people to the program. The Oregon Health Services Commission, established to prioritize the treatments, drew public input at numerous hearings. Although Medicaid recipients were not well represented at the hearings, their advocates were. To date, complaints about the prioritization have been few (Bodenheimer 1997a, 1997b). Of course, this was done within the confines of a health care system that still denies coverage to a significant portion of the population and gives little voice to those unable to pay. Full coverage is still a long way off.

Another recent development in participatory health care is the creation of virtual communities of those who have contracted various diseases. Sufferers from hundreds of diseases have found that web sites and discussion lists can be used for a variety of purposes. In some particularly rare diseases, such web sites have permitted the identification of sufficient numbers of cases to make drug trials and controlled medical interventions possible. In some cases they have even gone so far as to become involved in designing treatments for the diseases. Consider just a few of them.

The website for the Creutzfeldt-Jakob Disease Foundation (1998) is typical of many of these sites. It was founded by relatives of persons who died of the disease and a physician interested in the subject. It contains a statement in lay language of the etiology of the disease as well as its known incidence and hypothesized causes. It also provides a reference list of both popular press and technical publications for those who wish to dig deeper. Links are provided to other websites having additional material on the disease. A message board permits the posting of comments, questions, and additional information.

Wide Smiles (1998) is a similar organization run by and for persons with cleft lips and palates. It provides the complete text of over six hundred articles on various aspects of cleft lips and palates, including advice to parents, problems with feeding newborn children, concerns about insurance, speech problems, and statistics on the prevalence of the problem. Its board of directors includes both physicians and laypersons (mothers of children with cleft palates and related problems). A substantial portion of the site is devoted to before and after photos. Particularly novel is a children's story about a child with a cleft palate.

Somewhat different is the Intersex Society of North America (ISNA) (1998), a "peer support, education, and advocacy group founded and operated by and for intersexuals: individuals born with anatomy or physiology which differs from cultural ideals of male and female." It maintains a large web site complete with information about hermaphrodites, discussions of the potential problems associated with surgery, recommendations for treatment, and bibliographies of both the popular press and the medical literature. It also issues a newsletter, *Hermaphrodites with Attitude,* and supplies a video on the subject. Several medical practitioners are also associated with the organization. While offering medical information, ISNA challenges the widely held belief that hermaphroditism must in all cases be treated as a medical problem.[4]

Finally, Little People of America (1998) is "An Organization for People of Short Stature" founded in 1957. It claims over five thousand members, all under four feet ten inches tall. Its website provides information on a variety of issues associated with dwarfism. In addition to providing support for short persons, it helps parents deal with raising children affected by various forms of dwarfism and a special newsletter and chat room for teens. Like Wide Smiles, it contains a picture gallery of people of short stature, thereby emphasizing that such persons are not unusual and can lead fulfilling lives.

Yet, as in other aspects of social life, participation in health care systems is a complex and difficult task. A recent review of the literature on participation in health care planning shows the complexity of the problem (Perlstadt, Jackson-Elmore, Freddolino, and Reed 1998). Participation in health care planning has been mandated since the 1960s, but often it has been limited by inadequate knowledge of the system, limited support staff, and huge time commitments that bias participation toward those who are well-educated and hold professional or managerial positions. But as in other areas of social life, participation must start with immediate issues and move to those more abstract or distant later on. Put differently, participation is not impossible—but it takes a little longer.

ARTS

The arts provide powerful ways of participating in society. The arts were once conceived of as sources of truth as well as beauty, of power as well as entertainment. Today, they are often viewed across the political spectrum as frills, as ornamentation, as gingerbread decoration that covers the serious business of society. As a result, in the United States the arts have been impoverished.

The motion picture industry personalizes the political through many of the films it makes. Key events are described as if they were mere backdrops for love stories. In the absence of real enemies, fictitious ones are created. Events are interpreted by mainstream films as the result of the actions of particular heroic individuals. While heroes exist, Hollywood goes far beyond the occasional hero to describe entire historical epochs as the result of the actions of a few persons. At the extreme, the so-called action movies starring Bruce Willis and Arnold Schwarzenegger, among others, give the viewer the feelings of power and control that are often missing from daily life at the same time as they glorify violence.

Furthermore, in fields as diverse as music, dance, and painting, a "winner take all" approach prevails such that a handful of stars dominate, thereby impoverishing the rest of us (Frank and Cook 1995). Those artists, musicians, filmmakers, actors, dancers, and the like who are not able to attract huge audiences are left with a choice between a life on the margins or dropping out of the arts entirely. Public schools pay little attention to the arts, viewing them as a luxury that we can ill afford. In practice, this means that only a handful of persons will become successful artists; artists who cannot speak to the (somewhat mythical) mainstream are denied any voice at all.

But this need not be the case. Indeed, despite the difficulties in raising funds, some two hundred independent media arts centers exist across the nation (Trend 1997). At their best, they offer minorities and the poor the opportunity to express their grievances, to participate in political debates, and to celebrate their own understandings of daily life. They include Appalshop in Kentucky and Women Make Media in New York City. But most of these organizations are struggling to make ends meet. Most are not supported either by private foundations, who prefer to fund established arts groups, or by public monies, which are usually channeled in ways unlikely to disturb the powers that be. We have a long way to go to produce arts that are democratic.

MEDIA

It is a truism that an informed citizenry is necessary to the functioning of a democracy. However, the media not only inform the public about what is occurring in the world, but also actively form public opinion, public attitudes, and public behavior. There is no way we can separate the formation of opinion from the provision of information, since the very decision that certain information will be reported while other information is ignored is itself formative of opinion. Thus, even if every effort is made to achieve reporting that is objective and unbiased, the necessary selectivity of the media will itself bias the public.

Authoritarian societies typically keep the media under very close control. That way only the facts that the government wants revealed and only the interpretations that are politically acceptable reach the public. In a democracy, presumably we would want the reverse to happen. We would want what has traditionally been called a free press.

Yet, despite the fact that the U.S. media are privately owned, they tend to present a very narrow, carefully selected view of the world. Despite the market enthusiasts' belief that private ownership leads to choice, the American media do little to satisfy critics on both the left and the right. Indeed, it is not absurd to say that both the Right and the Left are simultaneously correct in their judgments about media bias.

Media ownership in the United States is highly concentrated. Among newspapers, local monopolies are the rule. Fewer than thirty U.S. cities have more than one newspaper. Television combines both local and national oligopolies: a handful of channels and a handful of networks in any given viewing area. Cable television has loosened the grip slightly, but often only to provide us with reruns of programs made for the networks. Six motion picture companies now control more than half the industry (Albarran and Chan-Olmsted 1998). The book market is even more concentrated. Five companies now control 80 percent of book publishing (Schiffrin 1999).

Nor should it be forgotten that the media are no longer distinct. Books may be published on the web. Motion pictures are broadcast on television. Television news is broadcast on the web. Both television and telephone cables deliver the Internet to one's doorstep. New digital technologies and relaxed government control make it easy for conglomerates to control the full spectrum of media. The technologies have permitted joining of expertise across previously diverse industries. Relaxed government control has permitted large corporations and conglomerates to vastly increase their holdings. In 1938 no one could own more than one AM station. A number of legislative changes after 1989 have not so gradually eased those rules, based on the conflation of competition with diversity of speech (Price and Weinberg 1996). Today, by one estimate a mere twenty-three corporations control most of the media (Barber 1996). As communications professor Herbert Schiller puts it, "The present condition can be stated simply. What does it mean to allow the formative elements of public consciousness to be in the hands of private image and message factories?" (1996:263).

Moreover, corporate sponsorship of the media tends to encourage a view of the world that is particularly friendly to corporations, either by direct censorship or, more often, by fear of offending sponsors (Barber 1996). At the same time, corporate public relations and advertising departments tell the public how wonderful corporations are. Everyone loves to shop at WalMart. Archer Daniels Midland is the "supermarket to the world" (although several of its officers were found guilty of price-fixing). Even public television has succumbed to the lure of corporate dollars. Originally established to air controversy and promote debate, the Public Broadcasting System now receives 23 percent of its programming budget from corporate donors (read "sponsors"). Moreover, it has rejected several award-winning documentaries, perhaps because they might offend its corporate donors (Bullert 1998).

Furthermore, in recent years, starting with the Reagan administration, the media have been deregulated. Thus, there are few limits to the quantity or content of television advertising. There are few requirements for public service announcements. The requirements for quality children's television have been gutted. Deregulation has hardly brought further competition to the media; it has brought greater mediocrity and greater competition for the same "mainstream" markets, that is, the markets most likely to capture large sums of advertising revenue. Nowhere was this more evident than in the endless reporting of the so-called Monica Lewinsky affair. Day and night, television reporters and their guests debated the various "spins" that one might put on what scanty evidence was made public. At any given time, a cable television viewer could find several stations endlessly repeating the same hearsay. At the same time, major issues facing the nation—poverty, crime, education, health care—received little or no serious analysis. But there is little doubt that by appealing to the prurient interests of the viewers, advertising revenue could be and was increased.

At the same time, the media are obsessed with an ideology of "balance." Thus, mirroring the poverty of the two major political parties, each issue is discussed as if there were *only* two relatively balanced points of view along a continuum (Figure 6.1). This view is reinforced by our obsolete two-party, winner-take-all system of representation, as noted above. In point of fact, however, on virtually every issue facing us as citizens of neighborhoods, communities, regions, or nations, there are thousands of points of view and thousands of suggestions for improving the situation. Moreover, these points of view are not found on any continuum, but are interrelated in complex ways as a network of relations as shown in Figure 6.1.

Consider just one issue: health care. There are far more than two options: public and private care. There is a full gamut of alternatives—cooperatives, HMOs, government hospitals and clinics, private physicians' practices, reimbursement schemes, prepayments, and so on. Boiling all of this down to a two-minute sound bite destroys the very nature of the democratic process by giving the impression (as do the rational choice theorists) that all decisions are merely bargaining sessions in which preferences of the parties concerned are fixed and immutable. Such media posturing impedes rather than advances the search for imaginative alternatives that satisfy a range of desires and needs.

Related to this is the illusion that a mainstream exists and that it must exist if there is to be political stability. Those not accepting one or the other "balanced" view are deemed extremists, radicals, reactionaries. But both the (organized) Right and the Left believe that their view is the correct one and that it must be shared in its entirety by all supporters. Heterodox

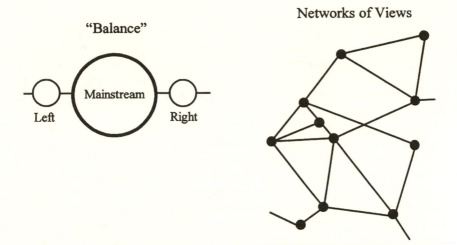

Figure 6.1. Two views of the media.

opinion is ruled out as irrational, unworkable, or just plain stupid. This vanguardism of both the Right and the Left diminishes the space for democratic participation and debate throughout society. And it is for these reasons that the Right and the Left both find the media to be biased in the opposite direction. Neither view is represented adequately and each side sees the maintenance of political orthodoxy as essential to its objectives. One obvious solution to this problem is to have a wide range of media that report based on differential evaluations of the salience of information.

FAMILY

Most discussions of democracy do not mention the family except in passing. In contemporary America, and in much of the rest of the Western world, families are treated as private places far removed from the politics of the outer world. However, if we are not born into the world as atomized individuals, if we are indeed dependent on others even to judge the accuracy of our thoughts, then families must play a central role in teaching about democracy.

Indeed, the family as a purely private space is itself a relatively recent notion, created in part as protection against the rationalized world of the marketplace. Before the beginnings of industrialization, families were multiform, fluid in their boundaries, and usually only vaguely distinct from the workplace. The family was first and foremost an economic unit, (1) in the sense that it joined together two larger families through marriage, (2) in that it often included apprentices, boarders, hired hands, servants, and / or other persons not tied by blood or marriage, and (3) in that most work took place in or near the home and included all members of the family. However, by the 1870s U.S. families were redefined so as not to include unrelated individuals and, with the notable exception of farm families, most ties to the workplace were ended (Berthoff 1971).

Much effort was expended to create the seemingly natural nuclear family. It required the severing of other ties that linked families to the rest of the community. For example, child labor laws and compulsory schooling eliminated the ties to the workplace that were common in the nineteenth century and before and that still are commonplace in the less industrialized world today. Mothers' Day, a holiday originally proposed to celebrate mothers' activities *outside* the home and family, was institutionalized as a celebration of domesticity. Zoning laws restricted the numbers of unrelated persons who could occupy a dwelling. Welfare laws prohibited aid to families that lived communally. During the Great Depression, New Deal legislation treated all men as wage earners and all women as homemakers; in twenty-six states married women were prohibited from working (Coontz 1992).

World War II brought large numbers of women into the workforce, many in highly paid jobs in manufacturing. But the end of the war was marked by successful actions on the part of management to remove those same women from the workforce. Tremendous pressure was put on women to marry, become mothers, raise families, and stay at home. Since single mothers were not supposed to exist, premarital sex that resulted in pregnancy was often dealt with by irresistible social pressure to marry. In one documented extreme case, women who did not want a domestic "career" were confined to mental hospitals and subjected to electroshock treatment. Conversely, men were supposed to have housewives in order to gain promotions. As Stephanie Coontz puts it, "Caring for others was confined to women, and personal autonomy was denied them; personal autonomy was reserved for men, and caring for others was either denied them or personalized" (1992:44).

Yet, minority and poor families were never included in the ideal nuclear families. They were more often than not the victims of family policy because they failed in one way or another to live up to the white middle-class standards of what a family was supposed to be. Those in inner cities, in particular, have been victimized by the nuclear family ideal. As industries fled the cities and public transit was reduced or abandoned, they were blamed for their laziness, lack of discipline and lack of "family values."

Today, the range of family types is once again growing. In addition to the "complete" families of the 1950s situation comedies, we now see single-parent families (usually headed by women), gay and lesbian families, and a host of other forms. But all too often families tend toward violence, hierarchy, and authority. Moreover, these tendencies are quite pronounced, perhaps all the more so due to our insistence on the privacy of the family.

Of most obvious significance, families are places where gender matters. Yet, as is evident to virtually everyone, gender relations are hardly equal. Of particular import is the emancipation of women. Paradoxically, the increased ability to choose one's career, itself the product of greater educational opportunity, has led to destabilization of life courses for both women and men. Whereas previously many, perhaps most, women expected to stay home and focus their lives around housework and child rearing, this now appears as only one career option. Similarly, men who expected that they would be the "breadwinner" in the family now find themselves having to negotiate gender roles in the household (Beck 1992). Thus, what was once taken for granted, even if oppressive for men and (especially) women, is a matter of discussion: Who should change the baby's diaper? Who should work and for how many hours? Who should clean the home? Birth control devices make it possible now to ask when children *should be* born. Furthermore, the increase in life expectancy means that most people outlive their child-raising responsibilities, leaving many years of family life with an "empty nest." These and other issues, which were not even questions fifty years ago, are now the subject of intense emotional debate.

If these are difficult issues for the middle class, they are even more difficult for the poor. Today, more than 20 percent of American children live in poverty and one-eighth of children under twelve go hungry, while one hundred thousand are homeless on any given night. Many of these children live in single-parent households, almost always headed by a woman. Moreover, only two nations in the Western hemisphere have higher infant mortality rates than the United States: Haiti and Bolivia (Coontz 1992). Indeed, infant mortality rates for some U.S. ethnic and racial groups are equal to or higher than those of the some of the world's poorest nations.

In our privatized families, it appears that only love can hold couples together in the face of the centrifugal forces pulling them apart. Thus, couples often attempt to resolve marital problems by elevating love to a new plane. It is here that expressing dependence on others is seen as legitimate, acceptable, even encouraged. Yet, since work lives are organized around the demands of the labor market, this strategy usually meets with only partial success. Ulrich Beck and Elisabeth Gernsheim-Beck explain: "While men and women are *released* from traditional norms and can search for 'a life of their own,' they are *driven* into seeking happiness in a close relationship because other social bonds seem too tenuous or unreliable" (1995:24). The situation is in some ways reminiscent of Johan Huizinga's description of life in the late Middle Ages. In the midst of war and social chaos, chivalric love was the haven from society: "To formalize love is, moreover, a social necessity, a need that is more imperious as life is more ferocious. Love has to be elevated to the height of a rite" (1954:108). If in late medieval times love was the respite from war, in our contemporary society, love is the sole place where the rules of the market do not apply. It is the one place where instrumental, calculating behavior is not rewarded. Thus, all of the demands for emotional attachment, for meaning, for escape from materialism are focused on familial love. Given the enormous—and unrealistic—demands placed on them, it is no wonder that so many marriages end in divorce, that so many relationships that appear solid melt away.

In sum, the emancipation of women makes democracy in the family not merely a luxury but a necessity. Yet, democracy and justice in the family are not *faits accomplis;* they are something yet to be won. The family is a place where children are raised, where moral values are learned, where there is no neutral moral ground. As Susan Moller Okin puts it, "While its forms are varied, the family in which a child is raised, especially in the earliest years, is clearly a crucial place for early moral development and for the formation of our basic attitudes to others. It is, potentially, a place where we can *learn to be just*" (1989:18; emphasis in original).

Alternatively, it can be a place where we learn to be unjust. Families are often places where relations of domination and subordination are learned, rather than places where democratic values are fostered. They are places where unpaid work—housework, child care, care of adult parents—takes place, but where it is rarely shared equally. They are places where spousal and child abuse are all too common and where much of the violence of life is experienced (Okin 1989).

Moreover, it is ironic that the very private character of the family often creates many of the problems that prohibit or constrict democratic family life. Typically, in both philosophical treatises and social science research, families are treated as black boxes. In these closed units, concepts such as democracy and justice either are said not to apply or are taken for granted as places where shared understandings and mutual respect inhere. But this is very rarely the case. Families are contested spaces where negotiations over who will do what, how children will be raised, when family events will be scheduled, how (or whether) nonfamilial obligations will be integrated into family life go on continuously.

In addition, the privateness of families, or the lack of it, is the result of government. Both positive law and jurisprudence have changed the nature of families over time. Whereas in the past, slaves, women, and children were seen as family property to be dealt with as necessary by male property owners, today we see such practices as barbaric. But at the same time, we are still far more tolerant of family violence than we are of other kinds of violence.

In times past, and in many non-Western cultures today, the distinction between work and family was and is far less rigid. In contrast, since Western (and especially American) families are regarded as private spaces, few businesses take into account the needs of their employees *as family members*. For hourly workers, despite some move toward flextime, workplace rules generally make it difficult to manage pregnancy, child care, children's doctor visits, care for elderly parents, and other personal activities. For managers, time is somewhat more flexible, but working hours are often considerably longer and social pressure to sacrifice family to work is strong. This is particularly the case for men, leading to a reinforcement of stereotypical gender roles both in the family and elsewhere.

In short, despite the fact that the two-wage-earner family is now the norm, business continues to operate as if there is a housewife behind each and every worker. As Beck and Gernsheim-Beck (1995) suggest, from the vantage point of our market society, the ideal employee is not a family member at all, but a social isolate willing and able to spend long hours at work and utterly divorced from other activities. Indeed, the issues are so touchy that *Business Week* had difficulty in getting companies to participate in a recent survey of work-family relationships. McDonald's refused categorically to participate, while another unnamed company was removed from the survey when most of the completed questionnaires were found to have identical answers (Hammonds 1996).

Yet, in addition to the benefits to families, attempts to alter workplace relations so as to make them more family friendly actually pay off in terms of productivity. Not surprisingly, workers who find their employers willing to accommodate their family and personal needs are less likely to be absent, more likely to stay on the job and are more productive (ibid.).

Of course, a democratic family is not likely to be one in which issues are put to a vote. More likely, a democratic family is one in which debate, dialogue, discussion are the norm in decision-making and in carrying out those decisions. Adult family members need to bear equally the responsibilities that come with family life: child rearing, housework, care for elderly parents. Clearly, both partners must have an equal say in family matters. But children bring special problems and special obligations. The very obvious dependency of infants makes it impossible to incorporate them into all decisions. But as children mature, as they develop the ability for moral reasoning, they need to become full members of the family unit, participating in decision-making and learning both their responsibilities and their rights. There is no simple formula for raising children democratically, but clearly highly authoritarian family relations are antithetical to democracy. Democratic families are not likely to end negotiations over family matters, but they are likely to put all parties to those negotiations on a more equal footing. They are likely to reproduce democratic values in their children.

But families cannot be expected to produce children schooled in democratic values by themselves. The structure of the family is in part the result of events and decisions taken outside the family, by the state, the community, the workplace, and other social institutions. Without workplace flexibility and democratic schools and communities, without laws that grant equal rights to all members of families, democratic families are unlikely to thrive. As Ulrich Beck puts it: "What remains central is that *the equalization of men and women cannot be created in institutional structures that presuppose their inequality*" (1992:109; emphasis in original).

LAW

Only a few countries, mainly within the Anglo-American tradition, prescribe or require jury trials for most criminal cases. Juries are among the very few places where ordinary citizens can come together to deliberate over an important issue. While they are hardly perfect institutions, juries tend to act quite responsibly, undertaking their appointed tasks with great seriousness. It appears that relatively few criminals brought to trial go unpunished, while relatively few innocent persons are punished.

Moreover, juries provide an alternative model both to legal authority (the judge) and to the election of representatives. In juries, ordinary citizens chosen nearly randomly (although with significant input from counsel) deliberate, debate, and discuss the evidence and arrive at a conclusion—often a conclusion of significant moral import. In some cases unanimity is required, while in other cases a simple or substantial majority is necessary to decide a case. We need not concern ourselves with the specific details here. What is important is that juries are an example of direct participation by ordinary citizens in state affairs.

Nevertheless, juries are relatively constricted in their functioning by the peculiar character of the court system. Judges usually instruct the juries on points of law, determine what evidence they may or may not hear (even determining what constitutes evidence). In some cases, judges may overrule juries to find a defendant innocent. More recently, experiments have been made with giving juries greater authority. For example, Heuer and Penrod (1996) report the results of a study of trials in which jurors were allowed to ask questions of the witnesses and take notes on the proceedings. They conclude that such participatory procedures—in both civil and criminal trials—are desired by jurors and help to clarify issues, especially in

complex legal proceedings. Clearly, more experiments of this sort are needed, both to increase participation and to better ensure that justice is served.

PUTTING IT ALL TOGETHER: NETWORKS OF DEMOCRACY

In no society could we expect that all people would want to participate
in all the domains of human endeavor described above. Nor would we expect that one form of democracy would or should be found in all domains,
in all places, or at all times. Indeed, requiring such participation, even
through informal norms, would be oppressive. It would create another
Leviathan. Moreover, as political scientist Ian Shapiro (1996) has argued,
participation is not a primary but a secondary good. It is important because
it leads to other goods. Those goods include self-realization, autonomy, responsibility, caring. Doubtless, there are others. But if this is so, then how
might a more democratic society actually work? And how do we get from
here to there?

I submit that a truly democratic society would be one in which there
would be overlapping networks of democracy. Such networks would explicitly include not only humans but all of the myriad things we interact
with on a daily basis. As sociologist Bruno Latour (1987, 1993) has argued,
such "actor networks" would recognize that while things may have no volition, they do act upon us (or resist our interventions). They are part and
parcel of our *social* life. For example, a flood is not a natural disaster; it is
the result of our being in the path of an overflowing river. We need to decide collectively when (if ever) to place cities in flood plains. Similarly, cel-
lular telephones do not merely make it possible to call someone from an
automobile; they transform social relations—sometimes so much as to
contribute to automobile accidents. We need to decide collectively when
and where (if at all) it is appropriate to use such technologies. In short, the
introduction of new things into social life transforms social relationships.
If we are to build networks of democracy, we can no longer afford to consider things as passive or neutral (cf. Heidegger 1977; Scott 1995). Far too
much is at stake, for in our technoscientific society most social relations are
mediated by things.

In the democratic society I envision, all adults would be free to participate in shaping as few or as many of these networks to the extent that they
wished. Thus, I might participate actively in shaping networks related to
the workplace, science and technology, family, and education. But I might
at the same time decide to let others participate in shaping networks of
health care and the arts. Over time I might change my choices, based on
different needs and interests during my life. Others would make different
choices. In each of these instances, I would be involved in debate and dia-

logue about what kind of world we want. Depending on the nature of the issue, that world might be our home, our neighborhood, our city, our nation, or the entire planet. In fact, the location and nature of those boundaries themselves would be part of the debates.

These networks would be overlapping. By this I mean that within each network I would not only debate, argue, and discuss different issues, but I would do it with (at least some) different persons. Figure 6.2 describes in somewhat idealized form what I mean. Network A is a singular network. In a community such as that depicted by network A, all social relations are funneled through the same channels, as represented by the single type of line connecting the nodes (persons and things). Such a community might be an isolated small society, a "utopian" village of the sort common in the United States of the nineteenth century or a highly despotic society such as the one that Ceauşescu attempted to create in Romania (see Chapter 3). Either way, dominance in one aspect of social life, what Boltanski and Thévenot (1991) would call one world, what Walzer (1983) would call one sphere, would mean de facto dominance in all other spheres. The pressure to conform to community norms in such a network would be overwhelming. Such norms might be open and flexible, providing many opportunities for disagreements to surface, but they could also be highly oppressive and stifling. In contrast, B consists of overlapping networks as represented by the different kinds of lines connecting the various nodes. A relationship in one network would not necessarily involve the same persons and things as a relationship in another network. While not fully independent, each network would have a certain level of autonomy vis-à-vis the others. Thus, domination in one network would not necessarily lead to domination in others. In fact, the reverse effect might ensue; domination in one network might well result in mobilization of the other networks to end the domination. In such a network, my leadership position in the network represented by the solid line would have little effect on my position in the networks represented by the broken lines. To be more concrete, my wealth in the market sphere would not give me a significant advantage in the political sphere. Similarly, your political position would not provide you with significant advantages in the sphere of education.

Clearly, B offers greater autonomy for persons than does A. Moreover, B is far more likely to be self-correcting than A. Individuals in A are likely to find that everyone with whom they come into contact has similar views, while those in B are more likely to hear diverse views. Thus, debate in B will be more open and more animated, but less likely to result in sudden social upheaval. At their best, the extant liberal democracies begin to resemble B, but they have far to go to achieve more than a resemblance.

In sum, by building networks of democracy, we can begin to resolve the problem of order in a manner that creates individual autonomy while

A. A Single Network   B. Overlapping Networks

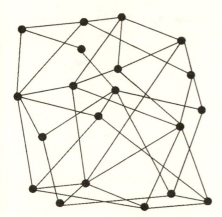 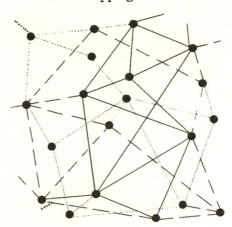

Figure 6.2.   Networks of democracy.

defining and reaching for the common good, in a manner that embeds moral responsibility in the networks rather than in either individuals or structures. Such networks can avoid both the placement of moral responsibility on some Leviathan where it becomes unbearably light as well as on individuals where it becomes crushingly heavy. But they will not resolve all the problems of the world. They will not lead us to a utopian world in which conflicts no longer exist. They will not guarantee that only right and just decisions are made. They will not ensure against the possibility that occasionally majorities will act in irresponsible ways. They will not enthrone some idealized model of reason. Indeed, it is those who put their faith in science, the state, or the market who are the true utopians. They believe that technical wizardry, a great leader, or the magic of the market can accomplish tasks that require the participation of us all.

What networks of democracy can do is to put before us the key problems of the day in a manner in which they may be addressed by informed citizens. They can help citizens become informed through participation in the networks. They can ensure that all citizens have an opportunity (without being forced) to engage in deliberation, discussion, and debate about the issues affecting their lives. They can use science, market, and state as necessary to achieve socially desired ends—ends defined as socially desirable through the very process of debate. Perhaps most importantly, they can provide us with an image of the future that is ever-changing as we make a never-ending attempt together to grapple with Tolstoy's questions: Who are we? How shall we live?

NOTES

1.   Denis Wrong (1994) notes that if Hobbes's state of nature had actually existed, then humans would have had little interest in each other rather than engaging in a war of each against all.

2.   Sagoff goes on to note that efficiency has no basis even in utilitarian philosophy as it focuses on expectations that precede a transaction rather than consequences that follow it.

3.   This is not to suggest that scientific findings are merely the opinion of biased observers. It is to suggest that scientific knowledge claims, like all other knowledge claims, are always partial and tentative. They may be subject to revision at a later time or in another place. As Hull (1988) suggests, objectivity is not a characteristic of scientists, but of scientific communities.

4.   For a treatment of this issue that examines sexual identity in light of the problem of order see Dreger (1998).

REFERENCES

Abir-Am, Pnina G. 1987. "The Biotheoretical Gathering, Trans-Disciplinary Authority and the Incipient Legitimation of Molecular Biology in the 1930s: New Perspective on the Historical Sociology of Science." *History of Science* 25:1–70.

Agnew, Bruce. 1998. "NIH Embraces Citizens' Council to Cool Debate on Priorities." *Science* 282:18–19.

Albarran, Alan B., and Sylvia Chan-Olmsted. 1998. "The United States of America." Pp. 19–32 in *Global Media Economics*, edited by Alan B. Albarran and Sylvia Chan-Olmsted. Ames: Iowa State University Press.

Althusser, Louis. 1997. *Reading Capital*. London: Verso.

American Management Association. 1997. "Electronic Monitoring and Surveillance." http://www.amanet.org/survey/elec97.htm

Amy, Douglas. 1996. "Elections in Which Every Vote Counts." *Chronicle of Higher Education*, January 12.

Aries, Philippe. 1962. *Centuries of Childhood: A Social History of Family Life*. London: Jonathan Cape.

Arnold, Thurman. 1937. *The Folklore of Capitalism*. New Haven, CT: Yale University Press.

Arrow, Kenneth J. [1951] 1963. *Social Choice and Individual Values*. New York: John Wiley.

Atkinson, Anthony B., Lee Rainwater, and Timothy M. Smeedling. 1995. *Income Distribution in OECD Countries: Evidence from the Luxembourg Income Study*. Paris: Organisation for Economic Cooperation and Development.

Avery, Natalie, Martine Drake, and Tim Land. 1993. *Cracking the Codex: An Analysis of Who Sets World Standards*. London: National Food Alliance.

Ayres, Clarence Edwin. 1927. *Science: The False Messiah*. Indianapolis: Bobbs-Merrill.

Ayres, Clarence Edwin. 1944. *The Theory of Economic Progress*. Chapel Hill: University of North Carolina Press.

Babbage, Charles. 1835. *On the Economy of Machinery and Manufactures*, 4th ed. London: Charles Knight.

Babbage, Charles. [1830] 1970. *Reflections on the Decline of Science in England and Some of Its Causes*. New York: Augustus M. Kelley.

Bacon, Francis. [1603] 1964. "The Masculine Birth of Time." Pp. 59–72 in *The Philosophy of Francis Bacon*, edited by Benjamin Farrington. Chicago: University of Chicago Press.

Bacon, Francis. [1607] 1964. "Thoughts and Conclusions." Pp. 73–102 in *The Philosophy of Francis Bacon*, edited by Benjamin Farrington. Chicago: University of Chicago Press.

Bacon, Francis. [1605/1626] 1974. *The Advancement of Learning and the New Atlantis*. Oxford: Clarendon.

Bacon, Francis. [1620] 1994. *Novum Organum*. Chicago: Open Court.

Bailes, Kendall E. 1974. "The Politics of Technology: Stalin and Technocratic Thinking among Soviet Engineers." *American Historical Review* 79:445–69.

Bailes, Kendall E. 1977. "Alexei Gastev and the Soviet Controversy over Taylorism." *Soviet Studies* 29:373–94.

Bailes, Kendall E. 1978. *Technology and Society under Lenin and Stalin: Origins of the Soviet Technical Intelligentsia*. Princeton, NJ: Princeton University Press.

Barber, Benjamin R. 1984. *Strong Democracy*. Berkeley: University of California Press.

Barber, Benjamin R. 1996. *Jihad vs. McWorld: How Globalism and Tribalism Are Reshaping the World*. New York: Ballantine.

Barr, Robert B., and John Tagg. 1995. "From Teaching to Learning: A New Paradigm for Undergraduate Education." *Change*:13–25.

Barrett, Amy. 1998. "New Teeth for Old Patents." *Business Week* 3606:92, 94–95.

Bathe, Greville, and Dorothy Bathe. 1935. *Oliver Evans: A Chronicle of Early American Engineering*. Philadelphia: Historical Society of Pennsylvania.

Baum, L. Frank. 1939. "The Wizard of Oz." Hollywood, CA: MGM.

Baum, L. Frank. [1907] 1979. *Dorothy and the Wizard in Oz*. New York: Ballantine.

Beardsley, Edward H. 1969. *Harry L. Russell and Agricultural Science in Wisconsin*. Madison: University of Wisconsin Press.

Beck, Ulrich. 1992. *Risk Society: Towards a New Modernity*. London: Sage.

Beck, Ulrich, and Elisabeth Gernsheim-Beck. 1995. *The Normal Chaos of Love*. Cambridge: Polity.

Bellah, Robert, Richard Masden, William M. Sullivan, Ann Swidler, and Steven Tipton. 1985. *Habits of the Heart: Individualism and Commitment in American Life*. Berkeley: University of California Press.

Benjamin, Martin. 1990. *Splitting the Difference: Compromise and Integrity in Ethics and Politics*. Lawrence: University of Kansas Press.

Berlan, Jean Pierre, and Richard Lewontin. 1986a. "The Political Economy of Hybrid Corn." *Monthly Review* 38:35–47.

Berlan, Jean-Pierre, and Richard Lewontin. 1986b. "Breeders' Rights and Patenting Life Forms." *Nature* 322:785–88.

Berle, A. A., and C. G. Means. [1932] 1968. *The Modern Corporation and Private Property*. New York: Harcourt, Brace, and World.

Bernal, J. D. 1952. "The Engineer and the State." Pp. 25–30 in *Man Conquers Nature: Text of Speeches at Battersea Town Hall Meeting, January 13, 1952*. London: Society for Cultural Relations with the USSR.

Bernstein, Aaron. 1999. "All's Not Fair in Labor Wars." *Business Week* 3638:43.

Berry, Wendell. 1977. *The Unsettling of America: Culture and Agriculture*. San Francisco: Sierra Club.

Berthoff, Rowland. 1971. *An Unsettled People: Social Order and Disorder in American History*. New York: Harper and Row.

Blanksten, George I. 1953. *Perón's Argentina*. Chicago: University of Chicago Press.

Blumberg, Paul. 1968. *Industrial Democracy*. New York: Schocken.

Bodenheimer, Thomas. 1997a. "The Oregon Health Plan: Lessons for the Nation. Part 1." *New England Journal of Medicine* 337:651–55.

Bodenheimer, Thomas. 1997b. "The Oregon Health Plan: Lessons of for the Nation. Part 2." *New England Journal of Medicine* 337:720–23.

Boltanski, Luc, and Laurent Thévenot. 1991. *De La Justification: Les Economies de la Grandeur*. Paris: Gallimard.

Boston Globe. 1999. "North Korea Puts Death Toll from Famine at about 220,000." May 11:A2.

Bourdieu, Pierre. 1998. *Contre-Feu: Propos pour Servir à la Résistance Contre l'Invasion Néo-liberale*. Paris: Liber-Raisons d'Agir.

Bourke, Austin. 1993. *"The Visitation of God"? The Potato and the Great Irish Famine*. Dublin: Lilliput.

Braudel, Fernand. 1973. *Capitalism and Material Life, 1400–1800*. New York: Harper.

Bremner, Brian. 1998. "Last Chance for the Yen?" *Business Week* 3585:46–47.

Bromley, Daniel W. 1997. "Rethinking Markets." *American Journal of Agricultural Economics* 79:1383–93.

Bromley, Daniel W. 1998. "Transitions to a New Political Economy: Law and Economics Reconsidered." Cambridge: Department of Land Economy, Cambridge University.

Bullert, B. J. 1998. "Public TV: Safe Programming and Faustian Bargains." *Chronicle of Higher Education* 45(4):B7.

Burawoy, Michael. 1979. *Manufacturing Consent*. Chicago: University of Chicago Press.

Burawoy, Michael. 1985. *The Politics of Production: Factory Regimes Under Capitalism and Socialism*. London: Verso.

Bureau of Labor Statistics. 1999. "BLS Career Information." http://stats.bls.gov/oco/ocos159.htm

Burke, Edmund. [1795] 1881. "Thoughts and Details on Scarcity." Pp. 133–69 in *The Works of the Right Honorable Edmund Burke*. Boston: Little, Brown.

Busch, Lawrence. 1996. "Bringing Nature Back In." *Centennial Review* 30:491–500.

Bush, Vannevar. 1945. "Science, the Endless Frontier." Washington, DC: US Office of Scientific Research and Development.

Butler, Declan. 1997. "Eugenics Scandal Reveals Silence of Swedish Scientists." *Nature* 389:9.

Buttel, Frederick H., and Jill Belsky. 1987. "Biotechnology, Plant Breeding, and Intellectual Property: Social and Ethical Dimensions." *Science, Technology, and Human Values* 12:31–49.

Byrne, John A. 1995. "Management Meccas." *Business Week* 3442:122–33.

Byrne, John A. 1996. "And You Thought CEOs Were Overpaid." *Business Week* 3490:34.

Callahan, Raymond E. 1962. *Education and the Cult of Efficiency: A Study of the Social Forces that Have Shaped the Administration of the Public Schools*. Chicago: University of Chicago Press.

Callon, Michel. 1998. "Introduction: The Embeddedness of Economic Markets in Economics." Pp. 1–57 in *The Laws of the Markets*, edited by Michel Callon. Oxford: Basil Blackwell.

Campbell, Christiana McFayden. 1962. *The Farm Bureau and the New Deal*. Urbana: University of Illinois Press.

Campbell, James. 1999. *Recovering Benjamin Franklin: An Exploration of a Life of Science and Service*. Chicago: Open Court.

Cardwell, D. S. L. 1971. *From Watt to Clausius*. Ithaca, NY: Cornell University Press.

Carlyle, Thomas. [1829] 1878. "Signs of the Times." Pp. 187–96 in *Critical and Historical Essays*. New York: Appleton and Company.

Center for Responsive Politics. 1998. "Influence, Inc." http://www.crp.org/lobbyists/

Chapman, Stephen. 1996. "Preserving Corporate Welfare As We Know It." *Chicago Tribune*. October 20:21.

Chernow, Ron. 1998. *Titan: The Life of John D. Rockefeller, Sr*. New York: Random House.

Chun, In-Young. 1997. "The Reality of Human Rights in North Korea." Pp. 111–64 in *Understanding Human Rights in North Korea*, edited by Sung-Chul Choi. Seoul: Institute of Unification Policy, Hanyang University.

Clinton, William Jefferson. 1997. "Science and Technology: Shaping the Twenty-First Century." http://www.whitehouse.gov/WH/EOP/OSTP/SNTletter.html

Clinton, William Jefferson. 1999. "Economic Report of the President: Transmitted to the Congress, February, 1999." Washington, DC: US Government Printing Office.

Cloud, John. 1998. "The KGB of Mississippi." *Time* 151(12):30.

Coase, Ronald H. 1976. "Adam Smith's Views of Man." *Journal of Law and Economics* 19:529–46.

Coase, Ronald H. 1988. *The Firm, the Market and the Law*. Chicago: University of Chicago Press.

Colden, Cadwallader. [1727] 1902. *The History of the Five Indian Nations*. New York: New Amsterdam.

Coleman, James S. 1990. *Foundations of Social Theory*. Cambridge, MA: Belknap.

Cook, Noble D. 1998. *Born to Die: Disease and New World Conquest, 1492–1650*. Cambridge: Cambridge University Press.

Coontz, Stephanie. 1992. *The Way We Never Were: American Families and the Nostalgia Trap*. New York: Basic Books.

Corporation for Enterprise Development. 1998. "Bidding for Business: Are Cities and States Selling Themselves Short?" http://www.cfed.org/cfedpublications/bidding.htm

Country Life Commission. [1909] 1911. *Report of the Commission on Country Life*. New York: Sturgis and Walton.

Cox, James. 1999. "Not Quite Land of Free Trade: Tariffs Shield Some U.S. Products." *USA Today*. May 6:1B.

Coy, Peter. 1998. "Social Security: Let It Be." *Business Week* 3606:34–35.

Creutzfeldt-Jakob Disease Foundation. 1998. "Creutzfeldt-Jakob Disease Foundation." http://members.aol.com/crjakob/index.html

Crosby, Alfred W. 1986. *Ecological Imperialism*. New York, NY: Cambridge University Press.

Curtis, Julie. 1991. "Introduction." Pp. vii–xxi in *Diaboliad* by Mikhail Bulgakov. London: Harvill.

Dahl, Robert A. 1989. *Democracy and Its Critics*. New Haven, CT: Yale University Press.

Dahlberg, Kenneth A. 1980. *Beyond the Green Revolution*. New York: Plenum.

Danbom, David B. 1979. *The Resisted Revolution*. Ames: Iowa State University Press.

Daniels, Roger. 1994. "The Decisions to Relocate the North American Japanese: Another Look." Pp. 1–7 in *The Mass Internment of Japanese Americans and the Quest for Legal Redress*, edited by Charles McClain. New York: Garland.

Dapper, Olfert. [1660] 1975. "Benin at the Height of Its Power." Pp. 122–30 in *Nigerian Perspectives: An Historical Anthology*, edited by Thomas L. Hodgkin. New York: Oxford University Press.

Deletant, Dennis. 1995. *Ceauşescu and the Securitate: Coercion and Dissent in Romania, 1965–1989*. Armonk, NY: M.E. Sharpe.

Deutscher, Irwin. 1969. "Looking Backward: Case Studies on the Progress of Methodology in Sociological Research." *American Sociologist* 4:35–41.

Dewey, John. 1927. *The Public and Its Problems*. New York: Henry Holt.

Dewey, John. [1916] 1961. *Democracy and Education*. New York: Macmillan.

Dilthey, Wilhelm. 1961. *Pattern and Meaning in History*. New York: Harper and Row.

Dreger, Alice D. 1998. *Hermaphrodites and the Medical Invention of Sex*. Cambridge, MA: Harvard University Press.

Dulles, Foster Rhea, and Melvyn Dubofsky. 1993. *Labor in America: A History*. Arlington Heights, IL: Harlan Davidson.

Dunman, Jack. 1952. "Agricultural Aspects of the Schemes." Pp. 10–14 in *Man Conquers Nature: Text of Speeches at Battersea Town Hall Meeting, January 13, 1952*. London: Society for Cultural Relations with the USSR.

Durant, Will. 1939. *The Life of Greece*. New York: Simon and Schuster.

Durkheim, Emile. [1893] 1964. *The Division of Labor in Society*. New York: Free Press.

Duster, Troy. 1995. "Symposium: The Bell Curve." *Contemporary Sociology* 24:158–61.

Dvorak, John C. 1998. "The Software Protection Racket." *PC Magazine* 17(15):87.

Dworkin, Terry M. 1997. "It's My Life—Leave Me Alone: Off the Job Employee Associational Privacy Rights." *American Business Law Journal* 35:47–99.

East, Edward M. 1923. *Mankind at the Crossroads*. New York: Charles Scribner's Sons.

Eco, Umberto. 1983. *Travels in Hyperreality*. New York: Harcourt, Brace, Jovanovich.

Edmunds, John C. 1996. "Securities: The New World Wealth Machine." *Foreign Policy* 104:118–33.

Einhorn, David A. 1998. "Shrink-Wrap Licenses: The Debate Continues." *IDEA: Journal of Law and Technology* 38:383–401.

Ellul, Jacques. 1964. *The Technological Society*. New York: Vintage.

Engineers Joint Council. 1961. *The Training, Placement and Utilization of Engineers and Technicians in the Soviet Union*. New York: Engineers Joint Council.

Evans, Oliver. 1795. *The Young Mill-Wright and Miller's Guide*. Philadelphia: Author.

Eyzaguirre, P., and M. Iwanaga. 1996. *Participatory Plant Breeding: Proceedings of a Workshop on Participatory Plant Breeding, 26–29 July*. Rome: International Plant Genetic Resources Institute.

Falcoff, Mark, and Ronald H. Dolkart (Eds.). 1975. *Prologue to Perón: Argentina in Depression and War, 1930–1943.* Berkeley: University of California Press.

Feddersen, Timothy, and Wolfgang Pesendorfer. 1998. "Convicting the Innocent: The Inferiority of Unanimous Jury Verdicts under Strategic Voting." *American Political Science Review* 92:23–35.

Federico, P. J. 1945. "The Patent Trials of Oliver Evans." *Journal of the Patent Office Society* 27:586–613, 657–81.

Fedorov, Nikolai F. 1990. *What Was Man Created For? The Philosophy of the Common Task.* London: Honeyglen.

Feenberg, Andrew. 1995. "Subversive Rationalization: Technology, Power, and Democracy." Pp. 3–22 in *Technology and the Politics of Knowledge,* edited by Andrew Feenberg and Alastair Hannay. Bloomington: Indiana University Press.

Fei Shaotong. [1948] 1992. *From the Soil: Foundations of Chinese Society.* Berkeley: University of California Press.

Ferguson, Eugene S. 1980. *Oliver Evans: Inventive Genius of the American Industrial Revolution.* Greenville, DE: Hagley Museum.

Feyerabend, Paul. 1978. *Science in a Free Society.* London: New Left Books.

Fisher, Donald. 1990. "Boundary Work and Science: The Relation between Power and Knowledge." Pp. 98–119 in *Theories of Science in Society,* edited by Susan E. Cozzens and Thomas F. Gieryn. Bloomington: Indiana University Press.

Fitzgerald, Deborah. 1990. *The Business of Breeding: Hybrid Corn in Illinois, 1890–1940.* Ithaca, NY: Cornell University Press.

Fitzgerald, Deborah. 1996. "Blinded by Technology: American Agriculture in the Soviet Union, 1928–1932." *Agricultural History* 70:459–86.

Fleischmann, Glen. 1971. *The Cherokee Removal, 1838.* New York: Franklin Watts.

Food Marketing Institute. 1998. "Supermarket Facts: Industry Overview 1997." http://www.fmi.org/food/superfact.html

Foreign Agricultural Service. 1998. "The Competition in 1997." http://www.fas.usda.gov/cmp/com-study/1997/comp97-us.html

Foust, Dean, and Jonathan Drew. 1999. "Can Red Hat Stay Red-Hot?" *Business Week* 3636:85, 88.

Frank, Robert H., and Philip J. Cook. 1995. *The Winner-Take-All Society.* New York: Penguin.

Fraser, Stephen. 1998. "Canada-United States Trade Issues: Back from Purgatory? Why Computer Software 'Shrink-Wrap' Licenses Should Be Laid to Rest." *Tulane Journal of International and Comparative Law* 6:183–234.

Freedland, Jonathan. 1997. "Master Race of the Left." *Guardian.* August 30:1–2.

Friedman, Milton. 1962. *Capitalism and Freedom.* Chicago: University of Chicago Press.

Friedman, Milton. 1998. "The Solution: Parental Choice." http://www.friedman-foundation.org/index.html

Frome, Michael. 1971. *The Forest Service.* New York: Praeger.

Fuller, Steve. 1988. *Social Epistemology.* Bloomington: Indiana University Press.

Galbraith, John Kenneth. 1967. *The New Industrial State.* Boston: Houghton Mifflin.

Gardner, William, and Joseph Rosenbaum. 1998. "Database Protection and Access to Information." *Science* 281:786–87.

Garland, Susan B., and Emily Thorton. 1998. "Justice's Cartel Crackdown." *Business Week* 3588:50–51.

Garten, Jeffrey E. 1999. "Megamergers Are a Clear and Present Danger." *Business Week* 3613:28.

Gebert, Konstanty. 1993. "'Shock' Crock: Poland's Overrated Reforms." *Washington Post*, May 2:C1.

General Secretariat. 1999. "General Secretariat of the Dutch Scienceshops." http://www.bu.tudelft.nl/wetensch/lsw/ehome.htm

Gerber, Theodore P., and Michael Hout. 1998. "More Shock Than Therapy: Market Transition, Employment, and Income in Russia, 1991–1995." *American Journal of Sociology* 104:1–50.

Gert, Bernard. 1991. "Introduction." Pp. 3–32 in *Man and Citizen (De Homine and De Cive)* by Thomas Hobbes. Indianapolis: Hackett.

Giddens, Anthony. 1994. "Living in a Post-Traditional Society." Pp. 56–109 in *Reflexive Modernization: Politics, Tradition and Aesthetics in the Modern Social Order*, edited by Ulrich Beck, Anthony Giddens, and Scott Lash. Cambridge: Polity.

Giedion, Siegfried. [1948] 1975. *Mechanization Takes Command*. New York: W.W. Norton.

Gilbert, Daniel R. 1996. "The Prisoner's Dilemma and the Prisoners of the Prisoner's Dilemma." *Business Ethics Quarterly* 6:165–78.

Goonatilake, Susantha. 1982. *Crippled Minds: An Exploration into Colonial Culture*. New Delhi: Vikas.

Gorz, André. 1973. *Socialism and Revolution*. Garden City, NY: Doubleday.

Habermas, Jurgen. 1971. *Knowledge and Human Interests*. Boston: Beacon.

Habermas, Jurgen. 1998. *Between Facts and Norms: Contributions to a Discourse Theory of Law and Democracy*. Cambridge, MA: MIT Press.

Halliburton, R., Jr. 1975. *The Tulsa Race War of 1921*. San Francisco: R and E Research Associates.

Hammonds, Keith H. 1996. "Balancing Work and Family." *Business Week* 3493: 74–80.

Hansmann, Henry. 1990. "When Does Worker Ownership Work? ESOPs, Law Firms, Codetermination, and Economic Democracy." *Yale Law Journal* 99:1749–1816.

Haraway, Donna. 1995. "Situated Knowledges: The Science Question in Feminism and the Privilege of Partial Perspective." Pp. 175–94 in *Technology and the Politics of Knowledge*, edited by Andrew Feenberg and Alastair Hannay. Bloomington: Indiana University Press.

Hardin, Charles M. 1955. *Freedom in Agricultural Education*. Chicago: University of Chicago Press.

Harding, Sandra. 1991. *Whose Science? Whose Knowledge? Thinking from Women's Lives*. Ithaca, NY: Cornell University Press.

Hauser, Robert J. 1995. "Symposium: The Bell Curve." *Contemporary Sociology* 24:149–53.

Hawkes, J. G. 1994. "Origins of Cultivated Potatoes and Species Relationships." Pp. 3–42 in *Potato Genetics*, edited by J. E. Bradshaw and G. R. Mackay. Wallingford, Oxon: CAB International.

Hays, Samuel P. 1959. *Conservation and the Gospel of Efficiency*. Cambridge, MA: Harvard University Press.

Heidegger, Martin. 1977. *The Question Concerning Technology and Other Essays*. New York: Harper and Row.

Heilbroner, Robert L. 1961. *The Worldly Philosophers*. New York: Simon and Schuster.

Hellweg, Eric. 1998. "Coding for Freedom." *Business 2.0* 3:114–16.

Herrnstein, Richard J., and Charles A. Murray. 1994. *The Bell Curve: Intelligence and Class Structure in American Life*. New York: Free Press.

Heuer, Larry, and Steven Penrod. 1996. "Increasing Juror Participation in Trials Through Note Taking and Question Asking." *Judicature* 79:256–62.

Hirschman, Albert O. 1970. *Exit, Voice, and Loyalty: Responses to Decline in Firms, Organizations, and States*. Cambridge, MA: Harvard University Press.

Hirschman, Albert O. 1977. *The Passions and the Interests*. Princeton, NJ: Princeton University Press.

Hobbelink, Henk. 1987. *New Hope or False Promise? Biotechnology and Third World Agriculture*. Brussels: International Coalition for Development Action.

Hobbes, Thomas. [1651] 1991. *Leviathan*. Cambridge: Cambridge University Press.

Hobbes, Thomas. [1658/1642] 1991. *Man and Citizen (De Homine and De Cive)*. Indianapolis: Hackett.

Hofstadter, Richard. 1955. *Social Darwinism in American Thought*. Boston: Beacon.

Homans, George C. 1950. *The Human Group*. New York: Harcourt, Brace, World.

Horwitz, Morton J. 1977. *The Transformation of American Law*. Cambridge, MA: Harvard University Press.

Howard, Philip K. 1994. *The Death of Common Sense: How Law Is Suffocating America*. New York: Random House.

Huizinga, Johan. 1954. *The Waning of the Middle Ages*. Garden City, NY: Doubleday.

Hull, David L. 1988. *Science as a Process: An Evolutionary Account of the Social and Conceptual Development of Science*. Chicago: University of Chicago Press.

Huntington, Samuel P. 1996. *The Clash of Civilizations and the Remaking of the World Order*. New York: Simon and Schuster.

Illich, Ivan. 1976. *Medical Nemesis*. New York: Random House.

International Telecommunications Union. 1994. *African Telecommunication Indicators*. Geneva: Author.

Intersex Society of North America. 1998. "The Intersex Society of North America." http://www.isna.org/

Johnston, Arthur. 1974. "Introduction." Pp. vii–xx in *The Advancement of Learning and New Atlantis*, by Francis Bacon. Oxford: Clarendon.

Jones, C. R. [1916] 1917. "Scientific Management as Applied to the Farm, Home, and Manufacturing Plants." Pp. 108–15 in *Proceedings of the 30th Annual Convention of the Association of American Agricultural Colleges and Experiment Stations*. Published by Association of American Agricultural Colleges and Experiment Stations.

Jones, Gavin M., and R. M. Douglas. 1997. "Introduction." Pp. 1–12 in *The Continuing Demographic Transition*, edited by G. W. Jones, R. M. Douglas, J. C. Caldwell, and R. M. D'Souza. Oxford: Clarendon.

Jones, James H. 1981. *Bad Blood: The Tuskegee Syphilis Experiment*. New York: Free Press.

Josephson, Matthew. 1962. *The Robber Barons*. New York: Harcourt, Brace & World.

Kaplan, Abraham. 1964. *The Conduct of Inquiry*. Scranton, PA: Chandler.

Karier, Clarence. 1973a. "Liberal Ideology and the Quest for Orderly Change." In *Roots of Crisis: American Education in the Twentieth Century*, edited by Clarence J. Karier, Paul Violas, and Joel Spring. Chicago: Rand McNally.

Karier, Clarence. 1973b. "Testing for Order and Control in the Corporate Liberal State." In *Roots of Crisis: American Education in the Twentieth Century*, edited by Clarence J. Karier, Paul Violas, and Joel Spring. Chicago: Rand McNally.

Keller, Evelyn Fox. 1985. *Reflections on Gender and Science*. New Haven, CT: Yale University Press.

Kimmelman, Barbara A. 1983. "The American Breeders' Association: Genetics and Eugenics in an Agricultural Context, 1903–13." *Social Studies of Science* 13:163–204.

Kipling, Rudyard. 1899. "The White Man's Burden." *McClure's Magazine* 12(4):290–91.

Knight, Frank H. 1947. *Freedom and Reform: Essays in Economics and Social Philosophy*. New York: Harper and Brothers.

Kohler, Robert E. 1980. "Warren Weaver and the Rockefeller Foundation Program in Molecular Biology: A Case Study in the Management of Science." Pp. 249–93 in *Sciences in the American Context*, edited by Nathan Reingold. Washington, DC: Smithsonian Institution.

Kondro, Wayne. 1998. "Canada Opens Program to Community Groups." *Science* 282:1237–38.

Koutaissoff, Elisabeth. 1990. "Introduction." Pp. 11–30 in *What Was Man Created For? The Philosophy of the Common Task*, by Nikolai Fedorov. London: Honeyglen.

Kover, Arthur. 1967. "Models of Man As Defined By Marketing Research." *Journal of Marketing Research* 4:129–32.

Krohn, Wolfgang, and Wolf Schafer. 1983. "Agricultural Chemistry: The Origin and Structure of a Finalized Science." Pp. 17–52 in *Finalization in Science: The Social Orientation of Scientific Progress*, edited by Wolf Schafer. Dordrecht: D. Reidel.

Kuttner, Robert. 1996a. "Rewarding Corporations That Really Invest in America." *Business Week* 3464:22.

Kuttner, Robert. 1996b. "Unions Are Good For the U.S.—And Clinton Should Say So." *Business Week* 3496:23.

Kuttner, Robert. 1998. "Globalization's Dirty Little Secret." *Business Week* 3594:20.

Kuttner, Robert. 1999. "This Is a Tax Cut Whose Time Hasn't Come." *Business Week* 3619:24.

Latour, Bruno. 1987. *Science in Action: How to Follow Scientists and Engineers through Society*. Milton Keynes, England: Open University Press.

Latour, Bruno. 1993. *We Have Never Been Modern*. Cambridge, MA: Harvard University Press.

Latour, Bruno. 1996. *Petite Réflexion sur le Culte Moderne des Dieux Faitiches*. Paris: Sythélabo.

Laurie, Bruce. 1989. *Artisans into Workers: Labor in Nineteenth Century America*. New York: Hill and Wang.

Law, John. 1994. *Organizing Modernity*. Oxford: Blackwell.

Lenin, Vladimir I. [1917] 1932. *The Threatening Catastrophe and How to Fight It*. New York: NY: International.

Lenin, Vladimir I. 1937. *Selected Works*, Volume 7. London: Lawrence and Wishart.

Lenin, Vladimir I. 1938. *Theory of the Agrarian Question*, Volume 12, V. I. Lenin, Selected Works. New York: International.

Leonhardt, David. 1998. "One Big, Unhappy Family at United." *Business Week* 3584:6.

Leonhardt, David. 1999. "UAL: Labor Is My Co-Pilot." *Business Week* 3618:38.

Levenstein, Harvey. 1988. *Revolution at the Table: The Transformation of the American Diet*. New York: Oxford University Press.

Lewontin, Richard. 1976. "The Problem of Lysenkoism." Pp. 32–64 in *The Radicalisation of Science*, edited by Hilary Rose and Steven Rose. New York: Holmes and Meier.

Lindquist, Christopher. 1999. "A Windows-Free World: Linux." *PC/Computing* 12(6):192.

Lipton, Michael, and Richard Longhurst. 1989. *New Seeds and Poor People*. Baltimore: Johns Hopkins University Press.

Little People of America. 1998. "Little People of America." http://www.bfs.ucsd.edu/dwarfism/lpa.htm

Lynn, Frances M., and Jack D. Kartez. 1994. "Environmental Democracy in Action: The Toxics Release Inventory." *Environmental Management* 18:511–21.

MacPherson, C. B. 1962. *The Political Theory of Possessive Individualism*. Oxford: Clarendon.

MacPherson, C. B. 1985. "Introduction." Pp. 9–63 in *Leviathan by Thomas Hobbes*, edited by C. B. MacPherson. London: Penguin.

Madison, James, Alexander Hamilton, and John Jay. [1778] 1966. *The Federalist Papers*. New Rochelle, NY: Arlington House.

Mail & Guardian. 1997. "Mobutu Dies in Morocco." September 25:8.

Malthus, Thomas Robert. [1798] 1959. *Essay on the Principle of Population*. Ann Arbor: University of Michigan Press.

Mann, Charles C. 1998. "Who Will Own Your Next Good Idea?" *Atlantic Monthly* 282(3):57–82.

Marty, Martin E., and R. Scott Appleby. 1993. "Introduction: A Sacred Cosmos, Scandalous Code, Defiant Society." Pp. 1–19 in *Fundamentalisms and Society: Reclaiming the Sciences, the Family, and Education*, edited by Martin E. Marty and R. Scott Appleby. Chicago: University of Chicago Press.

Marx, Karl. [1844] 1964. *The Economic and Philosophic Manuscripts of 1844*. New York: International.

Marx, Karl. [1867] 1967. *Capital*. New York: International.

Matson, Floyd W. 1964. *The Broken Image*. New York: Braziller.

Maurer, Stephen M., and Suzanne Scotchmer. 1999. "Database Protection: Is It Broken and Should We Fix It?" *Science* 284:1129–30.

McClain, Charles. 1994. "Introduction." Pp. vii–xiv in *The Mass Internment of Japan-*

ese Americans and the Quest for Legal Redress, edited by Charles McClain. New York: Garland.

McConnell, Grant. 1953. *The Decline of Agrarian Democracy.* Berkeley: University of California Press.

McIntosh, Peggy. 1995. "White Privilege and Male Privilege: A Personal Account of Coming to See Correspondences through Work in Women's Studies." Pp. 76–87 in *Race, Class and Gender: An Anthology,* edited by Margaret L. Andersen and Patricia Hill Collins. Belmont, CA: Wadsworth.

Mcintyre, Richard. 1992. "Consumption in Contemporary Capitalism: Beyond Marx and Veblen." *Review of Social Economy* 50:40–60.

McNeill, William H. 1963. *The Rise of the West.* Chicago: University of Chicago Press.

Mead, George Herbert. 1962. *Mind, Self, and Society from the Standpoint of a Social Behaviorist.* Chicago: University of Chicago Press.

Melman, Seymour. 1981. "Alternative Criteria for the Design of the Means of Production." *Theory and Society* 10:325–36.

Merton, Robert. 1957. *Social Theory and Social Structure,* 2nd ed. New York: Free Press.

Merton, Robert. [1938] 1970. *Science, Technology, and Society in Seventeenth Century England.* New York: Harper and Row.

Moberg, David. 1992. "Union Busting, Past and Present." *Dissent* 39:73–80.

Mokyr, Joel. 1985. *Why Ireland Starved: A Quantitative and Analytical History of the Irish Economy.* London: George Allen and Unwin.

Montgomery, Susan Barbieri, and Robert Maisashvili. 1998. "UCC 2B Could Result In Ambiguous IP Rights." *National Law Journal:*C23.

Moore, Barrington, Jr. 1966. *Social Origins of Dictatorship and Democracy.* Boston: Beacon.

Moore, F. C. T. 1994. "Taking the Sting out of the Prisoner's Dilemma." *Philosophical Quarterly* 44:221–33.

Moore, Stephen, and Dean Stansel. 1995. "Ending Corporate Welfare as We Know It." http://www.cato.org/pubs/pas/pa225.html

Myrdal, Gunnar. 1944. *An American Dilemma: The Negro Problem and Modern Democracy.* New York: Harper and Brothers.

Nagel, Thomas. 1986. *The View from Nowhere.* New York: Oxford University Press.

Nakano, Takeo, and Leatrice Nakano. 1980. *Within the Barbed Wire Fence: A Japanese Man's Account of His Internment in Canada.* Toronto: University of Toronto Press.

Nathaniel-Isaacs, Neila. 1994. *Inner City Conflict: A Case Study of History and Planning in Overtown, Miami.* Master's Thesis, Community and Regional Planning, University of Nebraska, Lincoln.

National Center for Education Statistics. 1997. "Public Elementary and Secondary Expenditures per Student." http://nces.ed.gov/pubs/ce/c9752a01.html

Nelkin, Dorothy. 1984. *Controversy.* London: Sage.

New York Stock Exchange. 1998. *New York Stock Exchange Fact Book, 1997.* New York: Author.

Okin, Susan Moller. 1989. *Justice, Gender, and the Family.* New York: Basic Books.

Orléan, André. 1994. "Vers un Modéle Général de la Coordination Economique par les Conventions." Pp. 9–40 in *Analyse Economique des Conventions*, edited by André Orléan. Paris: Presses Universitaires de France.

Ormerod, Paul. 1994. *The Death of Economics*. London: Faber and Faber.

Pateman, Carole. 1975. "A Contribution to the Political Theory of Organizational Democracy." *Administration and Society* 7:5–26.

Pauly, Philip J. 1987. *Controlling Life: Jacques Loeb and the Engineering Ideal in Biology*. New York: Oxford University Press.

Pearce, Brian. 1952. "Some Industrial Aspects of the Schemes." Pp. 19–20 in *Man Conquers Nature: Text of Speeches at Battersea Town Hall Meeting, January 13, 1952*. London: Society for Cultural Relations with the USSR.

Peel, J. D. Y. 1971. *Herbert Spencer: The Evolution of a Sociologist*. New York: Basic Books.

Perkins, John H. 1997. *Geopolitics and the Green Revolution*. New York: Oxford University Press.

Perlstadt, Harry, Cynthia Jackson-Elmore, Paul P. Freddolino, and Celeste Reed. 1998. "An Overview of Citizen Participation in Health Planning: Lessons Learned from the Literature." *Civic Review* 87:347–67.

Pinstrup-Anderson, Per. 1982. *Agricultural Research and Technology in Economic Development*. London: Longman.

Port, Otis, and Inka Resch. 1999. "They're Listening to Your Calls." *Business Week* 3631:110–11.

Porter, Ed. 1987. "Foreign Involvement in China's Colleges and Universities: A Historical Perspective." *International Journal of Intercultural Relations* 11:369–85.

Premier Ministre. 1998. "Conclusions de la Conférence des citoyens sur l'utilisation des OGM en agriculture et dans l'alimentation." http://www.premier-ministre.gouv.fr/FAIT/JUILLET98/010798B.HTM

Presser, Harriet B. 1999. "Toward a 24-Hour Economy." *Science* 284:1778–79.

Prest, John. 1981. *The Garden of Eden: The Botanic Garden and the Recreation of Paradise*. New Haven, CT: Yale University Press.

Price, Monroe E., and Jonathan Weinberg. 1996. "United States (2)." Pp. 265–78 in *Media Ownership and Control*, edited by International Institute of Communication. London: IIC.

Prokofyev, V. V. 1933. *Industrial and Technical Intelligentsia in the U.S.S.R.* Moscow: Cooperative Publishing Society of Foreign Workers in the USSR.

Putnam, Robert D. 1995. "Bowling Alone: America's Declining Social Capital." *Journal of Democracy* 6:65–78.

Rachels, James. 1993. *The Elements of Moral Philosophy*. New York: McGraw Hill.

Raphael, D. D., and A. L. Macfie. 1982. "Introduction." Pp. 1–52 in Adam Smith, *The Theory of Moral Sentiments*. Indianapolis: Liberty Fund.

Rapp, Friedrich. 1985. "Soviet-Marxist Philosophy of Technology." *Studies in Soviet Thought* 29:139–50.

Rasmussen, David M. 1973. "Between Autonomy and Sociality." *Cultural Hermeneutics* 1:3–45.

Ravetz, Jerome. 1971. *Scientific Knowledge and Its Social Problems*. New York: Oxford University Press.

Reich, Leonard S. 1985. *The Making of American Industrial Research: Science and Business at GE and Bell, 1876–1926*. Cambridge: Cambridge University Press.

Reingold, Jennifer, and Ronald Grover. 1999. "Executive Pay." *Business Week* 3625:72–74, 78, 81, 84, 89–90.

Reiter, Ester. 1991. *Making Fast Food: From the Frying Pan into the Fryer*. Montreal: McGill-Queens University Press.

Replogle, R. 1987. "Personality and Society in Hobbes's Leviathan." *Polity* 19:570–94.

Restivo, Sal. 1988. "Modern Science as a Social Problem." *Social Problems* 35:205–25.

Ricoeur, Paul. 1967. "New Developments in the Phenomenology of Language in France." *Social Research* 34:1–30.

Ricoeur, Paul. 1974. *The Conflict of Interpretations*. Evanston, IL: Northwestern University Press.

Rosenberg, Charles E. 1967. "Factors in the Development of Genetics in the United States: Some Suggestions." *Journal of the History of Medicine and Allied Sciences* 22:27–43.

Rosenfeld, Stuart A., and Jonathan P. Sher. 1977. "The Urbanization of Rural Schools, 1840–1970." Pp. 11–42 in *Education in Rural America*, edited by Jonathan P. Sher. Boulder, CO: Westview.

Ross, Edward A. 1915. *Social Control*. New York: Macmillan.

Rostow, Eugene V. [1945] 1994. "The Japanese American Cases—A Disaster." Pp. 189–233 in *The Mass Internment of Japanese Americans and the Quest for Legal Redress*, edited by Charles McClain. New York: Garland.

Rostow, Walt Whitman. 1960. *The Stages of Economic Growth: A Non-Communist Manifesto*. Cambridge: Cambridge University Press.

Rowe, Jonathan. 1996. "Reinventing the Corporation: Corporate Responsibility." *Washington Monthly* 28(4):16.

Rufin, Jean-Christophe. 1991. *L'Empire et les Nouveaux Barbares: Rupture Nord-Sud*. Paris: Editions Jean-Claude Lattés.

Rukeyser, Walter Arnold. 1932. *Working for the Soviets: An American Engineer in Russia*. New York: Covici-Friede.

Rysavy, Tracy. 1998. "Mothers for Eco-Justice." *Yes! A Journal of Positive Futures* (Summer):24–26.

Sachs, Jeffrey. 1993. *Poland's Jump to the Market Economy*. Cambridge, MA: MIT Press.

Sagoff, Mark. 1988. *The Economy of the Earth: Philosophy, Law and the Environment*. Cambridge: Cambridge University Press.

Saint-Exupéry, Antoine de. [1939] 1965. *Wind, Sand, and Stars*. New York: Time-Life.

Salomon, Jean-Jacques. 1973. *Science and Politics*. London: Macmillan.

Samuels, Warren J. 1977. "The Political Economy of Adam Smith." *Ethics* 87:189–207.

Sanks, Terry M. 1998. "Database Protection: National and International Attempts to Provide Legal Protection for Databases." *Florida State University Law Review* 25:991–1016.

Sarewitz, Daniel. 1996. *Frontiers of Illusion: Science, Technology, and the Politics of Progress*. Philadelphia: Temple University Press.

Scherer, F. M. 1970. *Industrial Market Structure and Economic Performance*. Chicago: Rand McNally.

Schiff, Ashley L. 1962. *Fire and Water: Scientific Heresy in the Forest Service*. Cambridge, MA: Harvard University Press.

Schiffrin, André. 1999. "Publishers' Spring Catalogues Offer Compelling Reading About the Market for Ideas." *Chronicle of Higher Education* 45(28):B8–B9.

Schiller, Herbert. 1996. "United States (1)." Pp. 249–64 in *Media Ownership and Control*, edited by International Institute of Communication. London: IIC.

Schlosser, Eric. 1998. "The Prison-Industrial Complex." *Atlantic Monthly* 282(6):51–52, 54–58, 62–66, 68–70, 72–77.

Schutz, Alfred. 1970. *On Phenomenology and Social Relations*. Chicago: University of Chicago Press.

Science. 1998a. "Database Bill Worries Scientists." *Science* 280:1499.

Science. 1998b. "Science Shops in Canadian Universities." *Science* 280:1515.

Sclove, Richard E. 1995. *Democracy and Technology*. New York: Guilford.

Sclove, Richard E., Madeleine L. Scammell, and Breena Holland. 1998. *Community-Based Research in the United States*. Amherst, MA: Loka Institute.

Scott, James C. 1998. *Seeing Like a State: How Certain Schemes to Improve the Human Condition Have Failed*. New Haven, CT: Yale University Press.

Scott, W. Richard. 1995. *Institutions and Organizations*. Thousand Oaks, CA: Sage.

Sénat. 1998. "Conférence de citoyens." http://www.senat.fr/opecst/o980603.html

Shapin, Steven, and Simon Schaffer. 1985. *Leviathan and the Air-Pump: Hobbes, Boyle, and the Experimental Life*. Princeton, NJ: Princeton University Press.

Shapiro, Ian. 1996. *Democracy's Place*. Ithaca, NY: Cornell University Press.

Sher, Jonathan, and Rachel Tompkins. 1977. "Economy, Efficiency, and Equality: The Myth of Rural School and District Consolidation." Pp. 43–77 in *Education in Rural America*, edited by Jonathan P. Sher. Boulder, CO: Westview.

Shiva, Vandana. 1991. *The Violence of the Green Revolution*. London: Zed.

Shlapentokh, Dmitry. 1996. "Bolshevism as a Fedorovian Regime." *Cahiers du Monde Russe* 37:429–66.

Shlapentokh, Dmitry. 1997. "Life/Death—Cosmos/Eschatology: Nikolai Berdiaev and the Influence of the Fedorovian Vision." Pp. 301–52 in *Analecta Husserliana*, edited by A-T. Tymieniecka. Amsterdam: Kluwer Academic.

Shott, Susan. 1976. "Society, Self, and Mind in Moral Philosophy: The Scottish Moralists as Precursors of Symbolic Interactionism." *Journal of the History of the Behavioral Sciences* 12:39–46.

Smith, Adam. [1759] 1982. *The Theory of Moral Sentiments*. Indianapolis: Liberty Fund.

Smith, Adam. [1776] 1994. *An Inquiry into the Nature and Causes of the Wealth of Nations*. New York: Modern Library.

Sobel, Lester A. 1975. *Argentina & Peron: 1970–1975*. New York: Facts on File.

Solbakk, Aage. 1990. *The Sami People*. Karasjok, Norway: Sámi Instituhtta, Davvi Girji.

Spencer, Herbert. 1890. *State Tampering with Money and Banks*. New York: Worthington.

Spencer, Herbert. 1906. *The Study of Sociology*. New York: D. Appleton.

Spencer, Herbert. [1916] 1945. *The Man Versus the State*. Caldwell, ID: Caxton.

Spiro, Leah Nathans. 1998. "A $3.5 Billion Tranquilizer." *Business Week* 3598:42.

Spring, Joel. 1972. *Education and the Rise of the Corporate State*. Boston: Beacon.

Stalin, Joseph. 1932. *On Technology*. Moscow: Cooperative Publishing Society of Foreign Workers in the USSR.

Staudenmeier, John M. 1989. "Perils of Progress Talk: Some Historical Considerations." Pp. 268–98 in *Science, Technology, and Social Progress*, edited by Steven L. Goldman. Bethlehem, PA: Lehigh University Press.

Stiglitz, Joseph E. 1999. "Whither Reform? Ten Years of the Transition." Paper presented at the Annual Bank Conference on Development Economics, Washington, DC.

Swift, Jonathan. [1726] 1947. *Gulliver's Travels*. New York: Grosset and Dunlap.

Swinney, Dan. 1998. *Building the Bridge to the High Road: Expanding Participation and Democracy in the Economy to Build Sustainable Communities*. Chicago: Midwest Center for Labor Research.

Szreter, Simon. 1993. "The Idea of Demographic Transition and the Study of Fertility Change: A Critical Intellectual History." *Population and Development Review* 19:659–701.

Taylor, Frederick Winslow. 1911. *The Principles of Scientific Management*. New York: Harper.

Taylor, Howard F. 1995. "Symposium: The Bell Curve." *Contemporary Sociology* 24:153–58.

Taylor, Peter Leigh. 1994. "The Rhetorical Construction of Efficiency." *Sociological Forum* 9:459–90.

Teitelbaum, Michael S. 1975. "Relevance of Demographic Transition Theory for Developing Countries." *Science* 188:420–25.

Thiesenhusen, William C. 1971. *Technological Change and Income Distribution in Latin American Agriculture*. Paper No. 78, Land Tenure Center, University of Wisconsin, Madison.

Thompson, E. P. 1971. "The Moral Economy of the English Crowd in the Eighteenth Century." *Past and Present* 50:76–136.

Thompson, Paul. 1995. *The Spirit of the Soil: Agriculture and Environmental Ethics*. London: Routledge.

Thoreau, Henry David. [1854] 1997. *Walden*. Boston: Beacon.

Tickner, J. Ann. 1992. *Gender in International Relations*. New York: Columbia University Press.

Tierney, John. 1997. "Technology Makes Us Better." *New York Times*, September 28:Section 6, 46.

Tocqueville, Alexis de. [1835–1840] 1956. *Democracy in America*. New York: Mentor.

Trend, David. 1997. *Cultural Democracy: Politics, Media, New Technology*. Albany, NY: SUNY Press.

Tullock, Gordon. 1985. "Adam Smith and the Prisoners' Dilemma." *Quarterly Journal of Economics* 100:1073–81.

U.S. Arms Control and Disarmament Agency. 1999. "Value of Arms Transfer Deliveries, Cumulative 1994–1996 by Major Supplier and Recipient." http://www.acda.gov/wmeat97/wmeat97.htm

U.S. Congress. 1998. "Unlocking Our Future: Toward a New National Science Policy." http://www.house.gov//science/science_policy_report.htm

Ure, Andrew. 1835. *The Philosophy of Manufactures*. London: Charles Knight.

Useem, Andrea. 1999. "Wiring African Universities Proves a Formidable Challenge." *Chronicle of Higher Education* 45(30):A51–A53.

Useem, John, and Ruth Hill Useem. 1955. *The Western Educated Man in India*. New York: Dryden.

Van Alstyne, R. W. 1960. *The Rising American Empire*. New York: Oxford University Press.

Vanek, Jaroslav. 1970. *The General Theory of Labor-Managed Market Economies*. Ithaca, NY: Cornell University Press.

Veblen, Thorstein. 1912. *The Theory of the Leisure Class: An Economic Study of Institutions*. New York: Macmillan.

Veblen, Thorstein. 1921. *The Engineers and the Price System*. New York: B. H. Huebsch.

Vick, Karl. 1993. "Bittersweet Harvest." *St. Petersburg Times*, November 21:A1.

Wallerstein, Immanuel. 1974. *The Modern World-System. Capitalist Agriculture and the Origins of the European World-Economy in the Sixteenth Century*. New York: Academic.

Walzer, Michael. 1983. *Spheres of Justice: A Defense of Pluralism and Equality*. New York: Basic Books.

Ware, Steven J. 1996. "Employment Arbitration and Voluntary Consent." *Hofstra Law Review* 26:83–160.

Weber, Max. [1922] 1978. *Economy and Society*. Berkeley: University of California Press.

Wedel, Janine R. 1998. *Collision and Collusion*. New York: St. Martin's.

Wheat, Leonard F. 1973. *Regional Growth and Industrial Location*. Lexington, MA: Lexington.

Whitaker, Arthur P. 1975. "An Overview of the Period." Pp. 1–30 in *Prologue to Perón*, edited by Mark Falcoff and Ronald H. Dolkart. Berkeley,: University of California Press.

Whiteman, Darrell L. (Ed.). 1983. *Missionaries, Anthropologists and Cultural Change*. Williamsburg, VA: College of William and Mary Press.

Wide Smiles. 1998. "Wide Smiles." http://www.widesmiles.org/

Williams, William Appleman. 1969. *The Roots of the Modern American Empire*. New York: Random House.

Wilshire, Bruce. 1990. *The Moral Collapse of the University: Professionalism, Purity and Alienation*. Albany: State University of New York Press.

Wilson, Edward O. 1998. *Consilience: The Unity of Knowledge*. New York: Alfred A. Knopf.

Winner, Langdon. 1986. *The Whale and the Reactor*. Chicago: University of Chicago Press.

Wolf-Phillips, Leslie. 1987. "Why 'Third World'?: Origin, Definition, and Usage." *Third World Quarterly* 9:1311–27.

Wolff, Edward N. 1995. "How the Pie Is Sliced: America's Growing Concentration of Wealth." *American Prospect* 22:58–64.

Woodberry, Robert D., and Christian S. Smith. 1998. "Fundamentalism et al.: Conservative Protestants in America." *Annual Review of Sociology* 24:25–56.

Work in America. 1973. *Work in America*. Cambridge, MA: MIT Press.

Wrong, Dennis H. 1994. *The Problem of Order: What Unites and Divides Society.* Cambridge, MA: Harvard University Press.

Yoxen, Edward. 1981. "Life as a Reproductive Force: Capitalizing the Science and Technology of Molecular Biology." Pp. 66–122 in *Science, Technology, and the Labor Process,* edited by L. Levidow and R. M. Young. London: CSE.

INDEX